THE PERFORMANCE OF
MIDDLE ENGLISH CULTURE

Theatricality as a cultural process is vitally important in the middle ages; it encompasses not only the thematic importation of dramatic images into the *Canterbury Tales*, but also the social and ideological 'performativities' of the mystery and morality plays, metadramatic investments, and the ludic energies of Chaucerian discourses in general. The twelve essays collected here address for the first time this intersection, using contemporary theory and historical scholarship to treat a number of important critical problems, including the anthropology of theatrical performance; gender; allegory; Chaucerian metapoetics; intertextual play and *jouissance*; social mediation and rhetoric; genre; and the institutionality of medieval studies. The volume is a tribute to the distinguished medievalist MARTIN STEVENS, whose own work on Chaucer and the medieval drama is honoured here.

JAMES J. PAXSON is Associate Professor of English at the University of Florida; LAWRENCE M. CLOPPER is Professor of English at Indiana University; SYLVIA TOMASCH is Associate Professor of English at Hunter College, City University of New York.

THE PERFORMANCE OF MIDDLE ENGLISH CULTURE

Essays on Chaucer and the Drama in Honor of Martin Stevens

Edited by

JAMES J. PAXSON
LAWRENCE M. CLOPPER
SYLVIA TOMASCH

D. S. BREWER

First published 1998
D. S. Brewer, Cambridge

ISBN 0 85991 527 1

D. S. Brewer is an imprint of Boydell & Brewer Ltd
PO Box 9, Woodbridge, Suffolk IP12 3DF, UK
and of Boydell & Brewer Inc.
PO Box 41026, Rochester, NY 14604–4126, USA

A catalogue record for this book is available
from the British Library

Library of Congress Cataloging-in-Publication Data
The performance of Middle English culture : essays on Chaucer and the
drama in honor of Martin Stevens / edited by James J. Paxson,
Lawrence M. Clopper, Sylvia Tomasch.
      p.   cm.
   Includes bibliographical references.
   ISBN 0-85991-527-1 (acid-free paper)
   1. English literature – Middle English, 1100–1500 – History and
criticism. 2. Chaucer, Geoffrey, d. 1400 – Criticism and
interpretation. 3. Chaucer, Geoffrey, d. 1400 – Knowledge –
Performing arts. 4. English drama – To 1500 – History and criticism.
5. Drama, Medieval – History and criticism. 6. Performing arts –
England – History. 7. England – Civilization – 1066–1485.
8. Performing arts in literature. I. Paxson, James J.
II. Clopper, Lawrence M., 1941– . III. Tomasch, Sylvia.
IV. Stevens, Martin.
PR251.P47   1998
820.9′001 – dc21   98-24827

This publication is printed on acid-free paper

Printed in Great Britain by
St Edmundsbury Press Ltd, Bury St Edmunds, Suffolk

CONTENTS

CONTRIBUTORS

About the Contributors

Kathleen Ashley is Professor of English at the University of Southern Maine. She has edited a collection of essays *Victor Turner and the Construction of Cultural Criticism: Between Literature and Anthropology* (University of Indiana Press, 1990), co-edited with Pamela Sheingorn *Interpreting Cultural Symbols: St Anne in Late Medieval Society* (University of Georgia Press, 1990), and is completing books on *Moving Subjects: The Semiotics of Processional Performance* and *Writing Faith* (co-authored with Pamela Sheingorn).

Richard K. Emmerson is Professor and Chair of English at Western Washington University. Interested in the intersection of medieval literature, art, and religion with modern theory, he has published on drama, illuminated manuscripts, and visionary poetry. His books include *Antichrist in the Middle Ages* (University of Washington Press, 1981); *Approaches to Teaching Medieval Drama* (MLA, 1990); *The Apocalyptic Imagination in Medieval Literature* (University of Pennsylvania Press, 1992), with Ronald Herzman; and *The Apocalypse in the Middle Ages* (Cornell University Press, 1993), with Bernard McGinn. With David Hult he has recently published a translation and commentary on the Old French play, *Jour Du Jugement* for the Early European Drama in Translation Series. He is currently working on a book-length project, *Medieval Literacies: Image, Language, and Ideology in Late Medieval Manuscripts*.

Marlene Clark teaches English at Lehman College (CUNY). She is currently at work on a project historicizing the life-cycle of mature medieval and Renaissance women represented in drama.

Sharon Kraus studied medieval drama at the City University of New York Graduate Center and is now doing research on theories of gender, the Middle English morality plays, and critical feminism in contemporary theory. Her book of poems, *Generation*, was published by Alice James Books in 1997.

Pamela Sheingorn, a Professor of History at Baruch College and the Graduate Center (CUNY), has written numerous articles on the relationship of medieval art and drama. She is the author of *The Easter Sepulchre in England* (1987) and co-editor with Kathleen Ashley of *Interpreting Cultural Symbols: Saint Anne in Late Medieval Society* (1990). She has edited and translated *The Book of Sainte Foy's Miracles* (University of Pennsylvania Press, 1995), and is currently co-authoring with Kathleen Ashley an interpretive study of the cult of Sainte Foy. She is co-organizer of the Medieval Feminist Art History Project and is engaged in a study of the constructions of gender and the body in medieval visual culture.

Seth Lerer is Professor of English and Comparative Literature at Stanford, where he is currently Chairman of the Department of Comparative Literature. His most recent publications include *Chaucer and His Readers* (Princeton University Press, 1993; paperback, 1996), and *Courtly Letters in the Age of Henry VIII* (Cambridge University Press, 1997).

John M. Ganim has authored *Style and Consciousness in Middle English Narrative* (Princeton University Press, 1983) and *Chaucerian Theatricality* (Princeton University Press, 1990). He is Professor of English, University of California at Riverside, where he is also the coordinator of the Focussed Research Project on Architecture, Urbanism, and Theory.

Alfred David is Professor of English Emeritus at Indiana University. He is the author of *The Strumpet Muse: Art and Morals in Chaucer's Poetry* (Indiana University Press, 1976), co-editor of *The Minor Poems* for the Chaucer Variorum (University of Oklahoma Press, 1982), editor of *The Romaunt of the Rose* for the Riverside Chaucer, and editor of the Middle Ages in *The Norton Anthology of English Literature*.

Richard Daniels, Associate Professor of English at Oregon State University, has published poetry and fiction as well as articles on Chaucer, Medieval drama, and literary and critical theory.

Warren Ginsberg is Professor of English at SUNY Albany. He is author of *The Cast of Character: the Representation of Personality in Ancient and Medieval Literature* (University of Toronto Press, 1983) and editor of *Ideas of Order in the Middle Ages* (SUNY Press, 1990). He has also edited *Wynnere and Wastoure and the Parlement of the Thre Ages* (Middle English Text Series, 1992). Forthcoming is a book titled *Dante's Aesthetics of Being* from University of Michigan Press.

Robert W. Hanning, Professor of English and Comparative Literature at Columbia University, has authored *The Vision of History in Early Britain* (Columbia University Press, 1966), *The Individual in Twelfth-Century Romance* (Yale University Press, 1977), and co-edited *Castiglione: the Ideal and the Real in Renaissance Culture* (Yale University Press, 1983). He has translated and co-edited, with Joan Ferrante, *The Lais of Marie de France* (Dutton, 1978). He is now completing a book on the subject of social game, rhetoric, and mediation in Chaucer's *Canterbury Tales*.

Peter W. Travis is Professor of English at Dartmouth College. He has published articles on the medieval drama, Chaucer, and medieval literary theory and is author of *Dramatic Design in the Chester Cycle* (University of

Chicago Press, 1982). He is at present working on a book about Chaucer's *Nun's Priest's Tale*.

William McClellan is Associate Professor of English at Baruch College (CUNY). He has published articles on medieval rhetoric, textual criticism, and cultural theory. He is completing a book entitled *The Griselda Complex: Chaucer's "Clerk's Tale" and the Dialogics of Power, Knowledge, and the Subjugation of Women in Late Medieval English Culture.*

About the Editors

James J. Paxson is Associate Professor of English at the University of Florida. He is the author of *The Poetics of Personification* (Cambridge University Press, 1994) and is working on a book about master tropes in critical theory and the social construction of the critical institution. He has co-edited *Desiring Discourse: The Literature of Love, Ovid Through Chaucer* with Cynthia Gravlee (Susquehanna University Press, 1998), and is Associate Editor of *Exemplaria: A Journal of Theory in Medieval and Renaissance Studies.*

Lawrence M. Clopper, Professor of English and Director of the Medieval Studies Institute at Indiana University, is the editor of the dramatic documents of Chester for the *Records of Early English Drama* and author of *"Songes of Rechelesnesse": Langland and the Franciscans* (University of Michigan Press, 1997). Currently, he is the President of the Medieval and Renaissance Drama Society and recently received a Guggenheim Fellowship for work on a book on medieval drama.

Sylvia Tomasch is Associate Professor of English at Hunter College (CUNY). She has published articles on Dante, Chaucer, *mappae mundi*, and the alliterative revival. She has co-edited a collection from the University of Pennsylvania Press entitled *Text and Territory: Geographical Imagination in the European Middle Ages*, and is completing a book on medieval geography, cartography, and literature.

FOREWORD

This volume came together as part of an effort to celebrate the retirement in 1994 of Martin Stevens, who served the City University of New York as Distinguished Professor of English as well as Dean of Baruch College. He also held positions at the State University of New York at Stony Brook, Ohio State University, and the University of Louisville, where he taught many, many students in courses ranging from the medieval through the modern. He has published books, dozens of articles, and edited editions of medieval poets and play cycles that now serve as standards in the field of medieval studies.

To honor so long and varied a career, three of his former students – Lawrence Clopper, Jim Paxson, and Sylvia Tomasch – planned to accordingly speak to the stages in his career, a career shaped by a wealth of interests and marked by fine achievements, by assembling a collection of thematically and methodologically interconnected essays. Martin Stevens has contributed to studies in linguistics, Old English, medieval Latin, Chaucer, the Middle English drama, Shakespeare, and critical theory; he has also written on pedagogy, the teaching of college writing, and medieval iconography. Capturing so broad and profound a contribution in an honorary, representative volume has no doubt been difficult, perhaps impossible. Yet the essays collected in *The Performance of Middle English Culture* would not have been possible without both the intellectual and the personal impetus of Martin Stevens. Many of the contributors to this volume call Martin a personal friend; all acknowledge the special influence his intellectual work has had on their own scholarly productions and humanistic thinking.

After bouts of severe illness, and after a permanent move from New York to San Francisco, Martin continues to be a productive writer and thinker – working on projects ranging from the theory of manuscript editing in a postmodern era to personal memoirs that will take in stride escape from the Holocaust, a brief and tumultuous life in Israel, emigration to the United States, and the long ascent in academic life. With his wife Rose Zimbardo – whom we also praise as a co-survivor, a paramount scholar of the Middle Ages and Renaissance, a friend, an excellent and loving human being – he has achieved the *lof* and *dom*, in our minds and hearts, of only the rare and elect.

Introduction

James J. Paxson

Chaucerian Theatricalities

The Performance of Middle English Culture takes as its subject the theatrically charged world of late medieval England. By "theatrical" I of course refer to the persistent Middle English mystery and morality plays as well as the lavish public spectacles that occasioned every religious feast or civic observance. But I also mean the theatrical and performative sense that seemed to saturate the poetical contributions of late medieval England, especially the work of Chaucer. The *Canterbury Tales* and *Troilus and Criseyde* hinge on metaphors and images, explicit and implicit, of stage-craft, public spectacle, and histrionic or dramatic characterization; they often find grounding in urban and civic ritual consciousness; and they centralize the mutually connected themes of social negotiation, play, parody, suasion, and mediation.[1] Chaucerian theatricality mirrors the literal theatricality of Ricardian public culture.

Although Chaucer studies and medieval drama studies have managed of late to make conceptual links between the traditional "literary" Chaucer and the popular world of urban spectacle (with an attempt to rethink history as prime conceptual operator),[2] these newly composed essays offer for the first time a sustained collective look at this important cultural

---

[1] By "dramatic" characterization, however, I do not wish to invoke the modern, anachronistic, and metaphorical sense of the term that has been attached to Chaucer criticism under the rubric of "dramatic theory" ever since George L. Kittredge made what were really a set of narratological pronouncements about the primacy of the narrative frame in *The Canterbury Tales*. For a good survey of this entrenched dramatic theory and its institutional heritage, see C. David Benson, *Chaucer's Drama of Style: Poetic Variety and Contrast in the "Canterbury Tales"* (Chapel Hill: University of North Carolina Press, 1986), 3–25. John Ganim, *Chaucerian Theatricality* (Princeton: Princeton University Press, 1990), provides one of the most comprehensive treatments of the theatrical macrometaphor in Chaucer.

[2] See for example Paul Strohm, *Hochon's Arrow: The Social Imagination of Fourteenth-Century Texts* (Princeton: Princeton University Press, 1992), 4 for another version of this methodological manifesto.

1

intersection. The institutionally sanctioned canon in the field of Middle English literary studies once cut off the works of the great masters like Chaucer or Gower from the popular matrix of ceremonial processions or feast-day biblical pageantry; but the field now recognizes and explores the cultural interdependence and interpenetrability of expressive forms dominant especially in fourteenth- or fifteenth-century England. From the present forward, one's writing "critically" about Chaucer and his elaborate textual metapoetics must mean addressing the performative social cosmos of late Ricardian royal procession or monarchical entry; one's researching the extant Corpus Christi plays will mean moving with dexterity between the professional or political processes of the provincial English municipalities and the codified texts that once seemed to fix (through the efforts of the great, authoritative editors such as Furnivall or Hardin Craig) what are now taken to be variable and contingent public performances. As a collective attempt to represent such fresh work now being done on the literature, drama, art, and social configurations of late medieval England, *The Performance of Middle English Culture* follows the historicist trails blazed by innovators like Paul Strohm or David Aers, while it incorporates a range of anthropological thinking on ritual, theater, and the pervasive cultural macrometaphor of performance.

Medieval Performativities

Although this volume treats late medieval forms, the theorization of medieval cultural performativity has been spurred by the study of technical and latinate (rather than literary or vernacular) materials from the *early* Middle Ages. Much contemporary work on medieval grammatical or scholastic culture continues to assert, ever more strongly, that the semiotic and ideological constitutions of that culture, although *textual* in documentary form, cohere as *performative* realities. These two qualities – the textual and the performative – had long been taken in traditional medieval studies as mutually exclusive opposites or antinomies; they had joined the battery of binarisms traceable in part to Chaucer's philosophical pronouncements themselves and to modern categories of analysis as well: included here are hieratic vs. demotic, learned vs. *lewed*, authoritative vs. experiential, humanistic vs. popular, written vs. oral, and so on. But it has been shown that medieval "culture" germinates as a self-constituting, performed social process that is interdependent with textual (i.e. grammatical and rhetorical) modes of cognition. Medieval culture's social institutions are not prior or posterior to, or phenomenologically distinct from, the universe of prescriptive textuality. Martin Irvine's monumental study *The Making of Textual Culture* makes this case for official, didactic, or hieratic textual canons and communities: the *grammatica* brought into being the selfsame literate culture it proposed to serve or enable or describe. In accord with the Foucauldian sense of ideological formation, it was not just *prescriptive* of that encoded culture, nor just reflective of it. Rather, the *grammatica* was *constitutive* of medieval culture on all levels.[3]

This performative phenomenology of cultural production, in which idealized structural rules, textual documents, and public or popular expressions call one another into being while they are used or "uttered" by a people or culture, demonstrates how the term "performativity" has come a long way from its original use by J. L. Austin who, nearly forty years ago, proffered it in his revolutionary speech-act theory.[4] All utterances have ideological depth in that they are social acts. *The Performance of Middle English Culture* thus draws on this conceptual tradition as it collates and energizes two concepts of medieval performance – the histrionic and the ideologically constitutive. It treats each term's denotation, each's definition, as a metaphorical version of the other's: the literal performance or performative of the medieval stage becomes as constitutive as the figural performance of the *grammatica*, while both corollary versions or concepts find realization, again literally and figurally, in the exemplary production of Chaucer's poetics.

In this way, our volume also reveals a source of inspiration in an important essay published by Martin Stevens – to whom we dedicate *The Performance of Middle English Culture* – two decades ago titled "The Performing Self in Twelfth-Century Culture." The essay stakes the claims for the anthropologically resonant, performance-based model of scholastic cultural production now on the ascendancy in contemporary thinking.[5] It is a model that Stevens has sustained and nourished in recent years regarding his work on the creation of the Ellesmere manuscript or the Wakefield plays; and it is a model that has impelled the publication of at least one other innovative collection, guided by Stevens's hand, that treats an anthropologically reconstituted native English drama in the late Middle Ages and early modern era.[6]

In general, the pieces collected in this volume, which embody the drive to keep theorizing the Middle Ages, make a performative or institutional statement of their own. As Lee Patterson has argued in *Negotiating the Past*, the construction of "medieval studies" – as a domain of professional,

---

[3] Martin Irvine, *The Making of Textual Culture: 'Grammatica' and Literary Theory, 350–1100* (Cambridge: Cambridge University Press, 1994), 1–2, 15–17.
[4] J. L. Austin, *How To Do Things With Words* (Cambridge: Cambridge University Press, 1962).
[5] Martin Stevens, "The Performing Self in Twelfth-Century Culture," *Viator* 9 (1978): 193–218.
[6] See the recent issue of *Mediaevalia: A Journal of Medieval Studies* 18 (1995, for 1992), which is guest edited by Stevens and Milla Riggio and bears the subtitle *Drama in the Middle Ages and Early Renaissance: Reconsiderations*.

systematic inquiry with its focus on the hermeneutic articulation of canonical literary texts – has always involved a conservative drive towards
stability, nostalgia, and institutional compartmentalization.[7] That is to
say, medievalists have been as guilty as their fellow scholars in Classical,
Renaissance, or Modern studies for segregating or "ghettoing" both the
historical Middle Ages and the professional study of it. The mystique of
Latin mastery endemic to medieval studies, the certitude of philological
positivism (crystallized in the nineteenth-century European university), and
the adoption of an until-recently solidified canon of great writers (the
Fathers, the Scholastics, Dante, Chaucer, Chrétien, and so forth), have
coalesced to produce a conservative and self-circumscribing professional
field. Medieval studies comprises its own clerisy. The overcoming of this
institutional segregationalism is an ongoing effort, one directed not just at
non-medievalists but at conservative or recalcitrant persons inside the field.
The current retreat from theory (or the embracing of our present era of
"post-theory") makes for an odd turn of plot in the story of a field that had
for so long ignored or belittled theory; medieval studies among all fields of
literary or cultural study most heavily incurred what de Man decried as an
institutional resistance to theory.[8] Our recognition that this resistance is
itself a performance helps promote the vitality of theory in medieval studies
as well as the topical value of performativity's many metaphorical and
literal manifestations in the objects we study. Theory can serve medieval
studies, but only with keen regard for historical documentary substance – a
fusion all the essays in this volume insist on.

Chaucer and the Drama: Texts and Topics

The Performance of Middle English Culture takes off by following the
canonical bipartisanism that characterizes Middle English literary studies:
Chaucer, like Shakespeare, represents what Harold Bloom thinks of as the
indisputable "cognitive center of gravity" in the Western canon,[9] while the
Middle English mystery plays have attained, only in the last two or three
decades (through the promotional work of scholars like Arnold Williams,
Rosemary Woolf, Martin Stevens, and Glynne Wickham), increased measure as "cultural capital" in the academic process of canon-formation.[10] In

---

[7] Lee Patterson, *Negotiating the Past: The Historical Understanding of Medieval
Literature* (Madison: University of Wisconsin Press, 1987), esp. chapter 1.
[8] Paul de Man, *The Resistance to Theory* (Minneapolis: University of Minnesota Press,
1986), 3–20.
[9] Harold Bloom, *The Western Canon: The Books and School of the Ages* (New York:
Harcourt, Brace and Company, 1994), 45–75, 105–126.
[10] See John Guillory, *Cultural Capital: The Problem of Literary Canon Formation*
(Chicago and London: University of Chicago Press, 1993), passim, for Guillory's

vulgar terms, there's always been Chaucer and everything else. Although the volume divides into two broad areas – medieval drama studies and Chaucer studies – its segments promote the synthesis I promised above by comprising a shaded spectrum of topical categories. These categories include (1) new theoretical appraisal of prime problems in medieval drama studies with special attention to the issue of gender in a generically representative morality play; (2) the blending, as it were, of Chaucerian poetic issues and theatrical or dramaturgical ones (here the synthetic mission of this volume unfolds directly); (3) ludic issues in the historical, social, and rhetorical worlds of Chaucer's major texts and their sources; and (4) the multicultural response to the canonical Chaucer.

The foregoing categories thereby address late Middle English performativity which is taken up directly in individual essays. Kathleen Ashley's "Sponsorship, Reflexivity and Resistance: A Cultural Reading of the York Cycle Plays" particularizes the synthetic project of *The Performance of Middle English Culture* and as such serves as the volume's ideal opening piece. Ashley demonstrates how the York Plays, in a "multiply reflexive manner," involve a variety of producers, audiences, and social functions in a cultural structure far more complex than prior critical or historical models had allowed. Richard K. Emmerson's "Eliding the 'Medieval': Renaissance New Historicism' and Sixteenth-Century Cycle Plays" takes a step further back in inspecting the theoretical assumptions implicit in the study of medieval drama. He erects a sound cultural-poetical critique of New Historicism's segregation of the medieval drama in particular. Taking the lead from Lee Patterson's now indispensable institutional analysis of this general state of affairs, Emmerson suggests ways for revising our institutional configuration that has, until now, so marginalized important cultural products like the Corpus Christi cycles.

These two pieces – which take up the problem of how to theorize the material production as well as the historical circumscription of dramatical texts – are complemented by examinations of specific plays. In the essay " 'Se in what stat thou doyst indwell': The Shifting Constructions of Gender and Power Relations in *Wisdom*," Marlene Clark, Sharon Kraus, and Pamela Sheingorn explore the problem of gendered personification in terms of the play's historicized imaging of gender and power. Histrionic imaging, the rhetorical constitution of personified characters (central to morality play poetics), and female/male power relations exist via their mutual constructedness – that is, via the way the text performs them, the authors contend. The authority of allegory long seen to stand as the monolithic frame for the moralities finds challenge in this play about the disruptions of theatricalized gender.

sociologically-based theory, drawn from Pierre Bourdieu, concerning the "monetary" rise and fall of the main canonical texts in Western academic culture.

The city itself, *platea* or histrionic setting par excellence, figures prominently in late Middle English culture, and the interdependence of Chaucerian (meta)poetics and the discursive metaphorics of theatricality or populous habitation organize Seth Lerer's "The Chaucerian Critique of Medieval Theatricality." This study shows how the theatrical imagery of Nicholas' farcical plot in the *Miller's Tale* and of Theseus' staged solemnities in the *Knight's Tale* reflects contemporaneous suspicions about the power and pervasiveness of histrionic artifice in Ricardian lists and dedicatory pageants. Chaucer's tales inscribe the poetics of public spectacle constitutive of urban society.

The historical importance of urban society, which looms large in Lerer's essay, furnishes an exclusive theme in John Ganim's "The Experience of Modernity in Late Medieval Literature Urbanism: Experience and Rhetoric in Some Early Descriptions of London." Readings of William Fitz Stephen's *Descriptio* of twelfth-century London and of John Stow's sixteenth-century *Survey of London* prompt Ganim to ascribe a "modernist" ideology to the Middle English construction of the Urban. Such an ideological configuration turns out to be programmatic in the generation of texts like Chaucer's *General Prologue*.

The poetics of urban space worked out by Ganim and central to subsequent speculation on the public religious drama and on Chaucer represents a further secularization of late medieval hermeneutical theorization while it maintains an intimate link between Chaucer's brand of poetics and the social world of public drama and common entertainments. On anti-secular footing stands Alfred David's re-examination of typology and theatrical imagery in "Noah's Wife's Flood." David sifts iconographic materials in order to further evaluate the typological role of the quarrelsome wife referred to in Nicholas's mock-theatrics in the *Miller's Tale*. And if the poetic structures of traditional typology power up the Noahic subtext of the *Miller's Tale* for David, the semiotics of language's indulgent free play – especially as it has been theorized by Roland Barthes – inform Chaucer's great fabliau, according to Richard Daniels's "Textual Pleasure in *The Miller's Tale*." Daniels begins by providing a comparative reading of analogs to the Tale, and he then shows how excessive and radical departure from analogs affords Chaucer a strange, new work – one that is aesthetically innovative and filled with the startling *jouissance* or linguistic *plaisir* described by Barthes.

Theorization about such innovative departure from sources invests additional pieces, contributed by Warren Ginsberg, Robert W. Hanning, and Peter Travis, that treat other *Canterbury Tales* and *Troilus and Criseyde*. Ginsberg's "Petrarch, Chaucer and the Making of the Clerk" discusses, at times in terms of Bakhtinian dialogism, the various "competing discourses" that are drawn from Petrarchan romance lyric and humanistic writing only to be negotiated and reshaped by Chaucer. Hanning centralizes the theme of mediation itself – a theme that underwrites medieval theories of translation,

6

text transmission, cultural imitation, and personal social interaction – in his essay, "The Crisis of Mediation in Chaucer's *Troilus and Criseyde*." By juxtaposing materials including Chaucer, Boccaccio, John Trevisa (his *Dialogus inter dominum et clericum*), and Juan Ruiz (the *Buen Amor*), Hanning contextualizes the primary character relationships in the *Troilus* (with the Narrator and Pandarus serving as the main mediational figures) in terms of the concurrent historical problem of mediation in the fourteenth century, particularly as it was manifested in the crisis of clerical or sacerdotal "representation." And Peter Travis rethinks the inexhaustible subject of Chaucerian metapoetics along with the narratorial manipulation of pretextual, exemplary source materials in the *Nun's Priest's Tale*. His essay, "Reading Chaucer *Ab Ovo*: Mock-*Exemplum* in the *Nun's Priest's Tale*," argues for the *exemplum*'s constitutive centrality in the performative making of the Priest's astonishing narrative and of the *Canterbury Tales* overall – a productive critical motion that surpasses akin discussions of the Chaucerian "mock *exemplum*."[11]

These studies of medieval performativity, built upon the social semiotics of mediation, play, and exemplarity, point us to the performative situatedness of contemporary Chaucerian scholars themselves. The volume's final essay, "A Postmodern Performance: Counter-Reading Chaucer's *Clerk's Tale* and Maxine Hong Kingston's 'No Name Woman'," by William McClellan, explores the prospects of Chaucer being "counter-read" against the literary products of cultural others in the 1990s (like Maxine Hong Kingston) while it contextualizes the life of the contemporary Chaucerian scholar in terms of his or her circumscribing institutional or social environment. Through his or her activity, the scholar exists, like the Chaucerian narrator or the urban subject of the late fourteenth century, as a performative entity, an intersection of fashioned text and sociosphere. McClellan uses autobiographical meditation juxtaposed with the theories of Gianni Vattimo on postmodernity and the personal in order to better illuminate Chaucer's strange narrative of privation.

The Performance of Middle English Culture incorporates or responds to the latest advances in metapoetic or self-reflexive critical formalism, in anthropologically oriented critical historicism, in the poetics of gender and embodiment, and in the increasing interdisciplinarity (partial to iconography as well as to sociology) now well entrenched in medieval and Renaissance studies. Its essays work from a number of angles to clarify our view of two previously separated late medieval worlds, the poetic and the theatrical, and in so doing it promotes stronger institutional and theoretical self-awareness in the cultural study of the Middle Ages.

---

[11] See for instance Larry Scanlon, *Narrative, Authority, Power: the Medieval Exemplum and the Chaucerian Tradition* (Cambridge and New York: Cambridge University Press, 1994), especially 229–44.

Sponsorship, Reflexivity and Resistance: Cultural Readings of the York Cycle Plays*

Kathleen Ashley

This essay does not offer a single cultural reading, but "cultural read-ings," an exploration of the various ways that cultural theory can open up medieval dramatic texts to new kinds of scrutiny. By using the term "cultural"[1] I mean to signal that the plays will be regarded as performances with social implications rather than as purely literary texts or as moments in a narrow history of the theater. It implies that such cultural performances have socio-economic, political, and institutional functions but I would add it also implies that we cannot reduce the plays simply to such functions; in talking about the drama as cultural performance, we must also attend to aesthetic and semiotic modalities – not just *what* they do but *how* they do it.

As a way of focusing this rather large topic, the essay will explore the idea of the plays' sponsorship because it in turn involves both social production and social reception. In contradistinction to several current and past readings of production and reception of the plays, I will argue that both are multiply sited. Such cultural performances as York cycle do not have one producer or audience or one social function but are so situated as to require the involvement of many kinds of producers, elicit many kinds of responses, and serve a variety of social needs. They are able to do this in part because they are fundamentally *reflexive*: referential of themselves as plays being performed, of their city and their craft guilds, and of social norms and institutions. I see evidence for this reflexivity both in the play texts and in the performative frames of civic festival.

* The first version of this essay was given as the Inaugural Helen Ann Robbins Lecture at the University of Rochester in December 1993. I wish to acknowledge the invitation by Russell Peck, and helpful response by Tom Hahn. Crucial assistance in preparing this version of the essay has been ably and patiently provided by Michael Mulhall, Administrative Assistant in the English Department at the University of Southern Maine.

[1] The term "cultural" has come under much scrutiny itself recently. For an example, see Daniel Cottom, "Ethnographia Mundi," in his *Text and Culture: The Politics of Interpretation* (Minneapolis: University of Minnesota Press, 1989), pp. 49–102.

The effect of my cultural readings will be to problematize, though not totally disrupt, causal links that have sometimes been posited between the play and its social effects, or between producers and audience responses. I hope to suggest that using terms like "hegemonic ideology" or "popular resistance" is far too reductive. This may sound like a weak version of cultural theory but I will argue that it offers a more powerful model for understanding cultural performances like these plays which were – in ways we have recognized but had difficulty articulating – so central to urban cultures of the late Middle Ages.

Producers

Because of the "religious" content of surviving play texts from York and elsewhere in England, many early drama critics discussed the plays as if they were produced by ecclesiastical sponsors who used the drama for the religious education of the laity. Given the anti-clerical biases of many of these early drama scholars, their appreciation for the plays was consequently rather limited. Even where they were not hostile to the religious content, the critics' view that the plays were popularizing vehicles produced by a clerical elite for the masses discouraged reading for subtlety or complexity. Hardin Craig is perfectly typical when he writes that

> Indeed, the religious drama had no dramatic technique or dramatic purpose, and no artistic self-consciousness. Its life-blood was religion, and its success depended on its awakening and releasing a pent-up body of religious knowledge and religious feeling. . . . When it succeeded, its success came from the import of its message or from the moving quality of some particular story it had to tell.[2]

More recent work on the York records by Alexandra Johnston and others has shown very clearly that the major sponsors of the York plays were not clerics at all but the town government, which annually decided *whether* the "Corpus Christi play" would be performed, and *when* and *where*, and administered the overall control.[3] Records of Early English Drama (REED) research also shows that ecclesiastical authorities came into conflict with the secular authorities about which ritual performance would take precedence – the Corpus Christi procession, sponsored by the church, or the plays, sponsored by the town – since both were scheduled on the same day and virtually on the same route through York. Evidence suggests

[2] Hardin Craig, *English Religious Drama of the Middle Ages* (Oxford: Oxford University Press, 1955), pp. 4–5, 9.

[3] Alexandra F. Johnston, "The Guild of Corpus Christi and the Processions of Corpus Christi in York," *Medieval Studies* 38 (1976): 372–84.

that civic authority was more powerful since eventually the plays won out over the procession for the date and urban space. However, clerics remained involved in the productions, either as playwrights or as directors hired by the producer craft guild, so that one could say clerical sponsorship of a kind continued, even if it was subordinated to lay control.

During the 1980s, cultural historians of the late medieval town like Charles Phythian-Adams developed a fuller sense of sponsorship, which included the complex relations between the town council of the governing oligarchy and other socio-economic institutions like religious and craft guilds. Civic records of dramatic performance were interpreted as revealing how integral to the fabric of urban society these plays were; the festive and the religious were seen to have a total social role so that the sponsor of the plays might be said to be the "community."[4] Within *this* paradigm, there was little conflict that could not be mediated by the cycle's performance structure. Mervyn James, for example, argues that the production of the cycle play enabled the guilds to shift fortunes over time with minimal conflict, creating unity out of diversity. The plays' sponsorship was communal, and the image of the community was of an integrated organism.[5]

Most recently, new forms of cultural theorizing have disrupted the model whereby the medieval drama was in some positive and holistic way good for the society. The Marxist bent of much contemporary cultural studies, in particular, makes class differentiation a crucial component of any analysis of social power. According to such arguments, the town oligarchy is an oppressive elite which used the plays to disempower the artisan class. Medieval festive performances were mechanisms through which these elites voiced their ideologies and exercised their power, presumably complicit with clerical authorities. The audience for the drama was not the ignorant laity (as it was when the producers were believed to be ecclesiastical), but rather the lower classes. In general, however, the plays are portrayed as reluctantly as they were by critics who believed the church was the principle sponsor, since they are seen to enforce the values of their producers. Work based on these Marxist assumptions tends therefore to concentrate on the audience, the only possible site of resistance to elite hegemony as Claire Sponsler has argued in "The Culture of the Spectator: Conformity and Resistance to Medieval Performances."[6]

---

[4] Charles Phythian-Adams, "Ceremony and the Citizen: The Communal Year at Coventry, 1450–1550," in *Crisis and Order in English Towns, 1500–1700: Essays in Urban History*, ed. Peter Clark and Paul Slack (London: Routledge and Kegan Paul, 1972), pp. 57–85.

[5] Mervyn James, "Ritual, Drama and Social Body in the Late Medieval Town," *Past and Present* 98 (1983): 3–29.

[6] Claire Sponsler, "The Culture of the Spectator: Conformity and Resistance to Medieval Performances," *Theatre Journal* 44 (1992): 15–29.

As my all too cursory review of the plays' critical history makes clear, each of the preceding paradigms has assumed that the plays themselves articulate the ideology of their producers, which is forcefully if not exploitatively performed for some unresisting mass audience. The causal links between producer, dramatic product, and social effect are pictured as relatively uncomplicated and predictable: the dominant sponsor produces a hegemonic text which in turn produces certain effects in its (undifferentiated) audience. Obviously, I have used broad strokes in my portrait of other interpretations of the medieval drama, but I believe my exaggerations are not fundamentally inaccurate. What I would like to turn to now is a more nuanced argument about how we might discuss the sponsorship of the plays, their social roles, and their possible audience responses.

Play Texts

Such a nuanced cultural reading will need, in the first place, to take the surviving play texts seriously as evidence for sponsorship. Each of the three moments in the history of medieval drama criticism I just sketched found it difficult to deal with the plays themselves in any depth. Indeed, the only critical school to read the texts with any appreciation for their complexity was, predictably, the new critics of the 1960s and 1970s; however, they treated the plays as *literary* texts to be related to other written texts of theology and spirituality and did not attempt to relate the plays to social, political, or economic practices.

Rereading the surviving dramatic texts with an awareness of their situatedness as cultural performances should permit us to become more aware of their ideological multilayeredness. Just as social formations are usually complex and even contradictory, so too as verbal artifacts the plays are riven with mixed messages, incompatible world views and multiple voices. They do not express monolithic ideologies in coherent packages but are often unstable discursive and symbolic formations, neither under the control of their civic producers nor completely coercive of their audiences' responses.

To argue for ideological multilayeredness is not, however, to say that the plays have no sustained dramatic focus or no perceptible relation to performance circumstances. In the case of the York cycle, where abundant records of production as well as the cycle text survive, we can reread the plays for their culturally performative roles. I will begin with a fairly obvious example that has been discussed at some length by Martin Stevens in *Four Middle English Mystery Cycles*. As he notes, the Skinners' pageant of Jesus' Entry into Jerusalem – play 25 out of York's 48 – is the most developed Entry play in medieval drama and it may be seen as "the ultimate York play" in celebrating York's corporate identity and mirroring the city to

12

itself: "When Jesus enters Jerusalem, he enters York."[7] The play imitates a royal entry ceremony, a "highly developed genre of civic procession in York," as Stevens points out.[8] Moreover, as Pamela Tudor-Craig has noted, the York Corpus Christi play wagons followed the route of royal entries, so that a blurring of the boundary between the dramatic fiction of entry and the historical experience of entry would seem inevitable.[9] However, a comparison between one historical record of a royal entry and the play of Christ's Entry certainly complicates notions of "mirroring" between play and civic event, and it is precisely the issue of where sponsoring power rests that differentiates biblical play from historical record.

When King Henry, for example, announced his intention of visiting York at the end of July, 1487, the civic oligarchy made plans to greet the king outside the town gates, at the limits of its jurisdiction, and to escort the king into the city in procession. The recorded speech of welcome says, "The Mayor, aldermen, sheriffs and commune council with the whole body of this City as your true and faithful subjects welcome your most noble grace unto this city." Within the "barre of Mikilgate" on either side of the street the "communaltye" of every craft will stand in their best array along the processional route, "without any staffes bering, With due obeysaunce making unto the king his grace and crying of 'King Henry.' "[10] The record further notes that "the play of corpus christi by the kinges Commaundement Was played thrugh the Citie and his grace hering the same in Conyngstrete at Thomas Scot house."[11] Entertainments also included the beheading of a Roger Layton for treason (a crime against the king) upon the Pavement – the broad street in front of All Saints Church that functioned as a civic site for display of criminals, a market, and the end of the pageant route.[12] A second man scheduled to be beheaded was pardoned by the king (in a show of grace no doubt publicly performed as well).

According to these civic records, initiative for the performance of the plays comes from the king, and the obligatory but prominent political role of the town notables in responding to royal command is foregrounded in the detailed descriptions of ceremonial dress and processional movement of the civic elites. The craft guild members are reduced in this historical

---

[7] Martin Stevens, *Four Middle English Mystery Cycles: Textual, Contextual, and Critical Interpretations* (Princeton: Princeton University Press, 1987), p. 51.

[8] Stevens, p. 51.

[9] Pamela Tudor-Craig, "Richard III's triumphant entry into York, August 29th, 1483," in *Richard III and the North*, ed. R. Horrox, Studies in Regional and Local History 6 (Hull: University of Hull Centre for Regional and Local History, 1986), pp. 108–16.

[10] Alexandra F. Johnston and Margaret Rogerson, eds., *Records of Early English Drama: York*, vol. 1 (Toronto: University of Toronto Press, 1979), p. 154.

[11] *York Records*, vol. 1, p. 155.

[12] Eileen White, "Places for Hearing the Corpus Christi Play in York," *Medieval English Theatre* 9 (1987): 24.

account of the royal entry to mere street show, an undifferentiated mass of loyal subjects (the "communaltye"), choreographed to bow and cry out to the king at the behest of their betters. The performance of the York cycle joins the beheading and the processional decorum in displaying the city's political subjection – so that one *could* see this as a account of royal hegemony and even royal sponsorship of the plays. York's governing elites co-operated, although their allegiances were probably still to Richard III.[13] The explicit instruction that guild members were not to "bear staffs" – presumably to discourage violence and street fighting – suggests a level of social *coercion* rather than any internalizing of the city's political agenda by the ordinary craftsman. We do not see a truly "communal" involvement in this account, but elite control under royal command.

Turning to the York Entry play text, however, we gain an entirely different perspective – that of the citizen, who *is* wholehearted in his response to the entry of Christ the King into his city, and who is presented as orchestrating the town celebrations. In the cycle, the town elites are dramatized by a large group of "citezens" identified as "burgensis." These townsfolk discuss Jesus' healings, his preaching, and his claims to be the king prophesied. Burgenses number seven concludes this initial debate:

> Sirs, methynketh ȝe saie right wele
> And gud ensampelys furth ȝe bryng.
> And sen we þus þis mater fele
> Go we hym meete as oure owne kyng,
> And kyng hym call.
> What is youre counsaill in this thyng?
> Now say ȝe all.   (lines 169–175)[14]

The emphasis on group unanimity is striking, and when the group asks the porter or janitor for more information about the coming of Jesus, he tells them that he has lent Jesus "our common asse" for the entry ride. Richard Beadle's headnote to this episode in his modern spelling edition interprets the "common" as "for the use of the poorest in the medieval community,"[15] but it seems to me likely that the playwright emphasizes the animal as common property, a sign of the whole community's welcome of him.

Beadle also comments that there "seems to be no obvious connection between the content or presentation of the play and the daily activity of the Skinners, who dressed animal skins, pelts and furs,"[16] and are named as the

---

[13] See Stevens, p. 54.

[14] Citations are from Richard Beadle, ed., *The York Plays* (London: Edward Arnold, 1982).

[15] Richard Beadle and Pamela M. King, eds., *York Mystery Plays: A Selection in Modern Spelling* (Oxford: Clarendon Press, 1984), p. 106.

[16] *York Mystery Plays*, p. 106.

play's craft producers. However, Stevens more accurately notes that trade symbolism is a prominent feature of the play, since the Skinners were makers of furred garments (particularly associated with the making of civic ceremonial costumes) and therefore they were the appropriate producers of a play which dramatizes civic procession. Presumably the "actors playing the Aldermen were splendidly bedecked for their procession." Thus, the Skinners "obtrude prominently upon their own performance."[17] Through costume, the guild differentiates itself from the common mass of guildsmen and also from the undifferentiated group of civic elites.

In addition to flatteringly portraying citizen reaction to the entry of Jesus, and thus suggesting a wholehearted (and not just strategic) *civic* sponsorship of the event, the play publicizes the involvement in production of the Skinners' guild in particular. York's dramatic self-representation thus points to double sponsorship by town and guild. Based on the records, Alexandra Johnston makes a case for seeing the York cycle text as controlled by the guilds, not by the city council which nevertheless ordered a master copy (the "register") of the cycle in the 1460s or 1470s, initiated the overall performance each year, and adjudicated disputes between guild pageant producers.[18] I'd argue that it's not necessary to posit *one* sponsor, but rather to see both the city council and the craft guilds as co-producers of the plays in a complexly differentiated and highly significant cultural activity.

Such self-reference on the part of the Skinners' guild is *reflexivity*, which I see as a crucial mechanism by which the cycle plays functioned semiotically. The most extended discussion of the term "reflexivity" as it is used by philosophers, linguists, and social scientists has been made by Barbara Babcock, who defines it as "the capacity of language and of thought – of any system of signification – to turn or bend back upon itself, to become an object to itself, and refer to itself."[19] As she also points out:

> Statements by a member of a class about its own class tend to paradox. By confounding subject and object, seer and seen, self and other, art and life – in short, by playing back and forth across terminal and categorical boundaries and playing with the very nature of human understanding – reflexive processes redirect thoughtful attention to the faulty or limited structures of thought, language, and society.[20]

Clearly, in the Entry play of York, the dramatic text turns biblical characters into York citizens, the other into the self, though one might

---

[17] Stevens, p. 60.
[18] Alexandra F. Johnston, "The York Cycle and the Chester Cycle: What do the records tell us?" in A. F. Johnston, ed., *Editing Early English Drama* (New York: AMS Press, 1987), p. 128.
[19] Barbara Babcock, "Reflexivity: Definitions and Discriminations," *Semiotica* 30 (1980): 2.
[20] Babcock, "Reflexivity: Definitions and Discriminations," p. 5.

argue that in this play the self-reference is mainly celebratory and self-congratulatory, a flattering mirror of the city of York rather than a spotlight on the "limited structures" of this civic society.

Reflexivity can, however, be more interesting than simply self-reference or self-promotion, which most drama critics have seen in the plays. There has been a fair amount of attention to what is called the "trade symbolism" of the plays – an identity between the biblical episode and the guild producing a play.[21] The Bakers were given the Last Supper play at York and at Chester presumably because of what Mervyn James calls a "symbolic affinity" between the guild bread-baking activities and the bread broken in the eucharistic scene.[22] The Waterdrawers of the River Dee in Chester presented Noah's Flood while the Shipwrights had the Building of the Ark at York. Likewise, in York, Beverley, Newcastle and Norwich the Adoration of the (gold-bearing) Magi was assigned to the Goldsmiths' guild. Such a relationship between the craft and its play has been seen at the very least as an advertisement for the guild's goods or services (a kind of "trade propaganda") or – more positively – as a symbolic association which might have ritual efficacy by effecting a real "transfer of grace" to performers and producers, as Homan has argued.[23]

What I will call reflexivity, however, can entail a cognitive stance close to irony in its awareness of the limitations of a group's ideologies and practices, as Babcock suggests.[24] Within various York plays a range of attitudes toward York government and craft identity are explored, including both positive affirmations and negative possibilities. The plays' reflexivity thus exemplifies a common stance in game or play generally which, given their premises of make-believe, are media ideally suited to question or comment upon "the routine postulates of other realities," Don Handelman has noted. The "messages of play . . . take apart the clock-works of reality, and question their organization, and indeed their very validity as human and as cultural constructs. . . .Within play, the self-as-subject can regard itself and others as object."[25] Victor Turner too regards all performative

[21] See Alan D. Justice, "Trade Symbolism in the York Cycle," *Theatre Journal* 31 (1979): 47–58. Lucy Toulmin-Smith, along with other early editors of the plays, noted "a sense of appropriate calling in the occupations to the subject of the particular play assigned to each craft." Lucy Toulmin-Smith, ed., *The York Plays* (New York: Russell and Russell; reissued 1963), pp. xliii–xliv.

[22] James, p. 20.

[23] Richard Homan, "Ritual Aspects of the York Cycle," *Theatre Journal* 33 (1981): 314–15.

[24] See also Babcock's "Reflexivity" in Mircea Eliade, ed., *The Encyclopedia of Religion*, vol. 16 (New York: MacMillan, 1987).

[25] Don Handelman, "Reflexivity in Festival and Other Cultural Events," in Mary Douglas, ed., *Essays in the Sociology of Perception* (London: Routledge and Kegan Paul, 1982), p. 163.

genres such as ritual, ceremonial, carnival, festival, games, spectacles and sports as constituting "a set of meta-languages whereby a group or community not merely expresses itself but, more actively, tries to understand itself in order to change itself."[26] Geertz interprets his famous cockfight not as functionalist (reinforcing status discriminations) but as "metasocial commentary"; collective symbolic structures are not primarily "social mechanics," he says, but social "semantics" – a story a society tells about itself.[27] Although Geertz refuses to privilege the cockfight as "the" story for Balinese society, he shares with Turner and other symbolic anthropologists a tendency to see such reflexivity of cultural performances in benign or positive terms.

However, within the York cycle, there is a striking amount of reflexivity that cannot be described as innocuous, for it seems to critique the very values other parts of the play or cycle celebrate. In the Nativity play assigned to the Tilethatchers, for example, Joseph calls attention to the rain coming in through holes in the roof, which is presumably a thatched roof. Can this really be considered propaganda for the thatchers' guild? There was an iconographic and theological basis for the holes in the roof,[28] yet surely the ironic connection with the sponsoring craft was obvious. Similarly, to return to the Entry play with its model citizens hailing his coming, Jesus does not celebrate the city he enters but laments its fickleness: "I murne, I sigh, I wepe also / Jerusalem on the to loke. / And so may thou rewe that evere thou thi king forsuke / And was untrewe" (lines 470–74). His condemnatory speech, biblically authorized though it might be, is at odds tonally with the rest of the play, which portrays happy burgesses chanting "Hail" verses in aureate style from the moment Jesus stops prophesying to the end of the play. As they experiment with self-reference, both plays appear to retain multiple and even somewhat contradictory messages.

An even more contradictory play, semiotically, is *Christ Before Pilate I: The Dream of Pilate's Wife* where Pilate and his wife Percula are presented as decadent aristocrats, surrounded by luxury, and gently handled in contrast to the deprivations and rough handling of Christ. The language used to characterize them in the first part of the play is drawn from

---

[26] Victor Turner, *The Ritual Process: Structure and Anti-Structure* (Ithaca: Cornell University Press, 1977; first published 1969), p. 337.

[27] Clifford Geertz, "Deep Play: Notes on the Balinese Cockfight," *The Interpretation of Cultures* (New York: Basic Books, 1973), p. 448.

[28] As signifying the fallen world into which the redeemer was being born. Panofsky comments on the use of images of intactness vs. ruination to express the antithesis of Christianity and Judaism in the fourteenth through sixteenth centuries. In the fifteenth century, the symbolic ruin was common in Nativity and Adoration of the Magi scenes. See Erwin Panofsky, *Early Netherlandish Painting*, vol. 1 (Cambridge: Harvard University Press, 1953), pp. 135–39.

descriptions of the sins of lechery, gluttony and sloth, as well as pride. Thus, Pilate first boasts of their noble ancestry, and he and Percula conduct rituals of greeting and farewell, drinking and lovemaking as well as settling into their soft, coverlet-piled beds which mark them as effete and sinful. Rosemary Woolf urges that these scenes of courtly life be interpreted as moral *exempla*, for they establish Pilate and Percula as "an arrogant and luxurious couple."[29] The contrast with the humility and physical suffering of Christ is dramatic and obviously intentional on the part of the playwright, perhaps "the York Realist."[30]

As thus interpreted, one would assume that audience members must condemn these characters, for no other reception makes sense; however, this moral judgment is interestingly undercut by another dimension of the play – its production by the Tapiters' and Couchers' guilds that made upholstery, tapestries, and coverlets. Those guild wares would certainly have figured prominently in the staging of the bedtime scenes in *The Dream of Pilate's Wife* play, so that the courtly decor would take on a positive role as advertising for the sponsoring guild and as object of desire for upwardly mobile citizens. There is an undeniable contradiction between the negative valence such products must have within the drama of Christ's Passion and their social desirability for the bourgeois members of the audience. The Tapiters' and Couchers' guilds could be said to sponsor both meanings simultaneously, and both were available to an audience member watching the play. It is difficult to say in this case whether the disparity in interpretive possibilities is simply a matter of unreconciled messages or whether there might be some deliberate critique of the craft and its work through the visual and verbal signs.

York's particular emphasis on the theme of work has been noted, most recently by Sarah Beckwith.[31] In its dramatization of salvation history, York foregrounds the importance of work, or "deeds." Throughout the first seven plays of the cycle, which depict the Creation of the world and falls of Lucifer, Adam, Eve and Cain, God establishes the importance of work by describing himself as a perfectionist master craftsman, continually seeking recognition for his accomplishments. Without going into detail here, I would argue that the first seven plays of the York cycle articulate a theology of labor, which poses a frightening question for man; as Adam asks in the long and unique lamentation of the Expulsion play after his fall,

[29] Rosemary Woolf, *The English Mystery Plays* (Berkeley: University of California Press, 1972), p. 245.

[30] In "The York Cycle," Richard Beadle concisely reviews what we know about the cycle productions, and discusses arguments for and against attributing many of the York Passion plays to one dramatist.

[31] Sarah Beckwith, "Making the World in York and the York Cycle," in Miri Rubin and Sarah Kay, eds., *Framing Medieval Bodies* (Manchester: Manchester University Press, 1994).

"Gyffe I wirke wronge, who shulde me wys / Be any way?" (Play VI, lines 107–8). God is a master craftsman and even his labors of creation go awry, as the plays make explicit. What hope is there for man, who is only a creature and whose work is likely to go amiss?

The York cycle explores the problematics of the "worthy work" in numerous plays from its beginning to its end, an appropriate concern – one might argue – for a city of merchants and guildsmen seeking to justify their activities. The reflexivity is very specific in such plays as the *Building of the Ark*, produced by the Shipwrights, which ignores the popular exegetical and allegorical interpretations of the ark's dimensions to dramatize God as a no-nonsense master builder teaching an inept and insecure apprentice, Noah.[32] Played for comedy, the craft's self-representation in Noah, who says "of shippe-craft can I right noght" (Play VIII, line 67), is redeemed by simul-taneous craft identification with God. Where the falls of the first seven plays had provoked serious questioning of human potential, Play VIII has a happy ending, for Noah does receive the necessary direction from God and testifies that "þis werke I warand both gud and trewe . . .Thurgh techyng of God maister myne" (lines 111, 104). Noah finally prays for future guidance from "He þat to me þis craft has kende" (line 150). The York *Building of the Ark* is about a shipwright's craft guild who draw their sanction for labor from a divine exemplar, and see their vocation hallowed by the building of a vehicle of salvation for mankind at the flood. At the same time, however, Noah's potentially catastrophic and richly comic lack of shipbuilding skills reminds the craft producers and their audience that the craft is a learned activity, subject to the vicissitudes of human ignorance. The Noah play thus offers a benign version of reflexivity, one not riven by the kind of moral contra-dictions of the Pilate play or other plays in the Passion sequence of York.

Among the most interesting and problematic for our exploration of sponsorship and the paradoxes of reflexivity are two plays of the Passion: *The Road to Calvary* and the *Crucifixion* (plays 34 and 35). A number of critics have noted the appropriateness of the producing guild to the action in the play (the Shearmen for 34 and the Pinners for 35). As Martin Stevens comments, the Pinners were "makers of pins, fishhooks, mousetraps and

---

[32] On the allegory, see Don Cameron Allen, *The Legend of Noah* (Urbana: University of Illinois Press, 1963), pp. 66–90, 138–73.

Richard Beadle has analyzed the technical terms for shipwrightry used in the play in "The Shipwright's Craft," in Paula Neuss, ed., *Aspects of Early English Drama* (Cambridge: D. S. Brewer, 1983), pp. 50–61 and appendix of terms pp. 151–52. He notes the traditional symbolism of the ark's details in the York play (lines 211–212), but argues that "these and other symbolic aspects of the ark and its construction would have been for the most part accessible only to the learned members of the audience" (60). What we might say in the context of the present essay is that such allusions are left undeveloped; the play we have is about the activity of building ships and can function metadramatically as a comment on the shipwright's craft.

other small metallic objects" and "clearly they were associated in some way with 'the nailing Process itself' "; just as obviously, they were not elevated by the association, he says, alluding to the fact that the craft was in this case portraying itself as torturing and killing Christ.[33] Most critics have made sense of these dramatic actions by arguing that the audience would be lured into identifying with the soldiers and then realize their implication in sin, but the issue of where either producers or audience members found their subject positions in this play cannot be resolved so simply and constructively. Instead, I would emphasize the contradictions arising out of the plays' representation of the world of work, its workplace politics and its ethic of diligence and ingenuity. The soldiers see themselves as good workmen, worthy of praise for a job well done, ironically mirroring the God of creation scenes.

In the first play, the soldiers show an energetic determination to get on with their job: the crucifixion. They take care to assemble all their "gere" – the steps and rope, hammer, nails, and brads. When all is readied, they are relieved: "nowe are we right arraied. / Loke þat oure gere be redy grayed / To wirke whanne we come þore" (Play 34, lines 293–95). The play contrasts the soldiers "arraied" in their "gere" for the work of crucifying Christ with their victim, stripped and bound: "þis werke is wele nowe," (line 340) they say, "For he is boune as beeste in bande / That is demed for to dye" (lines 341–42). Dehumanizing Christ, treating him like a beast, their behavior seems cruel and their commitment to the job perverted. We expect something of the moral judgment on the workmen that we expected with Pilate and his wife.

Yet here the extensiveness with which the dynamics of the workplace are explored suggests that something else is going on than the simple moral choice of which character is good, which evil. Soldier 1 – to whom Pilate had given the work order – takes his job very seriously, while Soldier 2 is more laid back: "Pees, man, for Mahoundes bloode, / Why make ȝe such crying?" (lines 34–35). The foreman asks about a third worker, Wymond, who is off making the cross, and when Wymond returns quizzes him on whether he followed job specifications (lines 76–85). In Play 35, the four soldiers are all dedicated to their task and to avoiding shoddy work: "Thanne to þis werke us muste take heede, / So þat oure wirkyng be noght wronge" (lines 25–26). Jesus has two brief and pathetic speeches but otherwise action in the 300–line play centers on the four soldiers who are busy attaching Christ to the cross and raising it into place.

Critics have noted the single-mindedness of the crucifiers about their job, but have not drawn the conclusion that the work ethic itself might be under scrutiny in the play. That is, the very skills claimed by the producing guilds are shown here in a negative light; theories of trade symbolism or guild

---

[33] Stevens, p. 30.

propaganda alone seem irreconcilable with the theological potency of the dramatic moment of Christ's sacrifice on the cross. Unlikely, even perverse as it seems, I *am* arguing that we have an unstable discursive formation in this play, and the effect of this semiotic conflict is to force an exploration of the *idea* of work itself. When the skills specific to the pinners are taken out of the normal and everyday world, when a dedication to craft is taken out of the mundane and put into the perspective of sacred history, the skills and craft commitment can be examined in the abstract.

Clifford Geertz and other anthropological theorists have argued that "Any expressive form works . . . by disarranging semantic contexts in such a way that properties conventionally ascribed to certain things are unconventionally ascribed to others."[34] The Passion plays of York employ just such a disarrangement of semantic contexts by showing the torturers of Christ as conscientious and skilled workmen. The concern with craftsmanship, with using the proper tools and materials, and completing the job to specifications – which the guilds were organized to promote and monitor – is here displaced onto Christian history at its moment of greatest pain. The displacement of values from the medieval urban working world onto sacred history makes these plays more than simply popularizations. In Lévi-Strauss' terms, the dramatizations are "good to think with" for they allow members of the York audience to be reflexive about their own socio-economic or political arrangements.

I have traced some of the York cycle meta-messages concerning the work ethic and craft skills – foundations for the achieved status on which bourgeois citizens of York based their identities. It is important to note, however, that reflexivity is not a trait found continuously throughout every play of the cycle. It appears to be an option, one mode alternating with others, available to audience members depending upon their own situations and perspectives. We might ask, for example, what kind of identification a female member of the audience would have with craft representations of shipwrights or pinners or thatchers – crafts that women did not practice. Or, what was her response to Dame Percula in the Pilate play or to other misogynist characters or speeches? Was the reflexivity even available to a woman observer?

Audiences

Having talked at some length about the multiple sites of production of plays and the reflexivity of the texts, especially when performed on festive occasions, we must now turn to the audiences for the plays, which should be differentiated by gender, class, civic status, education, religious

---

[34] Geertz, p. 447.

commitment, economic profession and so on. Historical documentation for the task of tracing out multiple audience responses is skimpy indeed but worth attempting even if hypothetically, as in the case of our female member of the audience above. Contemporary cultural studies has been especially resourceful in theorizing the appropriation of culture. Cultural critics – most of whom study contemporary mass cultural products – have posited a fair amount of creativity and variety in the way individuals respond to the messages and images beamed at them. Critics like Jan Radway writing on women's romance or John Fiske on television or Michel de Certeau on the tactical appropriation of everyday life all emphasize the role of the culture consumer in making meanings.[35] Similarly, James C. Scott has analyzed power relations in *Domination and the Arts of Resistance: Hidden Transcripts*. His argument is that "every subordinate group creates, out of its ordeal, a 'hidden transcript' that represents a critique of power spoken behind the back of the dominant."[36] He thus disagrees that subordinate or powerless groups have internalized the ideologies of the powerful, but would argue that one can trace "patterns of disguising ideological insubordination." All these works theorize tactics by which audiences appropriate cultural practices and performances not intended by their producers for their benefit.[37]

In medieval and early modern Europe, festival occasions and festive forms provided popular sites for disguised resistance and critique. Whether that critique was contained by the official frame or led to its subversion appears to have depended on local circumstances and specific contingencies – and not to have been predictable in advance from the action itself. A late record from York (1572) registers a letter sent to the Mayor and Aldermen by six "loving ffrendes" who request the town authorities to prohibit future ridings of a couple of disguised persons called Yule and Yule's wife. Clearly stimulated by the Christmas seasonal festivity but *outside* authorized festive frames, the two revelers rode through the city on St. Thomas Day before Christmas. The letter complains that they rode "very undecently and uncomely drawyng great concurses of people after thym to gaise," committing great but unspecified "enormyties."[38] The letter asks to have such rides

[35] See Janice A. Radway, *Reading the Romance: Women, Patriarchy, and Popular Literature* (Chapel Hill: University of North Carolina Press, 1984); John Fiske and John Hartley, *Reading Television* (London: Methuen, 1978; rpt. 1985); and Michel de Certeau, *The Practice of Everyday Life*, trans. Steven Rendall (Berkeley: University of California Press, 1984).

[36] James C. Scott, *Domination and the Arts of Resistance: Hidden Transcripts* (New Haven: Yale University Press, 1990), p. xii.

[37] For a fuller exploration of these theories of audience appropriations, see my "Contemporary Theories of Popular Culture and Medieval Performances," *Mediaevalia* 18 (1995): 1–13.

[38] *York Records*, vol. 1, p. 369.

barred, presumably because of the danger of popular uprising as much as the reason given, which was "the prophanyng of that day appoynted to holy uses."[39] As James Scott points out, the powerful had disguised ways of speaking as much as the powerless.

My final point about the multiple sponsorship of the York cycle is that reflexivity on a comprehensive scale such as one can trace in these plays is particularly associated with festivals. Anthropologist Don Handelman has argued that large-scale festivals are typical of complexly differentiated and well-bounded societies (which Mary Douglas calls "high group/high-grid").[40] Within such societies' festival frames, the established order can be questioned on a grand scale

> because both cosmology and social structure have such a strong everyday hold on the self. Such systems of high social and moral control can allow the self a high degree of reflexivity precisely because the doubts evoked by festival-play have such a comparatively vast spectrum of scale and minutiae to question. The active freedom of the self in festival is complementary to its restriction and incorporation in everyday life.[41]

My point here is that forms of reflexivity and resistance may be wittingly or unwittingly sponsored by the city and the Corpus Christi festival, though whether such possibilities are perceived by members of the audience or lead to social effects would, as I have argued, depend upon a variety of factors in reception and local situation. In her discussion of Corpus Christi processions, Miri Rubin makes the point this way: "Processions, like all rituals, can mean different things to different people. In their construction of images of the world and in their incitement to action, processions can bear messages that are contradictory, volatile, and determined by context."[42]

My aim in this essay has been to unsettle the notions of sponsorship and resistance, to suggest that we need not fall into the "communal" fallacy – on the one hand – or adopt some form of socio/political determinism – on the other – in order to read the phenomenon of medieval urban drama. Rather, we need to re-examine our interpretive assumptions with regard to such performance events as the York cycle, for critics have rushed to premature conclusions in constructing analytic models for what was a complex,

---

[39] *York Records*, vol. 1, p. 369.

[40] See Mary Douglas, "Introduction to Grid/Group Analysis," *Essays in the Sociology of Perception* (London: Routledge and Kegan Park, 1982), pp. 1–8.

[41] Handelman, p. 172.

[42] Miri Rubin, *Corpus Christi: The Eucharist in Late Medieval Culture* (Cambridge: Cambridge University Press, 1991), p. 265. For a discussion of audience distance and reflexivity, see Bruce Kapferer, "The Ritual Process and the Problem of Reflexivity in Sinhalese Demon Exorcism," in John J. MacAloon, ed., *Toward a Theory of Cultural Performance* (Philadelphia: ISHI, 1984), pp. 179–207.

historically variable, cultural performance. Even if resistance was always possible it was not predetermined, and sponsorship was also likely to be multiply sited and far from coherent or univocal. If we *are* able to open up our inquiry, I suspect that these drama texts and records will have much to show contemporary cultural theory about both the workings of social power at specific cultural sites and the variability possible through symbolic constructions.

Eliding the "Medieval": Renaissance "New Historicism" and Sixteenth-Century Drama

Richard K. Emmerson

Medievalists have often considered historical research to be a primary step toward the critical analysis of literary texts. In a classic declaration of this well-established approach to medieval literature, Morton Bloomfield states that "I wish to save history; we cannot approach literature innocent and naked. We must know what a poem meant before we can fully know what it means."[1] This statement suggests that if we could only gain a good enough grasp on the historical setting in which a poem was composed, rather than approaching it as "innocent and naked," we would see the text fully clothed by its historical context and know what it originally "meant." Although seldom stated so forthrightly, this position is a theoretical tenet fundamental to historicist attempts to recreate the origins and intentions of literary works. Until recently it was rarely interrogated because it is integral to key assumptions regarding such binary categories as text/context and literary construct/historical reality, institutionalized within the academy as the domains of critical interpretation and scholarly research. Historians of the texts usually called "medieval drama" have embraced this positivist model of the relation between historical research and literary analysis, placing faith in the documentary approach by tracing the origins of the drama and gathering evidence for the performance of plays and other entertainments in the later Middle Ages.[2] As a result, medievalists – as is evident in their conference presentations, histories, and research projects – give paramount importance to the discovery and recording of historical documentation. Context and historical "background" may receive greater

---

[1] Morton W. Bloomfield, *Essays and Explorations: Studies in Ideas, Language, and Literature* (Cambridge, MA: Harvard University Press, 1970), 278. Bloomfield's comments are from his review of Kenneth Sisam's *The Structure of Beowulf*, originally published in *Speculum* 41 (1966): 368–71.

[2] For a critique of this tendency in medieval drama scholarship, see Theresa Coletti, "Reading REED: History and the Records of Early English Drama," in *Literary Practice and Social Change in Britain, 1380–1530*, ed. Lee Patterson (Berkeley: University of California Press, 1990), 248–84.

emphasis than dramatic texts and editing documents becomes more important than synthesizing and marshalling them to interpret the plays that are
the "foreground" being studied. A most welcome departure from such
emphases is Martin Stevens's impressively synthetic and critically acute
study of the four "cycles," *Four Middle English Mystery Cycles: Textual,
Contextual, and Critical Interpretations*, which brings a whole range of
documentary as well as codicological evidence to bear on the literary
interpretation of the four great "cycles" of plays.[3] For some time Martin
Stevens has been concerned with the difficulties inherent in the historical
study of medieval drama, so it is appropriate to contribute some thoughts
on these issues to a volume in his honor.[4]

The present emphasis on the documentary in scholarship is one response
to the decontextualized "readings" that characterized New Critical
approaches to medieval drama in mid century. Alexandra Johnston has
rightly chided critics who have been "too quick to generalize, too anxious to
assume that the surviving texts are all we need to consider, too content to
spin our literary, critical, and theological webs independent of the factual
context of the drama."[5] We can all point to examples of such thinly spun
"webs." Nevertheless, we must also recognize that determining "the factual
context of the drama" is highly problematic. To begin with, it is difficult to
establish the provenance and date of most medieval plays, yet such basic
documentation is crucial if we are to conduct serious historical research,
because it is no longer possible to speak of "medieval drama" as if it were a
coherent, unified body of literature, or of the "late Middle Ages in
England" as if it were a static, stable society. John Coldewey has emphasized the close connection between economic conditions and the full range of
dramatic performances, arguing that "The shifting medieval economy was
related materially, thematically, and ideologically to theatrical practices."[6]
But such a recognition only underscores the need to situate the plays more
carefully, for, as Coldewey also notes, economic conditions in late medieval

---

[3] *Four Middle English Mystery Cycles: Textual, Contextual, and Critical Interpretations*
(Princeton: Princeton University Press, 1987). As I note in "Dramatic Developments:
Some Recent Scholarship on Medieval Drama," *Envoi: A Review Journal of Medieval
Literature* 1 (1988): 31–36, I consider Stevens's book to be one of the most important
studies of medieval drama published in the past twenty years.
[4] Stevens organized the session on "The Uses of History in the Study of Medieval
Drama" for the 1989 convention of the Modern Languages Association (Washington,
D.C.), at which an early version of this essay was presented. His helpful comments on
my paper then and the insightful suggestions made more recently by my colleague Marc
Geisler are gratefully acknowledged.
[5] Alexandra F. Johnston, "What if No Texts Survived? External Evidence for Early
English Drama," in *Contexts for Early English Drama*, ed. Marianne G. Briscoe and
John C. Coldewey (Bloomington: Indiana University Press, 1989), 12.
[6] John C. Coldewey, "Some Economic Aspects of the Late Medieval Drama," in
Contexts, ed. Briscoe and Coldewey, 80.

England varied not only through time, but also from region to region and from town to town in any given region. Similarly, Lawrence Clopper has shown the very close relationship existing between the system and traditions of government in a town and the type of drama or ceremonial it sponsored.[7] What we need now are more detailed analyses focusing on various regions and towns that draw upon and synthesize the work of social and economic as well as cultural historians.[8]

In the renewed attention to history, however, we must beware the danger of becoming so absorbed in collecting facts that we forget the dramatic texts motivating our search. Such a confusion of priorities has been the bane of literary historical scholarship, a problem that motivated the New Critical attack on historicism at mid century. More recently, Dominick LaCapra has warned against "archival fetishism," an historicism unaware that documents are not simple but complex, "texts that 'process' or rework 'reality' and require a critical reading. . . ."[9] We need to be particularly wary in pondering the relationship between literature and history. As Hayden White admonished more than twenty years ago, critics tend to speak of the context of a literary work as if

> this context – the "historical milieu" – has a concreteness and an accessibility that the work itself can never have, as if it were easier to perceive the reality of a past world put together from a thousand historical documents than it is to probe the depths of a single literary work that is present to the critic studying it.[10]

Thus, although most would agree with Bloomfield that history needs to be "saved," we must avoid the naive assumption that simply establishing the historical context of a literary text – no matter how particular the investigation and "thick" the description – will lead to insightful interpretation and a clear sense of "meaning."

It is especially misleading to perceive a dramatic text as an instrument that primarily "reflects" or "mirrors" history. This understanding of the

---

[7] Lawrence M. Clopper, "Lay and Clerical Impact on Civic Religious Drama and Ceremony," in *Contexts*, ed. Briscoe and Coldewey, 111.

[8] Good models are provided by Gail McMurray Gibson, *The Theater of Devotion: East Anglian Drama and Society in the Late Middle Ages* (Chicago: University of Chicago Press, 1989); and John Coldewey's "The Non-Cycle Plays and the East Anglian Tradition," in *The Cambridge Companion to Medieval English Theatre*, ed. Richard Beadle (Cambridge: Cambridge University Press, 1994), 189–210.

[9] LaCapra, *History and Criticism* (Ithaca: Cornell University Press, 1985), 19–20.

[10] Hayden White, "The Historical Text as Literary Artifact," in *Tropics of Discourse: Essays in Cultural Criticism* (Baltimore: Johns Hopkins University Press, 1978), 89; the paper was first given as a lecture to the Comparative Literature Colloquium at Yale, 24 January 1974. In *Negotiating the Past: The Historical Understanding of Medieval Literature* (Madison: University of Wisconsin Press, 1987), 41–74, Lee Patterson makes similar arguments, applied specifically to medieval historicism.

relationship of literature and history propels even the most recent scholarship on medieval drama. Historical events and political and religious formulations are posited as the "reality" reflected in the literary "mirror," the "aboutness" of the play and a key unlocking its "meaning." For example, in the commentary volume accompanying their monumental edition of the Chester Cycle, Robert Lumiansky and David Mills gloss the scene in the Chester *Coming of Antichrist* in which Antichrist rewards his newly converted Four Kings with various European principalities (XXIII.241–44) as follows: "The references here suggest a composite Antichrist-manifestation embracing Lutheranism, the Turkish threat and the papal involvement in the Franco-Spanish war, all suggestive of events in the 1530s and later."[11] Then these ideological and geographic references are explained as if the play mirrors European power relations existing during the middle third of the sixteenth century. But if the *Coming of Antichrist* is a mirror of such power relations, it is an opaque mirror that refracts contemporary events through the formulations of a 600 year-old apocalyptic tradition and of a theatrical convention that portrays tyrants and worldly lords as geographical bullies.[12] Furthermore, even if the scene did recall such contemporary events for the citizens of Chester in the 1530s – which is unlikely – what might it suggest to audiences when it was staged in later decades? This is a question of primary importance, since the meaning of the play resides as much in the responses of its audience as it does in its "text."[13]

It would be more useful to investigate the ways in which *The Coming of Antichrist* participates in history, particularly since during the sixteenth century, under the influence of Reformation theology, the figure of Antichrist was polemicized and identified with a specific enemy, as is suggested by the promise in the Late Banns to "bring out" Antichrist and a Doctor to "expownde / Whoe be Antechristes. . . ."[14] How did later productions both

---

[11] R. M. Lumiansky and David Mills, *The Chester Mystery Cycle*, vol. 2, Early English Text Society, s.s. 9 (London: Oxford University Press, 1986), 339.

[12] The character of World in *The Castle of Perseverance* is a good example; see Richard K. Emmerson, "The Morality Character as Sign: A Semiotic Approach to *The Castle of Perseverance*," in *Medieval and Early Renaissance Drama: Reconsiderations*, ed. Martin Stevens and Milla C. Riggio, *Mediaevalia* 19 (1995, for 1992). For *The Coming of Antichrist* in its apocalyptic tradition, see Richard Kenneth Emmerson, *Antichrist in the Middle Ages: A Study of Medieval Apocalypticism, Art, and Literature* (Seattle: University of Washington Press, 1981), 180–87.

[13] See Marvin Carlson, "Theatre Audiences and the Reading of Performance," in *Interpreting the Theatrical Past: Essays in the Historiography of Performance*, ed. Thomas Postlewait and Bruce A. McConachie (Iowa City: University of Iowa Press, 1989), 82–98.

[14] *Records of Early English Drama: Chester*, ed. Lawrence M. Clopper (Toronto: University of Toronto Press, 1979), 246. On the representation of Antichrist in a work contemporary with the revision of Chester, see Richard K. Emmerson, "Wynkyn de Worde's *Byrthe and Lyfe of Antechryst* and Popular Eschatology on the

resist and participate in the reformulation of Christianity's greatest enemy? How did they manipulate traditional apocalyptic expectations and respond to new theological formulations? How did they shape, and how were they shaped by, their audiences' awareness of contemporary events? Such questions, moreover, may be applied to the entire cycle, since each performance made "history." The text is only a trace of a complex historical event that involved players and assistants, civic and religious authorities, citizens and visitors, an event driven by and shaping a wide range of social, political, economic, and religious motivations. In short, it is a trace that does not mirror but only hints at a social event charged with all the complexity one would expect in a mobilized community. We will misunderstand the cycle – any medieval play, in fact – if we assume a simple one-to-one relationship between history and dramatic text.

Thus historical research should not only situate the dramatic texts more accurately, but also explore how they participate in, rather than just "reflect," history. Texts need to be understood "not as finalized 'sources' but as argumentative and interpretative documents in their own right, as historical contestants and as objects of contestation," according to Paul Strohm.[15] We have long known that medieval plays were "part of tremendous enterprises where civic or parish stakes were high,"[16] but we have not always appreciated the ways in which they did not simply "reflect" their times or propagate the ideology of their producers but were also intrinsically involved in reshaping events and critiquing dominant belief systems.[17] Here medievalists may learn from the practice of our colleagues studying Renaissance drama, especially from those whose theoretical position is loosely labelled "New Historicism." One popularizer of this approach claims that "today no bastion of literary scholarship has managed to exclude New Historicism,"[18] but in fact it has had little impact on

---

Eve of the English Reformation," *Mediaevalia* 14 (1991 for 1988): 281–311; for early Reformation views and representations of Antichrist, see Emmerson, *Antichrist in the Middle Ages*, 204–37.

[15] Strohm, *Hochon's Arrow: The Social Imagination of Fourteenth-Century Texts* (Princeton: Princeton University Press, 1992), 9, writing about somewhat earlier medieval texts. Strohm's book exemplifies sophisticated historicist analysis applied to medieval literature; see especially the introduction, "False Fables and Historical Truth," 3–9.

[16] Coldewey, "Some Economic Aspects," in *Contexts*, ed. Briscoe and Coldewey, 97.

[17] C. Clifford Flanigan, "Liminality, Carnival, and Social Structure: The Case of Late Medieval Biblical Drama," in *Victor Turner and the Construction of Cultural Criticism: Between Literature and Anthropology*, ed. Kathleen M. Ashley (Bloomington: Indiana University Press, 1990), shows how the marriage of Mary and Joseph in the Wakefield Annunciation "simultaneously affirms and undercuts the inherited social and theological order" (61).

[18] H. Aram Veeser, ed., *The New Historicism* (New York: Routledge, 1989), xiii. The essays introduce and critique the assumptions and practice of New Historicism. For its place in the recent "turn toward History" in American literary studies, see *New Historical*

medievalists, especially on those studying drama. This is unfortunate because certain features that characterize New Historicist critical practice can provide useful models for the study of medieval drama. Its recognition of the reciprocal nature of literary and other texts – "the historicity of texts and the textuality of history,"[19] to cite Louis Montrose's elegant formulation – and its insistence that literary texts are not only products of historical determinants but also shapers of the historical intertext are particularly insightful. According to Montrose, we must recognize that literature is not only socially produced but also "socially productive – that it is the product of work and that it performs work in the process of being written, enacted, or read" (23). Such an understanding of drama, the most public literary form, is necessary to investigate its multifarious social roles from the fourteenth through the sixteenth centuries.

Unfortunately, New Historicists studying Renaissance drama are unlikely to direct their critical skills toward the full range of this theatrical activity, because they seem unaware of "medieval" dramatic forms, even those staged late into the sixteenth century. This blindness results from a major flaw in their assumptions that medievalists may help remedy: their failure to interrogate a key assumption of the old historicism, the period distinction rigidly drawn between the Middle Ages and Renaissance. As Patterson notes

> New Historicism, despite its laudable self-consciousness, in fact operates largely according to a traditional historiographical scheme that not only sets the Renaissance over against the Middle Ages but understands the opposition in terms originally established by nineteenth-century liberal philology.[20]

This historiographical scheme, of course, is not limited to the New Historicism, but is fully embedded in most humanistic scholarship, which is influenced by two nineteenth-century studies, Huizinga's *The Waning of the Middle Ages* and Burckhardt's *The Civilization of the Renaissance in Italy*. Although medievalists have repudiated much of Huizinga, Renaissance scholars have re-embraced Burckhardt to re-establish "the inherited idea of the Renaissance. . . ."[21]

What underlies both books and others tracing the medieval-Renaissance

---

Literary Study: Essays on Reproducing Texts, Representing History, ed. Jeffrey N. Cox and Larry J. Reynolds (Princeton: Princeton University Press, 1993), 3–16.

[19] Louis A. Montrose, "Professing the Renaissance: The Poetics and Politics of Culture," in Veeser, ed., *New Historicism*, 20.

[20] Patterson, *Negotiating the Past*, 68.

[21] William Kerrigan and Gordon Braden, *The Idea of the Renaissance* (Baltimore: Johns Hopkins University Press, 1989), xi. On Huizinga and the pervasive "deprecatory view of the drama" in modern scholarship, see Martin Stevens, "Medieval Drama: Genres, Misconceptions, and Approaches," in *Approaches to Teaching Medieval English Drama*, ed. Richard K. Emmerson (New York: Modern Language Association, 1990), 44–46.

distinction is the assumption that the dominant – usually understood as hegemonic – ideology of the Middle Ages was bankrupt by the fifteenth century. Medieval culture then died a natural death and was replaced by the reborn classicism and free-thinking individualism found in humanist writings and by the explosion of creativity evident in the Italian masters. Inculcated through popular textbooks, which may include a chapter devoted to the "Proto-Renaissance" – that is, to *trecento* figures such as Giotto and Dante who are too "progressive" to be left stranded in the Middle Ages – this model shapes every student's misunderstanding of European culture.[22] Although usually not made explicit, the value judgments implicit in the model are obvious: the Middle Ages were traditional, naive, illiterate, close-minded, religious, and dead, whereas the Renaissance was progressive, experienced, literate, free-thinking, secular, and reborn.[23] The model leads to bald generalizations, such as the following written by a popular historian, which reinscribes for another generation of students and general readers the unexamined caricature of medieval literature:

> With a few lonely exceptions – Petrarch's *De viris illustribus*, Boccaccio's *Decameron* – medieval Europe's contributions to world literature had been negligible. Japan had been more productive, and the Stygian murk of the Dark Ages is reflected in the dismal fact that Christendom had then published nothing matching the eloquence of the infidel Muhammad in his seventh-century Koran.[24]

The model, originally formulated by art historians to describe developments in fourteenth- and fifteenth-century Italian culture, has been transferred quite unselfconsciously by literary historians to England, although in crossing the Channel its characteristic features are recalibrated and delayed from the fourteenth to the sixteenth century, when the Renaissance "flowered" in England. By tracing a "new" influence of Italian culture – especially of Petrarch – on English literature, the model both informs and conforms to "the pervasive and apparently ineradicable *grand récit* that

---

[22] Typical of such textbooks is William Fleming's *Arts and Ideas*, 6th ed. (New York: Holt, Reinehart and Winston, 1980), a widely assigned text for humanities courses in high school and college. For example, it traces the development of the Gothic and "gloomy, threatening medieval world view" (185) into "The Early Italian Renaissance Style" – which includes Dante, Giotto, and even St. Francis – by noting how "the icy intellectualism of the medieval universities was bound to thaw in the warmth of Franciscan emotionalism" (189). This revisionist chronology would take Bonaventure and other Franciscans by surprise.

[23] On similar binary categories see Anne Middleton, "Medieval Studies," in *Redrawing the Boundaries: The Transformation of English and American Literary Studies*, ed. Stephen Greenblatt and Giles Gunn (New York: Modern Language Association, 1992), 25.

[24] William Manchester, *A World Lit Only by Fire: The Medieval Mind and the Renaissance* (Boston: Little, Brown, 1993), 99–100.

organizes Western cultural history, the gigantic master narrative by which modernity identifies itself with the Renaissance and rejects the Middle Ages as by definition premodern."[25] Now fully institutionalized in English departments in the "field-coverage model of departmental organization,"[26] it is rarely questioned by literary historians, most of whom were trained to work within "periods." As a result, with a few important exceptions – such as Martin Stevens's NEH seminar on "Shakespeare and the Native Dramatic Tradition" – specialists in Renaissance drama have rarely dealt with medieval drama nor have many scholars considered seriously the issues of dramatic continuity and change.[27]

Lord Acton long ago urged historians to "Study problems, not periods," but as Thomas Postlewait notes, "the way we divide and analyze history *is* the problem."[28] This is particularly true of the segregation of "medieval" from "Renaissance" drama. Although now liberated from a Darwinian model tracing the "evolution" of an inchoate "pre-Shakespearean" ritual theatre into the "mature" drama of the Elizabethan "golden age," "medieval" drama remains ignored and misunderstood by Renaissance specialists. That this situation continues long after O. B. Hardison's groundbreaking work of the 1960s is troubling, particularly since New Historicists claim to substitute "for the diachronic text of an autonomous literary history the synchronic text of a cultural system."[29] But their synchronic studies of Renaissance drama do not include "medieval" forms, partly because a rigid historical periodization obscures the fact

---

[25] Lee Patterson, "On the Margin: Postmodernism, Ironic History, and Medieval Studies," *Speculum* 65 (1990): 92. Others have detailed the negative implications of this *grand récit* for medieval studies, including David Wallace, whose "Periodization/ Territorialization; Medieval/Renaissance" was read to a packed house at the 29th International Congress on Medieval Studies, Western Michigan University, on May 7, 1994. The present essay, though first presented in 1989, takes up Patterson's challenge to confront and remedy "the massive indifference to the realities of medieval culture displayed by colleagues in other fields" (104).

[26] Gerald Graff, *Professing Literature: An Institutional History* (Chicago: University of Chicago Press, 1987), 6.

[27] Two important exceptions are David M. Bevington, *From "Mankind" to Marlowe: Growth and Structure in the Popular Drama of Tudor England* (Cambridge, MA: Harvard University Press, 1962); and Robert Weimann, *Shakespeare and the Popular Tradition in the Theater: Studies in the Social Dimension of Dramatic Form and Function*, ed. Robert Schwartz (Baltimore: Johns Hopkins University Press, 1978). For papers from Stevens's NEH seminar, see *Medieval and Early Renaissance Drama: Reconsiderations*, ed. Martin Stevens and Milla Riggio, *Mediaevalia* 18 (1995, for 1992).

[28] Postlewait, "The Criteria for Periodization in Theatre History," *Theatre Journal* 40 (1988): 317.

[29] Montrose, "Professing the Renaissance," in *New Historicism*, ed. Veeser, 17. For Hardison's criticism of the Darwinian model, see *Christian Rite and Christian Drama in the Middle Ages: Essays in the Origin and Early History of Modern Drama* (Baltimore: Johns Hopkins University Press, 1965).

that numerous "medieval" plays – such as the mystery cycles staged into the 1570s – date to the sixteenth century. As a result histories and handbooks still popularize historical misinformation and emphasize the "new" developments in Renaissance drama. It is not unusual, for example, to read how "By the early sixteenth century, the great cycles of mystery plays spanning Christian history from Creation to Doomsday had begun to die a natural death,"[30] a comment blatantly ignoring the dramatic records.

The treatment of "medieval" drama in the two volumes of *The Revels History of Drama in English* devoted to the Renaissance exemplifies this problem. Volume two, surveying the years 1500 to 1576, includes a brief chapter on the suppression of the cycle plays, but fails to indicate their important roles or continuing performances. Its detailed chronology, listing such "theatrical events" as Queen Elizabeth's attendance at plays, fails to mention the rich variety of parish, civic, and other "medieval" plays produced during this period, citing only two items related to the cycles: "Last performance of York miracle cycle" (1569); and "Mayor of Chester summoned for permitting performance of miracle cycle" (1575).[31] Once again the demise of "medieval" forms is emphasized rather than their continuity and vitality into the third quarter of the century. Given such partial treatment of these urban popular plays, it is not surprising that the next *Revels* volume can then identify a "new" development of the 1570s and 1580s: a change in the locale of drama "from its longstanding environment of palaces and noble households . . . to the city and its environs."[32] But this change appears "new" because the *Revels History* has ignored the full range of sixteenth-century drama, which includes much that is non-aristocratic and urban. This ignorance is only too common in studies of Renaissance drama, which suffer from a problem noted by Brook Thomas: "Too often period specialists have such a narrow sense of history that they are prone to make exaggerated claims about the changes occurring within their period."[33]

Rather than combating this problem, New Historicists have usually simply elided "medieval" dramatic forms, perhaps because these historically minded critics are themselves misinformed or do not consider such

---

[30] Murray Roston, *Sixteenth-Century English Literature*, History of Literature Series (New York: Schocken Books, 1982), 55. The errors in this book are startling, but it is by no means alone in propagating misinformation regarding "medieval" drama to students of sixteenth-century literature. For a more recent example, see Robert N. Watson, "Tragedy," in *The Cambridge Companion to English Renaissance Drama*, ed. A. R. Braunmuller and Michael Hattaway (Cambridge: Cambridge University Press, 1990), 310.

[31] Norman Sanders, Richard Southern, T. W. Craik, and Lois Potter, *The Revels History of Drama in English*, vol. 2, *1500–1576* (New York: Methuen, 1980). For "The Suppression of the Mystery Cycles," see 7–11; for the chronology, xvi–xxxvii.

[32] J. Leeds Barroll, *The Revels History of Drama in English*, vol. 3, *1576–1613* (London: Methuen, 1975), 29.

[33] Brook Thomas, *The New Historicism and Other Old-Fashioned Topics* (Princeton: Princeton University Press, 1991), 14.

forms relevant to the study of Renaissance drama. Evident throughout their vast output, this situation is exemplified by Stephen Greenblatt's *Representing the English Renaissance*, a collection of studies – including some brilliant essays on drama – originally published in the most prominent New Historicist journal, *Representations*. The entries in the volume's index are telling. For "Drama" the reader is directed to "*See* Elizabethan theater; Shakespearean drama; *names of individual dramatists*."[34] The neat assumption that Renaissance drama may be divided into Elizabethan theater or Shakespeare or is limited to known playwrights allows no place for sixteenth-century plays continuing "medieval" dramatic forms, which, by their communal nature, don't fit a notion of the individual genius implied by the index. The entry for "Theater" (372) is more promising in that it does not refer readers to entries that automatically exclude the "medieval." But one remains disappointed, for the entry on theater "and society" deals with Jacobean England, and the entry on "regulation of" theater cites only the Privy Council order of 1597 suppressing plays in London. The important social roles played by the cycle plays during the sixteenth-century and the significance of their suppression during the period are not mentioned. In fact, the London theatre, the role of the individual artist, and the capitalist structures of "early modern" England are the primary interests of these critics, as is evident in the "theatre" entries on "authorship," "literary marketplace," "literary property," and "printing and publication." Needless to say, none of these deal with the theater outside of London or with the continuity of "medieval" dramatic forms.

One wonders why traditional distinctions based on unexamined historical periodization are so widely accepted by scholars who claim to take history seriously. There is no single answer, but the assumptions and praxis of New Historicists suggest at least four reasons. The first is evident in the difficulty they have in understanding ideologies that take religion seriously and see it as basic to human social activity. Although exploring such topics as ecclesiastical politics, heresy, religious polemic, and witchcraft, New

---

[34] Stephen Greenblatt, ed., *Representing the English Renaissance* (Berkeley: University of California Press, 1988), 366. A more recent example is Richard Wilson and Richard Dutton, *New Historicism and Renaissance Drama* (New York: Longman, 1992). David Aers, "A Whisper in the Ear of Early Modernists; or Reflections on Literary Critics Writing the 'History of the Subject'," in *Culture and History, 1350–1600: Essays on English Communities, Identities, and Writing*, ed. David Aers (Detroit: Wayne State University Press, 1992), 177–202, unfortunately came to my attention after the present essay was completed. A compelling essay, it shows how New Historicists and other more recent "radical" critics have constructed the same understanding of an "idealist" Middle Ages that Robertsonians and other conservative critics described in the past. Although concerned with different aspects of these critical schools, Aers and I reach many of the same conclusions. Regarding their failure to take religion seriously, for example, see Aers, 195–96.

Historicists rarely focus on the social life of religious groups, who may seem a remnant of the old "medieval" *mentalité*. The relative unimportance of religion is made explicit by Montrose, whose explanation of the "heterogeneous and unstable" nature of ideology delineates how "an ideological dominance is qualified by the specific conjunctures of ethnic, gender, class, profession, age, and other social positions occupied by individual cultural producers," a list eliding religion, an important social "position" in sixteenth-century England.[35] Thus the religious nature of much "medieval" drama may eliminate it from New Historicist analysis.

Related to this refusal to take religion seriously are the assumptions held by the economic, social, and historical theorists who have most influenced New Historicism – Marx, and especially Bakhtin and Foucault.[36] Religious belief is rarely treated sympathetically by these thinkers, who also firmly hold to the medieval-Renaissance distinction. Foucault, for example, despite stressing the *long dureé*, clearly sees the sixteenth century – "the moment of the Renaissance" – as a major dividing point in European history and the originary moment for those processes and structures of power that characterize the modern world.[37] Along with many of his disciples, Foucault exemplifies how "historicism, a product of the modern imagination, assumes that history will always be made new."[38] Ironically,

---

[35] Louis Montrose, "New Historicisms," in *Redrawing Boundaries*, ed. Greenblatt and Gunn, 404. In "Professing the Renaissance," in *New Historicism*, ed. Veeser, Montrose provides a related clue that explains their indifference toward medieval drama when he describes New Historicist rejection of "History" for "histories." In the category "History" Montrose places "the great code of Christian figural and eschatological history . . ." (20), the code, as is well known, that structures the cycle plays.

[36] Thomas, *New Historicism*, 37, notes Greenblatt's indebtedness to Foucault and Bakhtin. New Historicists also take their bows toward Marx – often as retheorized by Raymond Williams – but his influence has been less pervasive on American practitioners. See James Holstun, "Ranting at the New Historicism," *English Literary Renaissance* 19 (1989): 203–206. Marx, though, is crucial to the related British "Cultural Materialists." See Antony Easthope, *Literary into Cultural Studies* (London: Routledge, 1991), 119–23.

[37] Foucault often understands the sixteenth century to be a dividing point, emphasizes discontinuity and rupture in history, and pinpoints events, structures, and concepts that he believes take place for "the first time" and represent "a point of departure." See Foucault, "What Is Enlightenment?" in Paul Rabinow, ed., *The Foucault Reader* (New York: Pantheon, 1984), 36; "Nietzsche, Genealogy, History," *Foucault Reader*, 88; "On the Genealogy of Ethics: An Overview of Work in Progress," *Foucault Reader*, 370; and "The Subject and Power," in *Michel Foucault: Beyond Structuralism and Hermeneutics*, ed. Hubert Dreyfus and Paul Rabinow (Chicago: University of Chicago Press, 1982), 213.

[38] Thomas, *New Historicism*, 32. "As a result," Thomas adds, "the history of historicism is marked by perpetual claims to newness." For such a claim typifying New Historicism, see Steven Mullaney, *The Place of the Stage: License, Play, and Power in Renaissance England* (Chicago: University of Chicago Press, 1988): "Eclipsing all other forms of the new–both from the vantage point of literary history, and from the perspective of the city itself – were the public playhouses of Elizabethan London" (27).

Bakhtin, so influential in focusing scholarly attention on the carnivalesque culture of the Middle Ages and in tracing its continuity into the Renaissance, also firmly divides medieval from Renaissance, now linking these historical categories to a hierarchy that contrasts "folk" to "official" culture, a "living" laughter to a "deadly" seriousness. Medieval folk culture was dynamic and festive, in contrast to "the static, unshakable hierarchy" and "the spirit of the Gothic age, with its one-sided seriousness based on fear and coercion" that controlled medieval official culture.[39] Not until the Renaissance did laughter "flower" beyond medieval folk culture to enter "the sphere of great literature and high ideology" and "play an essential role in the creation of such masterpieces of world literature as Boccaccio's *Decameron*, the novels of Rabelais and Cervantes, Shakespere's dramas and comedies, and others" (72). To Bakhtin the periods also help distinguish "low" and "high" art. Medieval folk culture – for example, "the miracle and morality plays," which "acquired to a certain extent a carnivalesque nature," and "the mystery plays," which were "penetrated" by "laughter" (15) – could not "grow and flower" into "great literature" (96) before the Renaissance.

As is evident in Bakhtin's comments, the issue of canonicity is crucial to the medieval-Renaissance distinction. That medieval drama is not considered "great literature" and is largely excluded from the canon may therefore be a third reason for its elision by New Historicism. This situation pinpoints a fissure between theory and practice, though, since New Historicists claim to extend the kinds of texts worthy of serious critical attention and take pride in erasing canonical boundaries. As Leah Marcus states, critics no longer need to emphasize authorship and the humanist notion of literature as the "'golden' achievement of the human spirit" and may now "explore a vast panorama of 'nonauthorial' writings as part of our study of literature."[40] Yet, in practice, New Historicists focus not only on the authorial but on the authors who occupy the center of the literary canon, a focus excluding forms of sixteenth-century drama that are anonymous and non-

---

[39] Mikhail Bakhtin, *Rabelais and His World*, trans. Hélène Iswolsky (Bloomington: Indiana University Press, 1984), 268. Similar statements characterize Bakhtin's essentialist picture of the Middle Ages and treatment of the carnivalesque, problems also noted by medievalists. See Flanigan, "Liminality," in *Victor Turner*, ed. Ashley, 54–58; and Strohm, *Hochon's Arrow*, 45.

[40] Leah S. Marcus, "Renaissance/Early Modern Studies," in *Redrawing the Boundaries*, ed. Greenblatt and Gunn, 46. Marcus notes that "The unexplored or underdeveloped territory within early modern studies includes a vast array of writings whose form and apparent function disqualified it as serious literature – pamphlets, romances, ballads, even popular drama, and, at the other end of the cultural spectrum, ephemeral forms like the court masque, which was disparaged by its learned authors as the mere illusion of a night" (47). Significantly, only popular drama is set off by the term *even*, which suggests the extent to which Marcus sees its study as groundbreaking, even radical.

canonical.[41] Greenblatt exemplifies this privileging of the canonical by New Historicists, despite their rhetoric to the contrary. In "Resonance and Wonder" he states that New Historicists "are as concerned with the margins as with the center," but near the end of the essay, discussing the transfer of "Impressionist and Post-Impressionist masterpieces" to the Musée d'Orsay, he reveals his preference for the "aesthetic masterpiece" with its ability to produce "wonder" over "lesser objects" that create "resonance."[42] His comments make explicit what is implicit in his criticism, which manipulates the marginal as various markers of cultural practices – labels, photographs, maps, explanatory texts, and other "lesser objects" – are used in a museum to focus attention on the "aesthetic masterpiece." Despite their fashionable concern with the "margins," Greenblatt and other New Historicists do not challenge the hierarchy of values at the root of the center/margin distinction. Crucial in constructing the canonical theater of the London "center" and the Protestant early modern Shakespeare, this distinction elides the popular theatre of the provincial town, which is "Catholic," "medieval," marginalized.

The fourth, and perhaps most important, reason for the elision of the "medieval" by Renaissance New Historicism is evident in its particular version of the *grand récit* outlining literary-historical periodization. If medieval historiography and drama exemplify the "alterity" of the Middle Ages by sectioning time into divinely sanctioned units made meaningful by events that link heaven and earth and that are "almost always *out* of the ordinary,"[43] New Historicists emphasize the *familiarity* of the Renaissance, which they often designate the "early modern."[44] As Jean Howard notes, New Historicists – influenced by self-conscious post-modernity – read the

---

[41] Montrose, "Professing the Renaissance," in *New Historicism*, ed. Veeser, acknowledges the canonical nature of New Historicist analysis, noting that its focus "has been upon a refiguring of the socio-cultural field within which canonical Renaissance literary and dramatic works were originally produced" (17).

[42] Stephen J. Greenblatt, "Resonance and Wonder," in *Learning to Curse: Essays in Early Modern Culture* (New York: Routledge, 1990), 168 and 180–81. For New Historicist use of nonliterary texts to focus on "the familiar canon of English literature," see Holstun, "Ranting at the New Historicism," 192–95.

[43] See Nancy F. Partner, "The New Cornificius: Medieval History and the Artifice of Words," in *Classical Rhetoric and Medieval Historiography*, ed. Ernst Breisach, Studies in Medieval Culture 19 (Kalamazoo: Medieval Institute Publications, 1985), 17.

[44] For the implications of the term "early modern," see Marcus, "Renaissance/Early Modern Studies," in *Redrawing the Boundaries*, ed. Greenblatt and Gunn, esp. 41–43. Both "Renaissance" and "early modern" rely on "a perception of historical rupture" with the Middle Ages (43). Middleton, "Medieval Studies," in *Redrawing the Boundaries*, also notes how the Renaissance/early modern sets up the Middle Ages "as a universal 'other,' against which modernity defines itself . . ." (15). Interestingly, both essays appear in a volume that, despite its fashionable attention to the "new" and the need to redraw boundaries, reinscribes the usual discredited periodization. That one of its editors is America's leading New Historicist may partly account for this curiosity.

present into the Renaissance past, seeing it "as a boundary or liminal space between two more monolithic periods where one can see acted out a clash of paradigms and ideologies . . . ."[45] As a result, according to Patterson, they accept "that most reactionary of accounts, a hierarchical Middle Ages in which not merely alternative modes of thought but thought per se is proscribed," a stereotyped account that is basically unhistorical.[46]

Stereotyping the Middle Ages is common in Renaissance drama studies. For example, Jonathan Dollimore stresses the break from medieval "Christian essentialism," without considering whether such essentialism characterizes medieval drama, and Steven Mullaney states that "Popular drama in Renaissance England was born of the contradiction between a Court that in limited but significant ways licensed and maintained it and a city that sought its prohibition," without recognizing other sixteenth-century dramatic traditions that were genuinely popular.[47] It is telling that Mullaney devotes more attention to classical Athens than he does to contemporary provincial English towns, and that Michael Bristol, who attacks several critical distortions in drama scholarship, is silent on its most pervasive, unexamined, and misleading assumption, the rigid medieval/ Renaissance distinction. Bristol instead registers several binary categories distinguishing "earlier" drama – the amateur theater of "homogeneous social groups" playing "within a well-defined and authorized social milieu" – and the public playhouses, a professional theater that is "an actual heteroglot institution in which the exchange of experience crosses every social boundary," is transgressive, experimental, unauthorized, and the source of "genuine political anxiety."[48] As a result of such unexamined assumptions, much New Historicist and other criticism ignores the full range of sixteenth-century drama. Here is where renewed historical research by medievalists can provide some balance.

Medievalists have tended to emphasize the diachronic study of drama, even while insisting that medieval drama is valuable in its own right and not simply a prologue to future greatness. We now need more synchronic

---

[45] Jean E. Howard, "The New Historicism in Renaissance Studies," in *Renaissance Historicism: Selections from English Literary Renaissance* (Amherst: University of Massachusetts Press, 1987), 6.

[46] Patterson, "On the Margin," 97. He adds, "The only thing more striking than the familiarity of these schemes is their lack of interest in the realm they purport to privilege: history" (98). Noting how Greenblatt ignores medieval texts, Patterson comments that "the Middle Ages is not a subject for discussion but the rejected object, not a prehistory whose shape can be described but the history – historicity itself – that modernity must reject in order to be itself" (99).

[47] Mullaney, *Place of the Stage*, vii; and Dollimore, *Radical Tragedy: Religion, Ideology and Power in the Drama of Shakespeare and his Contemporaries* (Chicago: University of Chicago Press, 1984), 155–56.

[48] Michael D. Bristol, *Carnival and Theater: Plebeian Culture and the Structure of Authority in Renaissance England* (1985; rpt. New York: Routledge, 1989), 122–23.

examinations along the lines of the session sponsored by the Medieval and Renaissance Drama Society at the 1988 MLA convention in New Orleans. This session included several short investigations into a wide range of theatrical activity during the 1520s – university and parish drama, civic spectacle and court entertainment, cycle and morality plays.[49] Similar investigations aimed at later decades of the sixteenth century are needed if we are to extend the limited synchronic studies of New Historicists. Directing attention to provincial cities as well as to London, such investigations would counteract the narrowing focus of Renaissance specialists on London and re-examine their conclusions on a larger, national scale. Such investigations might compare, for example, Mullaney's description of Elizabeth's procession through London with Martin Stevens's analysis of the York "Entry into Jerusalem." To both scholars, the processions transform city into stage. Yet Mullaney focuses on the theatricality of the ceremonial in contrast with the liminal, extra-mural nature of popular theater, which he understands to be in an agonistic relation to the city and to authority. Stevens, on the other hand, sees the York cycle as reversing traditional negative attitudes toward the earthly city: "By making the city the destination rather than the place of departure, the drama reflects a whole new view toward urban culture . . . ."[50] Assuming both analyses are cogent, are these differences in the relationship between theater and city due to differences between "medieval" and "Renaissance" theatrical forms? Are they due to differences in urban size and landscape, political and economic structures, literary genre and ideology? Or do they simply follow from differing historicist methodologies?

Medievalists could also provide a more nuanced understanding of the social and political role of theater than the present models based on simple binary oppositions, whether they be "authorized-liminal" or "elite-popular." Investigating a fuller range of theatrical performances in sixteenth-century England would identify counter-traditions that are neither exclusively popular nor elite, subversive nor hegemonic. Does not Greenblatt's comment that the Shakespearean theater "is manifestly the product of collective intentions" in which writing "is itself a social moment" and that "the theater manifestly addresses its audience as a collectivity" sound remarkably familiar to students of medieval drama?[51] A truly synchronic examination not limited to the canonical nor to the kingdom's central city would remind us that such "social moments"

---

[49] For the papers see John C. Coldewey, ed., "English Drama in the 1520s: Six Perspectives," *RORD* 31 (1992): 57–78.
[50] Stevens, *Four Middle English Mystery Cycles*, 51 and 64; see Mullaney, *Place of the Stage*, 10–11.
[51] Stephen Greenblatt, *Shakespearean Negotiations: The Circulation of Social Energy in Renaissance England* (Berkeley: University of California Press, 1988), 4–5.

continue English dramatic traditions that predate Shakespeare and extend far beyond London and its "licentious Liberties." And if we wish to comprehend how theatre could provide political resistance to established power – not just a source of "political anxiety" – Robert Knapp notes that there is no better example of resistance than "a town's trying to hold fast to its old plays despite the opposition of a reforming ecclesiastical establishment."[52]

By extending their diachronic analyses into the sixteenth century, medievalists could modulate the overemphasis on innovation and discontinuity. The Tudor Chester cycle provides an opportunity to study the intermingling of traditional and new, discontinuity within continuity. Since it was staged a half dozen times between 1521 and 1575, it may be possible to study the occasions of its performance, considering how it embodied the desire for "faith and prosperity" during a time of severe economic hardship,[53] and how it was both shaped by history and shaped history for the citizens of Chester facing religious, economic, and political crises. The entries in the Chester Mayors Lists when the cycle was challenged would be a good starting point.[54] Keeping in mind Clopper's insight that during the 1560s and 1570s "the struggle over whether to produce the plays was a struggle between two, perhaps more, Protestant factions" and Tessa Watt's reminder that, rather than being a "coherent and unchanging" entity, Protestantism was "inseparable from and constantly modified by" its cultural contexts,[55] this study could trace the ways the plays mediated the struggle between forces of tradition and change and became "historical contestants" as well as "objects of contestation."[56]

Recently theorists have challenged the tendency of historicist scholarship to focus on the innovative and avant-garde.[57] We must now recognize how

---

[52] Robert S. Knapp, "Resistance, Religion, and the Aesthetic: Power and Drama in the Towneley 'Magnus Herodes,' *Cambises*, and *Richard III*," *RORD* 33 (1994): 143–44.

[53] Lawrence M. Clopper, "Lay and Clerical Impact," in *Contexts*, ed. Briscoe and Coldewey, 103–104. For the records see *REED: Chester*, ed. Clopper; and Alexandra F. Johnston, "The *York Cycle* and the *Chester Cycle*: What Do the Records Tell Us?" in *Editing Early English Drama: Special Problems and New Directions*, ed. A. F. Johnston (New York: AMS, 1983), 123–24.

[54] The entries for 1571–72 exemplify the "textuality of history" in their silence regarding the mayor's motivation, varied explanations and sequencing of events, and differing attitudes toward the plays. See *REED: Chester*, ed. Clopper, 96–97.

[55] See Clopper, "Lay and Clerical Impact," in *Contexts*, ed. Briscoe and Coldewey, 103; and Tessa Watt, *Cheap Print and Popular Piety, 1550–1640* (Cambridge: Cambridge University Press, 1991), 325. Watt states that we should "see belief-formation as a process: not a simple replacement of Catholic with Protestant doctrine, but a gradual modification of traditional piety. The resulting patchwork of beliefs my be described as distinctively 'post-Reformation,' but not thoroughly 'Protestant' " (327).

[56] Strohm, *Hochon's Arrow*, 9.

[57] See Alan Woods, "Emphasizing the Avant-Garde: An Exploration in Theatre Historiography," in *Interpreting the Theatrical Past*, ed. Postlewait and McConachie, 166–76.

continuity and tradition are essential to theater history, especially if we investigate the role of the audience and its "horizon of expectations." Yet historical studies of drama need not return to earlier methodologies, but instead should enrich New Historicist synchronic analyses to include a range of dramatic forms and should extend traditional diachronic studies beyond the rigid periodization that has hampered the study of medieval drama.[58] Perhaps by practicing a renewed historicism that avoids archival fetishism and mystifying periodization, medievalists may engage colleagues studying Renaissance drama and provide a model for understanding the full range of sixteenth-century English drama.

---

[58] A model for diachronic studies is Eamon Duffy, *The Stripping of the Altars: Traditional Religion in England c.1400–c.1580* (New Haven: Yale University Press, 1992). Lawrence Clopper's chapter, "From Ungodly Ludi to Sacred Play: English Drama," in the forthcoming *Cambridge History of Medieval English Literature: Writing in Britain, 1066–1547*, ed. David Wallace, will similarly cut across traditional period boundaries by extending the discussion of medieval drama well into the sixteenth century.

"Se in what stat thou doyst indwell": The Shifting Constructions of Gender and Power Relations in *Wisdom*

Marlene Clark, Sharon Kraus, Pamela Sheingorn

In the visually memorable production of the English morality play *Wisdom* staged under Milla Riggio's direction at Trinity College in 1984, the actor playing the fallen Might Will shocked and delighted the audience when one of the appurtenances of the new "array" he wore to replace his monkish robe turned out to be an oversized pink phallus eagerly bobbing up and down beneath his fashionably short gown.[1] This staging decision fixed Will's sex as male and gender as masculine. The political implications of the play were also not lost on the impresarios behind the Trinity production, since the characters of Anima and Wisdom were staged as iconic state portraits, which assumed a specific kind of mid-fifteenth-century audience and patronage. Though some of our conclusions about the constructions of gender and power relations differ from those suggested by the Trinity production, we found it a crucial stimulus to our own engagement with *Wisdom*.

The sexed, physical body of Will in the Trinity restaging provoked us to explore the ways in which gender and power relations are constructed in *Wisdom*. Our premise is that in this play the personified female soul's, or Anima's, three constitutive, personified Mights, Mind, Will and Understanding, although materialized in male bodies, do not sustain uniform subjectivity gendered masculine. Rather, we will argue that in *Wisdom* Anima's three Mights explore and experiment with fluid configurations of gendered characteristics, exchanging, rearranging, and amplifying them in multivalent combinations. The allegorical figures in this drama show the "free play" possible when gendered characteristics, routinely "clustered" in "normative" sex and gender configurations, form and re-form alternate sex

---

[1] On this production see Milla B. Riggio, "The Staging of *Wisdom*," *Research Opportunities in Renaissance Drama* 17 (1984): 167–77; Theresa Coletti and Pamela Sheingorn, "Playing *Wisdom* at Trinity College," *Research Opportunities in Renaissance Drama* 17 (1984): 179–84.

and gender identities. Thus, *Wisdom* enacts the "constructed character of sexuality," to use Judith Butler's words, and thereby reveals an awareness of sexed positions as *denaturalized* and contingent,[2] even as the play proposes its own "naturalized" schema of masculine parts, Mind, Will, and Understanding, constituting a feminine whole, Anima.

Our reading examines as well *Wisdom*'s preoccupation with secular, political power structures, which, as the play emphasizes, paradoxically delegitimize while they constrain these subject constructions – consolidating in accordance with the heterosexual imperative while fragmenting the notion that a unified gender subjectivity is possible. We see the play, rooted in its temporal moment, to be lodging a specific, political critique through the personifications during their moment of corruption. Although their critique might appear to be "contained" – that is, wholly subsumed by and reintegrated into the dominant Christian ideology of fifteenth-century feudal England – we suggest that the symbolic order of *Christianitas*, masculinity, and normative power relations is destabilized in the play's temptation scene and never completely reconsolidated in the play's final reconciliation scene.

The action of the *Wisdom* play is at first glance a fairly straightforward dramatization of a soul's falling from purity into sin and then repenting, making confession, and rejoining the community of the spiritually pure. The play first introduces Wisdom, who is Christ enthroned, and Anima, a soul who is lovingly espoused to him. Anima's constitutive parts, her five female Wits and three male Mights, are then brought on stage and their interdependent relationships to her are set forth. Soon after this introduction, Lucifer announces his desire to pervert Anima and proceeds to tempt her Mights away from the intense rigors of an austere, possibly monastic, asceticism, and toward a less disciplined *vita mixta*. Accepting Lucifer's rationale, the Mights embrace worldly corruption as wholeheartedly as they had previously espoused worldly denial. The anti-masque mayhem of the Mights' temptation, subsequent fall, and internal dispute comprises nearly half the play; Wisdom then returns, facilitates Anima's repentance and confession, and presumably restores her to her original condition. As we will discuss more fully at the end of this paper, Anima's reintegration with her five Wits and three Mights is neither wholly satisfying nor entirely successful.

Since the bulk of our essay will be concerned with Anima's relationship to her three Mights, it is well worth noting here that the tripartite structure of the rational part of Anima's soul – represented in *Wisdom* by the allegorical figures Mind, Will, and Understanding – is likely derived from an Augustinian model which posits a trinitarian structure of the soul,

---

[2] Judith Butler, *Bodies That Matter: On the Discursive Limits of "Sex"* (New York: Routledge, 1993), 93.

composed of three powers, "memoria, intelligentia and voluntas, in the performance of their functions."[3] In contradistinction to Thomist faculty psychology, however, these powers do not perform distinct functions.[4] Rather, according to Augustine, "these three are one . . . for not only is each contained in each, but also each by each."[5] Consequently, the feminine gender of these nouns notwithstanding,[6] the trinitarian unity of Augustine's conception of the soul has often been read theologically as corresponding metonymically to the Holy Trinity of Father, Son, and Holy Spirit as subsumed under the Godhead;[7] traditionally, both "trinities" have been personified as male. But the unity of the soul in Augustine's schema is disrupted by a soul/body split. Even though the "soul acts with the body and in it, subjected divinely to its domination," Augustine further asserts that "whatever corporeal things are put into or taken out of this body from without, produce something not in the soul but in the body, which is either opposed to its work or agrees with it."[8] And as many scholars before us have pointed out, the body is often correlated metaphorically with the female. From the very opening of the play *Wisdom* we see several over-lapping slippages in typical gender configurations. For although we would contend that it is Anima, cast as the Soul, who metaphorically represents the body in this play, and that it is Wisdom who is a metonymic representa-tion of the Trinity, it is the three male Mights, paradoxically housed in Anima's flesh while simultaneously sharing a metonymic relationship with Wisdom, who actually fall into bodily corruption. Moreover, the play foregrounds a female whole, while declaring that "eche clene soule" in its three parts "ys symylytude of Gode abowe" (line 284).

It is, of course, theologically correct to argue, as Clifford Davidson does,

---

[3] Wolfgang Riehle, *The Middle English Mystics*, trans. Bernard Standring (London: Routledge and Kegan Paul, 1981), 143.

[4] *The Essential Augustine*, ed. Vernon J. Bourke (Toronto: New American Library of Canada, 1964), 68.

[5] *Essential Augustine*, 77.

[6] Grammar has been an important determinant of the sex of personifications; since most abstract nouns are feminine in Latin, personifications in both visual and verbal renditions have tended to be female. See Denis Baron, *Grammar and Gender* (New Haven: Yale University Press, 1986). However, in the pictorial arts this convention is susceptible to alteration when the cultural understandings of specific personifications shift. For an example see Michael Evans, "Allegorical Women and Practical Men: The Iconography of the *artes* Reconsidered," in *Medieval Women*, ed. Derek Baker (Oxford: Basil Blackwell, 1978), 305–29; plates 1–33.

[7] For a discussion of medieval rhetorical theory of personification, see Helen Cooper, "Gender and Personification," *The Yearbook of Langland Studies* 5 (1991): 40–41. Cooper notes that by the late thirteenth century, "personification allegory was able to define the nature of the human form its concepts might take without grammatical constraint" (33).

[8] *Essential Augustine*, 74.

45

that "the Three Mights and the various inward and outward senses represent Anima's freedom, for they are her means of obtaining information about reality or the world and of processing that information. They are the means also by which temptation can come to her."[9] In keeping with the prevalent medieval attitude that rational thought and action were characteristic of men, it may likely be equally correct to argue that the "freedom" required in mid-fifteenth-century England to "obtain information about reality or the world" necessitates that Anima's three Mights be sexed male. And since sexual identity is typically linked with the "appropriate" display of "normative" gender characteristics, the Mights' behavior as beings sexed male becomes unavoidably entangled with their masculine gendered identities. Once fallen, though, the Mights' abstract identities become more fluid as they slip from one personification to another (e.g., Will becomes Lust becomes Lechery), and in the process their sex/gender identities become equally amorphous.

It follows that it is the component parts, Anima's three male Mights, rather than Anima herself, who enact her temptation and fall. Davidson observes that "Anima seems to be undramatically passive, lacking control over her fate rather than representing any of the freedom normally accorded to the soul." And he quotes Mark Eccles: " 'Anima is a puppet who suffers rather than acts.' "[10] Charlotte Spivack, noting the connection between Anima's behavior and her sex, calls attention to "the silence and passivity of Anima. She is not directly tempted, but is victimized by her faculties, or powers. Pure and worthy of Christ at the beginning and again at the ending, her worldly sojourn is enacted in effect outside her own control."[11] Anima's passivity can be traced to the Aristotelian notions of male and female that dominated thought about these matters in the Middle Ages. As Thomas Laqueur has noted, "What we would take to be ideologically charged social constructions of gender – that males are active and females passive, males contribute the form and females the matter to generation – were for Aristotle indubitable facts, 'natural' truths."[12] The disfiguring of Anima by inappropriate male/masculine behavior substantiates the widely held notion that such behavior automatically sullies women; that is, that women's virtue is determined by the actions of the men with whom they associate, no matter how unstable these men's gender roles and sexual identities are. So clearly is Anima empty of

[9] Clifford Davidson, *Visualizing the Moral Life: Medieval Iconography and the Macro Moralities* (New York: AMS Press, 1989), 95–96.
[10] Davidson, 95.
[11] Charlotte Spivack, "Feminine vs. Masculine in English Morality Drama," in *Fifteenth Century Studies*, vol. 13: *Le Théâtre et la cité dans l'europe medievale* (Stuttgart: Hans-Dieter Heinz, Akademischer Verlag Stuttgart, 1988), 141.
[12] Thomas Laqueur, *Making Sex: Body and Gender from the Greeks to Freud* (Cambridge, MA: Harvard University Press, 1990), 28.

signification of her own that even when she is physically present in the drama her sins are personified by seven devils that run out from under her horrible mantle.

In contrast, Anima's three Mights are far from empty of signification, though their signification through dramatic representation is complex and conflicted. We would argue that even though "male bonding" is an apparently important aspect of the fallen Mights' material circumstances and appears to be constitutive of a "male" subjectivity in the play, their apparently masculine gender roles and identities are inexorably inflected by their associations with *women* – just as Anima's is constituted by her association with men – but in a way that underscores the historical difference of sexual difference. As Bruce Smith has shown, male slippage from "masculinity" to "femininity," from virility to effeminacy, is often a direct result not of men's connections with other men, but with women.[13] Our premise concerning the conflicts inherent in the sex/gender system of mid-fifteenth-century England parallels that of Eve Sedgwick when she argues

in any male-dominated society, there is a special relationship between male homosocial (*including* homosexual) desire and the structures for maintaining and transmitting patriarchal power: a relationship founded on an inherent and potentially active structural congruence. For histor-ical reasons, this special relationship may take the form of ideological homophobia, ideological homosexuality, or some highly conflicted but intensively structured combination of the two.[14]

It is Sedgwick's formulation of the "highly conflicted but intensively structured combination of the two" which we wish to explore further in this essay.

[13] Smith's argument, derived from classical notions of the homoerotic and applied to the early modern period, is that "[b]ehavior that we would label homosexual, and hence a rejection of maleness" was in fact an *aspect* of maleness (75). He continues: "What we are dealing with here is an idea of effeminacy very different from our own. . . . Their distinction seems to be, not between male and female as modes of self-identity, or even between male and female as postures in making love, but between sexual moderation and excess" (196). More to our point is Smith's contention that "[h]omosexual desire is not a matter of men wanting to *be* like women. Quite the contrary. It is too great an *interest in women* that makes a man become like them. Homosexuality is a matter of men desiring other men. The first evidence we have of homosexual acts being associated with *our* sense of effeminacy does not occur until the eighteenth century" (171, emphasis added, with the exception of final *our*). Our argument is that what Smith notices as operative differences in the sex/gender system of the early modern period are apparent even earlier in the *Wisdom* play. See Bruce Smith, *Homosexual Desire in Shakespeare's England: A Cultural Poetics* (Chicago: University of Chicago Press, 1991).
[14] Eve Kosofsky Sedgwick, *Between Men: English Literature and Male Homosocial Desire* (New York: Columbia University Press, 1985), 25.

As the action moves from Anima, who is universalized, generalized, and abstract, to the Mights, who are discrete, individualized, and concrete, we also move from the realm of the timeless to a specific political and historical moment. When the play turns from the celestial to the terrestrial, the protagonist Anima is temporarily replaced by the three Mights.

Mind, the personification whose role within the soul is "apprehension," introduces himself as "the veray fygure of þe Deyte" (184),[15] and explains that in his figure is contained wholeness, fairness, freedom, glory, and gentleness. But Mind is quick to acknowledge the "vnstabullnes" of his exalted state. Recalling the "yerys and dayes of my synfullnes" (198), his "oreble fallynge and freellnes" (200), Mind understands his dependence upon God's grace to rise above temptation.

The initial metaphor invoked by Mind when describing himself to the audience is that of the mind contemplating itself: "Wen in myselff I haue mynde and se . . ." (185). The intellectual, self-referential circularity of Mind's apprehension of himself through the Godhead is reinforced by his contention that in his sinful state, "mynde makyt me myselff to dyspyse" (204), and that only through his self-contemplative plea to his Savior, "Haue mynde of me" (208), can "mynde to mynde bryngth þat fawowre" (209) – the restoration of God's grace.

It is Mind whom Lucifer, disguised as a "goodly galont," first approaches in the temptation scene, since Mind must first apprehend Lucifer's suggestion before Understanding can be brought to delectation and Will can make confirmation. Addressing Mind as "Sir," Lucifer suggests that while prayer, fasting, and labor have their place, so do other more worldly concerns. In the first of several deictic maneuvers of the play, Lucifer points to a specific audience member – one with a wife, children, busy servants, and other "unspecified charges" – to illustrate his point. Despite the reference to possible illegitimate children, Lucifer offers this (male) audience member to Mind as an example of one whose life is like Christ's in eschewing the purely contemplative in favor of the *vita mixta*. With this model Lucifer claims to provide "informacyon / Ande example to man" (423–24).

Lucifer couples this analogy with a canny reminder of the risks attending the purely contemplative life – specifically, the extreme physical deprivation and mental isolation which can produce bodily and intellectual wasting and possibly induce despair and/or madness. His reminder likely capitalizes on monastic fear of incontinence brought on by the inability to withstand the rigors of religious life, a scenario understood to be more displeasing to God

---

[15] All citations are to Mark Eccles, ed., *The Macro Plays: The Castle of Perseverance, Wisdom, Mankind*, EETS 262 (Oxford and London: Oxford University Press, 1969). We are very grateful to Milla Riggio for allowing us to use her book, *The Play of Wisdom: Its Texts and Contexts*, prior to its publication.

than a well-balanced secular life. Lucifer's arguments hold; Mind "recognizes" their merit.

Once "fallen," Mind becomes quite the dandy. Expensively accoutered, he revels in his large, extended noble family, his fortune, and his "grace" (here social, rather than spiritual), all of which make him "sovereign." In another deictic move, Mind proclaims that "galontys *now* be in most fame / Curtely personys men hem proclame" (emphasis added; 598–99). Mind now represents the courtier, serving a decidedly secular "Lordship" through the maintenance of liveried retainers ready to fight at the king's request.

It is our contention that Mind, in his insistent references to maintenance and in his representation of debauchery ("lechery was neuer more vsande / Off lernyde and lewde in þis lande" [681–82]), poses a critique of the courtly excess bought and paid for by the maintenance system designed to buttress the shaky reigns of both Henry VI and Edward IV with its liveried armies.

Mind's all-male cast of anti-masque dancers, members of his "retinue," typify excesses in the irascible appetite. Such excesses – indignation, sturdiness (bravery under fire), malice, hastiness, wretchedness, and discord – were all hallmarks of the reigns of Henry VI and Edward IV. Both of these reigns were characterized by long periods of internecine warfare punctuated by skirmishes in France and Scotland. Lords maintaining troops for both the Lancastrian and Yorkist causes are known to have changed allegiances impulsively and often.

Gail McMurray Gibson, in her essay "The Play of *Wisdom* and the Abbey of St. Edmund," argues that the play *Wisdom* is likely a token of reconciliation offered by the clerics of Bury St. Edmunds to Edward IV after his displacement of the monklike Henry VI.[16] Edward, however, is described by the Croyland Continuator as "fond of boon-companionship, vanities, debaucheries, extravagance and sensual enjoyments."[17] He was also a very shrewd manipulator of the maintenance system; his wife, Elizabeth Woodville, came from a large family strategically located in the north of England not far from the equally large but much more wealthy and powerful Neville family.[18] Through his adroit use of members of the

---

[16] Gail McMurray Gibson, "The Play of *Wisdom* and the Abbey of St. Edmund," in *The Wisdom Symposium: Papers from the Trinity College Medieval Festival*, ed. Milla Cozart Riggio (New York: AMS Press, 1986), passim.

[17] Mary Clive, *This Sun of York* (New York: Knopf, 1974), 95.

[18] Clive, 112–15. Elizabeth Woodville came from a large but relatively impoverished north country family. While Edward avoided financial aggrandizement of the Woodvilles to the extent that it would arouse the competitive impulses of other large and powerful north country families, he nevertheless "used Elizabeth's sisters and her older son to block dynastic marriages which nobles might otherwise have arranged among themselves" (114), thereby maintaining a balance of sorts among aristocratic clans jockeying for position.

Woodville family, Edward kept the Nevilles in check. Nevertheless, Edward was hardly more able than his predecessor to curb abuses inherent within the system of aristocratic maintenance of liveried retainers.[19]

The feudal bonds between men were highly stratified. They were also, as Mind recognizes, both tenuous and fungible. He admits to Will and Understanding that the basis of the terrestrial "worschyppe" now accorded to him by his followers resides in *his* service to an even more "myghty lordeschyppe." Mind's connection to an even higher secular power, therefore, is the main source of the "grett tenderschyppe" of his retainers. But it is exactly this esteem, leached down to him through the strata of the aristocracy, that, Mind concedes, makes "moche folke me dredys" (632), just as one can imagine Mind likely has occasion to dread the power of his lord now and again. Moreover, Mind's retainers' loyalty is based mainly on his continued ability to finance their "schendeschyppe," or shameful conduct; Mind in turn depends on his lord for the continued financing of his courtly lifestyle.

Mind, then, performs within a homosocial matrix of local and national politics. Though he and his red-bearded dancers appear to be rampantly heterosexual and his bonds with other men primarily homosocial, buttressing the patriarchal system of feudal maintenance in service to a male lord, the flimsy nature of those highly stratified bonds, and Mind's nervous insistence on sustaining them no matter the cost, point out that the politics of his all-male retinue is problematized by Sedgwick's paradox of a "highly conflicted but intensively structured" combination of *ideological homophobia* and *ideological homosexuality*. The all-male power structure of the feudal maintenance system emphasizes what Smith calls the "homosexual potential" vested in a structure which values male bonds above all other emotional ties.[20] And yet, at one and the same time, the maintenance system is also ideologically homophobic, in that male bonds are charged with fears of rejection, betrayal, and loss.

Understanding also operates in a matrix of gender and class politics. Characterized in the temptation first as Covetousness and then as Perjury, this Might is represented as susceptible to delectation, sensuality, and bodily delight, all excesses of the concupiscent appetite and characteristics that are typically gendered female in medieval Christian and secular thought.

Significantly, Understanding's chief preoccupation is with power rela-

---

[19] Clive, 108 and 128. The parliaments of November, 1461; April, 1463; and June, 1467 all addressed problems with the maintenance of liveried retainers and/or sumptuary laws, emphasizing the period's preoccupation with proprieties regarding dress. Though both the parliaments of 1461 and 1463 forbade outright the retention of liveried retainers, the Barons' armies continued to flourish.

[20] Smith, 56.

tions. This is a sensible concern since, in his prior innocence, Understanding served Anima by recognizing the incomprehensible Godhead that resides within the human soul: "Thus by knowynge of me to knowynge of Gode I assende" (252). Where Understanding previously had been devoted to intuitively comprehending himself ("knowynge of me"), in his corruption he is consumed with the work of comprehending his position in relation to others. He dedicates himself to vying with all other authority figures (who go unnamed) for power ("Ryches makyt a man equall / To hem sumtyme hys souereyngys wer" [587–88]). He also wishes to be the most fashionable and desirable of his peers ("To be holde ryche and reyall" [585]; "Non thre be in so grett aqweynttance" [658]). As Covetousness/Perjury, this personification is devoted to power relations in a secular, homosocial order.

This Might also delights in the material security that wealth brings – he likes even the feel of money ("my joy ys . . . to handyll yt" [581–83]). He desires to control the law through money ("Wo wyll haue law must haue monye" [666]) and is associated with simony and usury. Of particular interest in this respect are Understanding's comments, "Truthe on syde I lett him slyppe" (565), "I [wyll euer hante] falsnes, to be passante" (610), and "Trowthe recurythe not for habundance" (654). The truthful word, the oath spoken in fealty, cannot, in an increasingly conflicted secular world, be counted upon. What can be counted upon is money. The homosocial order of the fifteenth-century manor, courtroom, and battlefield is bound less by allegiance than by currency, and though Understanding delights in his own position, his critique signifies nostalgia and desire for the formerly strong bonds of loyalty among men. Understanding's propensities point to tensions between the market economy, flourishing in fifteenth-century East Anglia, and bastard feudalism, which was in marked decline.

Understanding also explicitly critiques the current state of troubled legal affairs. His lines contain the play's more overtly topical references, citing the Westminster court (789), the Knight-Marshall's court (853), the Admiralty court (854), and twice mentioning the Quest of Holborn (721, 731). An inquest such as that of Holborn might well have provided opportunity for local abuses of power,[21] and in fact the monks of Bury

---

[21] Eccles, *The Macro Plays*, 168. Eccles cites William Smith, Rouge Dragon's "A Breeff Description of the Famovs Cittie of London, Capitall Cittie of this Realme of England, &c. Ann. 1588," which describes the Wardmote Enquest of London and which "shows what the Holborn [quest] ought to have done and been":
... The Aldermen of euery ward, causeth all ye Inhabitants thereof, to assemble at a Church . . .where is chosen out amongst them about 24 parsons, which are called The Wardmot Enquest. And these do sitt all ye Christmas Hollydaies till Twelfft Day. And call beffore them all such parsons (in their ward) as be noted (yea, or suspected) of any notable crime. . . . Also they go into every mans howse within the said ward, & peruse their weights & measures, which, if they ffynd not Iust: they breake them in peeces.

St. Edmunds' abbey would have had good reason to be concerned about Bury's disintegrating juridical structure, since "one of the most important sources of [the abbey's] power was control and maintenance of the judicial system."[22] The abbey had controlled Bury's courts since at least 1290, but during the mid-fifteenth century struggled to compete with extraordinarily violent magnates and burgesses for authority; as Phillipa Maddern puts it, "The whole system of lawful hierarchy had been upset."[23] Understanding can thus be seen as pointing to tensions between competing secular and ecclesiastic courts, and to the possibility of anarchy. Likewise, the play's anti-masque scene can be read as an enactment of the secular world's perceived devolution into chaos. What is particularly interesting here is that this collapse into disorder seems also to occur in the personifications' embodied genders. As Understanding's corruption proceeds, he falls further outside the pale of normative heterosexuality, shifting from feminized to homoerotic characteristics. Understanding's own dancers, like Mind's, are an all-male cast of "jorours in a sute" (s.d. following 724) and as such further advance the "relationship between male homosocial . . . desire and the structures for maintaining and transmitting patriarchal power."[24] Once the third personification's, Will's, dance is presented – the only dance to introduce normative femininity and actual female bodies into this segment of the play – the homosocial bonds among Mind, Will, and Understanding momentarily fracture.

Understanding and Mind, angry with Will for prizing other acquaintances over theirs, remind Will of all they have done for him:

Mynde: Ye may not endure wythowt my meyntenance.
Vndyrstondynge: That ys bought wyth a brybe of owr substance.

(761–62)

Then Understanding, desiring both to punish Will and to recapture his own former attachment to Mind and Will, simulates a physical attack. "þi longe body bare," he tells Will, "to bett I not spare" (770–71). The mingling of gender and power conflicts that Understanding enacts may point to monastic anxieties about sexuality that were becoming exacerbated as

Also they present euery man, at whose dore the Street is not well paued: also all Strumpetts, Baudes, Raylers, Skolders, & such Lyke, which being found faulty, are punished accordingly. And therfore euery baudy bacheler had nead to looke to hym selff.

[22] Phillipa C. Maddern, *Violence and Social Order: East Anglia, 1422–1442* (Oxford: Clarendon Press, 1992), 170.

[23] Maddern, 88. It may be worth noting the rather famous eyewitness account of those times, the Paston Letters. For example, John Paston III, writing ca. 1469, describes the region's climate of lawlessness to John Paston II: "for what so euyr they do wyth ther swordys they make it lawe . . ." (*Paston Letters* i.532.)

[24] Sedgwick, 25.

ecclesiastics more diligently attended to the regulation of lay sexuality.[25] We suggest also that Understanding's desire for absolute political power is connected within the drama to a desire for stable homosocial attachments, attachments which were faltering in mid-fifteenth-century East Anglia. Understanding's gender shift, his intensified homosociality/-sexuality, seems to coincide with the increasing threat of losing attachments – both political and secular, and internal and spiritual – among men. Loss of homosocial bonds is the situation dramatized in *Wisdom*'s anti-masque sequence; we see the corrupted Understanding as not only emblematizing a life led devoid of the Godhead but also embodying a critique of the disorder produced by local authority figures, within and outside the abbey, who failed to impose rule.

At a first reading, Will appears to be the Might least likely to reveal gender instability. In engineering Will's fall, Lucifer tempts him with heterosexual pleasure: "Lewe yowr nyse chastyte and take a wyff" (476). Yet the very appeal to the senses calls up the medieval identification of women with carnality and sensory pleasure. As Howard Bloch notes, "The patristic articulation of gender assumes a relationship of male to female built upon the analogy of the world of intelligence to that of the senses."[26] According to this analogy, "Man as mind and woman as sensory perception are mutually exclusive."[27] Will's susceptibility to sexual desire thus undermines his position as determined by the analogy and renders his masculine gender suspect. He has become susceptible through Understanding's weakness in relaxing his control over the five Wits in accordance with Lucifer's sugges- tion: "Yowr fyve wyttys abrode lett sprede" (453). Once these female Wits are open to experience, the situation grows perilous, for Wisdom has cautioned that if the Wits were not "spared" from the World, the Flesh, and the Fiend, their sensuality might induce the Mights to follow, and that is indeed what happens. The contamination affects Will to such an extent that when Lucifer addresses a question to Sensuality – "Better ys fayer frut þan fowll pollucyon / What seyeth sensualite to þis conclusyon?" (477–78) – Will is the one who answers. He is brought along in the temptation not only in that he begins to see that "Man may be in the worlde and be right goode" (486), but also in that his very experience of sensorial pleasure feminizes him.

The twentieth-century reader/spectator may easily accept Will's extreme lustiness as a key feature of exaggerated masculinity. Yet this is a play in which the characters are personifications, not human individuals, and Lust has a long history as a female personification in medieval art and thought.

---

[25] David F. Greenberg, *The Construction of Homosexuality* (Chicago: University of Chicago Press, 1988), 291.

[26] Howard Bloch, *Medieval Misogyny and the Invention of Western Romantic Love* (Chicago and London: University of Chicago Press, 1991), 29.

[27] Bloch, 29.

Embodying the abstraction Lust feminizes Will – he becomes effeminate from "too great of an interest in women"[28] as Will's frolic with his female dancers bears out – even as his lusty actions masculinize him. He does not speak in one gendered voice, but rather in the voice of desire. Will's self-described lightness and delight in beauty, as well as his (possibly self-referential) assertion, "A woman me semyth a hewynly syght" (573), reinforce his gender instability. And his statement "Lust is now comun as þe way" (652) both indicates the dramatic range of the personification as male subject and recalls the "comun" woman or harlot as object.

Perhaps the most striking indication of gender slipperiness in the character Will/Lust/Lechery appears in the group of dancers he calls forth. It is impossible to associate a stable set of gendered characteristics with "six women in sut, thre dysgysyde as galontys and thre as matrones, wyth wondyrfull vysurs congruent." Further, all their names are abstractions. In a rare example of female-to-male crossdressing in English medieval drama, we see half the women dressed as men dancing in deceptively heterosexual couples with the other women, and all are masked. In this whirl of erotic energy, gendered characteristics seem to be in free play rather than bound to sexed bodies.

The behaviors displayed by the three fallen Mights, therefore, undermine any model the *Wisdom* play may offer for appropriate secular or monastic masculine conduct. Furthermore, we suspect that the play's decision to sex its protagonist, Anima, female, yet constitute her of male Mights as well as female Wits, may also call into question the sex/gender uniformity of the Christian subject. After the three Mights accede to temptation, the boundaries protecting their sex/gender identities become permeable. Where they were previously sexed/gendered consistently male/masculine, the Mights now manifest an unstable array of sex/gender markers, ranging from a mix of gendered features, to oscillation between the "masculine" and the "feminine," to a defensively hyperbolic rearticulation of the heterosexual imperative. Through their fallen performance of a range of improper behaviors, the three Mights enact a shifting constellation of abject desires, which include the wish for absolute political power, however corrupt; the need for excessively strong homosocial ties which in turn exposes latent anxiety about the homoerotic potentiality of the homosocial; and an exaggerated sexual appetite which threatens to overrun all bounds. Such free play both underscores and destabilizes the normative heterosexuality commanded by political and spiritual structures of authority.

The play can therefore be seen as working through the position of the disobedient subject, as that theory is usefully elaborated in Butler's *Bodies That Matter*:

[28] Smith, 171.

Where the uniformity of the subject is expected, where the behavioral conformity of the subject is commanded, there might be produced the refusal of the law in the form of the parodic inhabiting of conformity that subtly calls into question the legitimacy of the command, a repetition of the law into hyperbole, a rearticulation of the law against the authority of the one who delivers it.[29]

Clearly, it is Anima whose uniformity as a subject under God and king and whose conformity to Christian and secular law is expected. The play, however, emphasizes her lack of uniformity by fragmenting her subjectivity into constituent parts. This splintering produces in the dramatized parts of the soul an accompanying *non*conformity with respect to "naturalized" laws of gender fixity and political rule. Refusal of the law – both secular and spiritual – is the subject of the drama. This refusal, though, belongs to the fallen constituent parts, her Mights, rather than to Anima herself. The Mights who perform this refusal of the law in *Wisdom* in fact "parodically inhabit" a range of secular roles (as well as gender roles), possibly to "call into question the legitimacy of" secular and ecclesiastic power structures.

We turn now to what we see as the failed gesture of reconciliation in the play's final scene. After Wisdom's reappearance has brought about Anima's contrition and confession, Anima returns "all in here fyrste clothynge" (s.d. after 1064), protectively surrounded by her Wits and Mights. Visually, she has not in fact been restored to her original, unitary state. Verbally, her female Wits continue their silence and her male Mights retain traces of the roles they occupied in the secular world of the anti-masque while, we suggest, they embody a newly sedimented masculinity. Whereas the Mights initially had emphasized their participation in and responsibility for the Soul's conduct, they now isolate her as the sole agent of their previous corruption, pointing their fingers at Anima, rather than binding themselves in solidarity with her. Mind scolds Anima, "Haue mynde, Soule, wat Gode hath do" (1117) and reminds her that *she* was "dammyde by synn endelesly" (1123). Similarly, Understanding chides her, "Take vundyrston-dynge, Soule . . . [that] Ye be reformyde in felynge, not only as a best, / But also in þe ouer parte of *yowr* reasun" (1125–30; emphasis added); and in spite of her contrition and presumably complete rehabilitation, Anima is chastised by Will: "Spoyll you of yowr olde synnys and foly" (1136). In their moralizing and stratified reaction to Anima, the Mights serve as a projection of the "truths" about power and gender that Anima is supposed to have internalized. However, the strident quality of the Mights' accusations suggests to us anxiety about and the potential for resistance of patriarchy.

Likewise, the relation of tender lovingness between Anima and Wisdom is not restored. He is no longer the loving spouse of the play's beginning. He

---

[29] Butler, 122.

does not here embrace her. Rather he now seems the distant patriarch; Anima addresses him as "O thou hye soueren Wysdam" (1144). And Wisdom refers to her former failures rather than to his restored love of her. Though Anima has already confessed, Wisdom continues to rehearse her failures and to complain of the pain she has caused him: "Ye haue wondyde my hert" (1085).

Accepting this restored yet revised reality, Anima's last speech confirms the new element of distance in her relationship with Wisdom when she acknowledges, "Timor Domini inicium sapiencie" ("The fear of the Lord is the beginning of wisdom" [1153]) – Love has been replaced by fear. Near the end of this summarizing statement, the final speech of the play, she proclaims, "Ande so to ende wyth perfeccyon" (1161), but we argue that the play does not attain the perfection it claims. The reconciliation scene between Wisdom and Anima gestures toward both a loving relationship and the Pauline paradigm of a patriarchal order (headed by a masculine figure and completed by a subservient figure), but both gestures ultimately fail. The spiritual ideal of the love relationship has been replaced by patriarchal hegemony. The former reciprocity of their earlier relationship has been superseded by Anima's willing participation in and acceptance of the male authority as indicated by her citation of "Sent Powle" (1148) and "Salamon" (1152). But the patriarchal structure of their new relationship also does not hold; it requires a normalizing of gender relations through what Judith Butler terms the "regulatory apparatus of heterosexuality." As Butler observes, in the heterosexual power structure of patriarchy, "one is compelled to live in a world in which genders constitute univocal signifiers, in which gender is stabilized, polarized, rendered discrete and intractable. In effect, gender is made to comply with a model of truth and falsity which not only contradicts its own performative fluidity, but serves a social policy of gender regulation and control."[30] This is the world in which Anima is compelled to live at the play's close: her very structure has been demonstrated to be mutable and multivocal, but she must now assiduously monitor herself for gender conformity; she must perceive sexuality itself as always potentially unbridled sinfulness (as her Mights' easy corruption attests) residing within her; and she must now occupy a position of fearful abjection, never able to eradicate her memory of Wisdom's displeasure and discipline. Thus the play proposes its own "naturalized" schema of a Pauline binarism of sex and gender roles, attempting both to impose a heterosexual power structure *and* to restore the materiality of the sexed/gendered body. But that materiality has been problematized in the antimasque sequence, which contaminates – leaks into – the final scene and

---

[30] Judith Butler, "Performative Acts and Gender Constitution: An Essay in Phenomenology and Feminist Theory," in *Performing Feminisms: Feminist Critical Theory and Theatre*, ed. Sue-Ellen Case (Baltimore: The Johns Hopkins University Press, 1990), 278.

subverts the attempt to put the Pauline paradigm in place. Surrounding Anima, the Mights function as material reminders of the gender slippage displayed in the anti-masque. Their disruption of the binary through the exchange and rearrangement of gender characteristics has indelibly established the fluidity of gender in relation to the sexed body, a fluidity that we see as characteristically medieval.[31] This combines with the medieval theatrical practice of males crossdressing to play female roles to heighten audience awareness that Wisdom, in speaking with Anima, is ultimately addressing a feminized representation which occupies a body sexed male. Operating out of a more fluid concept of sex and gender than our own, medieval audience members, we argue, were capable of deconstructing the binary; perceiving clearly the dual nature of Anima, they saw also that the normative pairing of sex and gender, along with its concomitant hierarchy, is a construction; that is, the construction deconstructs itself.

In his own writing and teaching, Martin Stevens has repeatedly and convincingly recognized continuity between "medieval" and "Renaissance" drama, in preference to the artificial boundary stubbornly in place. In our analysis of gender and power relations in *Wisdom*, which begins from this "de-periodized" perspective to what we agree is one dramatic tradition, we are working out of the enormous and lasting influence that Martin has had on us. This paper is a gesture towards repaying, if only in small measure, the great debt that we owe our beloved teacher, admired fellow scholar, and dear friend.

---

[31] See Peter L. Allen, "Male/Female/Both/Neither: Gender as Floating Signifier in the Literature of Medieval France," *Medieval Feminist Newsletter* 14 (1992): 12–16, for a parallel study. Allen "examine(s) the ways in which a variety of literary works (composed primarily in thirteenth-century France) break sex and gender, often quite unexpectedly, into a variety of free-floating parts that cause us to rethink those concepts as radically as do philosophical texts written centuries later" (13).

The Chaucerian Critique of Medieval Theatricality

Seth Lerer

Let me begin by stating that the phrasing of my title is not calculated to evoke the traditions of the anti-theatrical prejudice that had permeated late antique and medieval polemic from Tertullian and Augustine through the Lollards.[1] My concern is not to ally Chaucer with the condemnations of his near-contemporary author of the Wycliffite "Tretise on Miracles Pleyinge," that now familiar document of late medieval anger at the sacrileges of performance and the fear of crowds and spectacle.[2] Nor am I largely motivated here by recent critical attempts to locate Chaucer's *Canterbury Tales* in such performative environments as the facts of oral recitation, the fictions of the roadside drama, or the imaginations of the Bakhtinian carnivalesque.[3] My interest, rather, lies in the construction of literary authority, and in particular, how the theatrical forms and gestures embedded in the beginning of the *Canterbury Tales* define the aegis of vernacular performance and autonomy of the writer. Chaucer's references,

---

[1] For discussions of these early traditions, see Heiko Jürgens, *Pompa Diaboli* (Stuttgart: Kohlhammer, 1972), and H. A. Kelly, *Ideas and Forms of Tragedy from Aristotle to the Middle Ages* (Cambridge: Cambridge University Press, 1994). See, too, the general review in Jonas Barish, *The Antitheatrical Prejudice* (Berkeley and Los Angeles: University of California Press, 1980).

[2] The *Treatise* gained much currency in scholarly discussions of medieval drama through the compelling analysis of V. A. Kolve, *The Play Called Corpus Christi* (Stanford: Stanford University Press, 1966), and through the edition of Clifford Davidson, *The Tretise of Miracles Pleyinge* (Washington, D.C.: Associated University Presses, 1981). For a challenging rebuttal to the notion of this text as an antitheatrical polemic, together with a survey of many of the terms and contexts of medieval dramatic discussion, see Lawrence M. Clopper, "*Miracula* and *The Tretise of Miracles Pleying*," *Speculum* 65 (1990): 878–905.

[3] See, for example, Carl Lindahl, *Earnest Games: Folkloric Patterns in the Canterbury Tales* (Bloomington: Indiana University Press, 1987); Laura Kendrick, *Chaucerian Play: Comedy and Control in the Canterbury Tales* (Berkeley and Los Angeles: University of California Press, 1988); John M. Ganim, *Chaucerian Theatricality* (Princeton: Princeton University Press, 1990).

allusions, and citations to the species of late fourteenth-century theater, I propose, are calibrated not so much towards articulating the theatricality of his own project as they are towards locating that project among competing and potentially disruptive forms of dramatic public expression.

This is a paper about the politics of literary allusion: about how the *Canterbury Tales* situates authorial control within the contexts of royal patronage, civic sponsorship, and popular response, and furthermore, about how late medieval social institutions contoured their power through the adoption of particular literary forms. To these ends, my approach to Chaucer's critique of medieval theatricality centers on how he both voices and suppresses the dramatic impulses of court, city, and country. I would like to propose some new lines of inquiry into the ideologies of medieval display and spectatorship as well as into the methodologies of modern critical approaches to the historicity of literary forms and the viability of lines of influence. Put briefly, I will argue that theatrical allusions function in the *Canterbury Tales* as markers of political relations: that they constitute the places for aristocratic and popular self-legitimization.

My immediate focus will be on the well-known tensions – literary, social, and dramatic – that inform the opening of the Canterbury contest. The relations between the *Knight's* and *Miller's Tales* have long been understood under the rubric of what Chaucer calls "quiting": requiting, paying back, recasting, but more centrally to the Chaucerian project, the sense that literary response constitutes a form of literary criticism. The domesticities of the Miller's fabliau rewrite as much as they requite the epic archness of the Knight's Theban fantasy. The realisms of the former answer the classicisms of the latter, the world of the barnyard replaces the world of the court, and the colloquialisms of the Miller's characters – with their rude inversions culminating in the great fart that rumbles through the poem's final couplets – comically subvert the stately measures of the Knight's gods and heroes.

But Chaucer anticipates these critiques of theatricality before the Knight and Miller tell their tales. The portraits of the five Guildsmen in the *General Prologue* – long dismissed simply as the group limnings of an estate to whom Chaucer had neglected to assign tales – constitute, *in nuce*, a potential challenge to alternative forms of English literary authority. For I believe that Chaucer silences his Guildsmen not out of neglect but out of purpose, and that by denying them the chance for tale-telling performance, he effectively removes one source of competition for official literature. The Guildsmen, I posit at this paper's close, stand in the *Canterbuy Tales* as representatives not just of class, profession, or estate, but of a competing civic aegis for vernacular literary making: the literary making of the Corpus Christi drama. In short, the *Canterbury Tales* defines the cycle plays as radically other – provincial, civic, and communally produced – and it is that otherness that, I believe, challenges current methodologies of studying the place of medieval drama in the Chaucerian project.

I

It has long been known that in the *Knight's* and *Miller's Tales* Chaucer deploys the strategies of two forms of medieval theater for the purposes of political criticism or religious parody. The "listes" organized by Theseus and his constructions of a great amphitheater for the tournamentary encounter of the sparring lovers, Palamon and Arcite, have been understood as the locus for Chaucer's own reflections on the artifice of form controlling his verbal project, as both amphitheater and poem reflect the creative, controlling urge of the poet in the political world.[4] The construction of Theseus's arena has also been located in the making of the public Chaucer and as resonating with the tournamentary impulses of the court of Richard II. As Clerk of the Works, Chaucer himself had a hand in organizing that great spectacle of royal display, the Smithfield pageant of October 1390, in which King Richard sought to articulate his control over London's civic and mercantile authorities and, in turn, to match chivalric greatness with the King of France who, the year before, had held a tournament to celebrate the Anglo-French truce.[5] By contrast, the *Miller's Tale* has been appreciated for its parodies of the religious theater found in the guild-sponsored Corpus Christi cycles and morality plays that presented narratives of scriptural history in ways both humorous and poignant for the populaces of provincial towns. With its opening announcement that the Miller speaks "in Pilates voys," its narrative allusions to Noah's flood, and its overarching plot line of the crafty clerk Nicholas as dramaturge and stage director of the carpenter's cuckoldry, the *Miller's Tale* offers a fabliau narrative grounded in the mechanics of theatrical performance.[6]

At one level, the deployment of theatrical techniques or dramatic allusions in both *Tales* raises questions of authorial control in the production of public literature. Theseus's making of his amphitheater and his stagings of the conflicts celebrate the royal aegis for performance, and they affirm what might be thought of as the principles of political theatrics operating at the court of Richard II. Ricardian political theatricality is

---

[4] The most complete and compelling recent statement of this critical view (ultimately traceable to the New Critical studies of Charles Muscatine of the 1950s) is V. A. Kolve, *Chaucer and the Imagery of Narrative: The First Five Canterbury Tales* (Stanford: Stanford University Press, 1984); see his summary on p. 135. For the genealogy of this approach, see Patterson, *Chaucer and the Subject of History*, p. 170 n. 10.

[5] Sheila Lindenbaum, "The Smithfield Tournament of 1390," *Journal of Medieval and Renaissance Studies* 20 (1990): 1–20.

[6] Sandra Pierson Prior, "Parodying Typology and the Mystery Plays in the *Miller's Tale*," *Journal of Medieval and Renaissance Studies* 16 (1986): 57–73. See, too, Ganim's compelling reassessment of Chaucer's uses of the plays in *Chaucerian Theatricality*, pp. 38–41, 188–89.

always public and consolidative in polemic, classicizing and dynastic in theme. It operates by redefining the chivalric impulses of courtly perform-ance through specifically literary and mythological texts. Thebes and Troy become, in effect, the two poles of Ricardian state allusion. The former grants an ideal of dynastic control and moral valence central to such Thebiatic texts as the *Knight's Tale*. The latter grants an ideal of civic power and imperial control, articulated in the many documents of Trojan historiography that circulated in the late fourteenth century (Chaucer's *Troilus* being only the most obvious example) and enacted in such public acts of affiliation as Nicholas Brembre's supposed attempt to rename London *Parva Troia* (understood, in 1386, as an act of treason) and in Richard's own appropriation of the city as "la neufre troy" in 1390.[7]

The venues for such classicizing and dynastic gestures were the tournaments and spectacles deployed by Richard with great vigor during the late 1380s and 90s. Staged for specific occasions, often under pressure from competing governmental groups (for example, the guilds or the corporation of the city of London), they were designed to placate the opposition parties by proposing to include them in the making and witnessing of the shows. This is the ostensible purpose of the Smithfield tournament of 1390, a ceremonial attempt to bring together the recently displaced Lords Apellant with the young King's noble partisans soon after Richard had declared his own majority. It was, as the chronicler Henry Knighton put it, a gesture of "good love, unity, and agreement"[8] staged among King, nobles, aristocrats, and civic leaders, though as Sheila Lindenbaum has recently shown, there was a wide gap between the official claims of social inclusion and the facts of courtly and chivalric control that governed the event.

> An urban tournament created expectations of a communal and partici-patory festival, but Richard produced a mere spectacle, a chivalric display

---

[7] Such, broadly speaking, is Lee Patterson's approach to Ricardian literary culture and Chaucer's role in its maintenance and critique (*Chaucer and the Subject of History* [Madison: University of Wisconsin Press, 1991], pp. 84–230; for specific discussions of the events named here, see pp. 93, 161). See, too, the characterization of London civic spectacle from Richard II through Henry VII in Lawrence M. Bryant, "Configurations of the Community in Late Medieval Spectacles: Paris and London during the Dual Monarchy," in Barbara A. Hanawalt and Katherine S. Ryerson, eds., *City and Spectacle in Medieval Europe* (Minneapolis: University of Minnesota Press, 1994), pp. 3–33, especially these remarks on p. 23: "English political relations were worked out in allegories in a way that they could not be in political practices. London operated within a politics of uneasy truce among volatile lords and nobles. The city shaped ceremonials for the king in order to accentuate the personal and symbolic ties between them."

[8] Henry Knighton, *Chronicon*, ed. Joseph Rawson Lumby (London: Her Majesty's Stationery Office, 1895), II:313, quoted in Lindenbaum, "Smithfield Tournament," pp. 3–4.

whose active participants were viewed at a distance by passive onlookers, unnecessary to the event.[9]

Lindenbaum's point is well taken, and she has made it clear that Richard's staging of the tournament systematically refigured an event, expected as a public festival, into an affirmation of exclusive chivalric control.[10] But what I think is central to the tensions of the Smithfield tournament (and, as I will note shortly, its connection to the *Knight's Tale*) is the fact that it is centrally an urban tournament: that is, it attempts to bridge the gap between the court and city and, in the process, defines the problematic of Ricardian theatricality for the early 1390s.

For what the King had sought, in effect, was a kind of common ground for court and city, and Smithfield, which as Lindenbaum notes was referred to in medieval documents as both the "king's field" and the city's "common ground," seemed to suit his purposes.[11] But there was also a symbolic valence to the setting, too. Almost a decade earlier, Smithfield had been the site of Wat Tyler's defeat and of the end of the Rising of 1381. It was a combat ground already deeply charged, in both the public and in the official mind, with the theatrics of royal power. The many chronicle accounts of Wat's last moments, while differing widely on sequences of action and points of detail, nonetheless all figure forth the rebel and the King as players in some pageant of rebellion. The version of Wat's death at Smithfield on June 15, 1381, recorded in London Corporation's official letter book, reads much like the description of a tournament, with its ranging of rebels and the defenders as if they were the matched lists of a public pageant, performed before the audience of King and court:

On this day God sent remedy for the same and His own gracious aid, by the hand of the most renowned man Sir William Walworth, the then mayor, who in Smithfield in the presence of our lord the king and those standing by him, lords, knights, esquires, and citizens on horseback, on the one side, and the whole of this infuriated rout on the other, most manfully by himself rushed upon the captain of the said multitude, Walter Tyler by name, and, as he was altercating with the king and the nobles, first wounded him in the neck with his sword and then hurled him from his horse, mortally pierced in the breast.[12]

So, too, in the *Anonimalle Chronicle*, there is a performative flavor to the capturing and killing of Wat, as his severed head is set upon a pole and

---

[9] Lindenbaum, "Smithfield Tournament," p. 10.

[10] See, too, Lindenbaum's restatement and development of this position in "Ceremony and Oligarchy: The London Midsummer Watch," in Hanawalt and Ryerson, eds., *City and Spectacle*, pp. 171–88.

[11] Lindenbaum, "Smithfield Tournament," p. 6.

[12] R. B. Dobson, *The Peasants' Revolt of 1381* (London: Macmillan, 1970), pp. 210–11.

displayed for the delectation of the king.[13] And in Froissart's account of the Rising in his *Chronique* – a narrative, as Margaret Aston has described it, that "characteristically dramatizes" its events – the dead Wat is "environed . . . all about" by his killers.[14] In these accounts, the hemming in, enveloping, and environing all about of Wat and his rebels signal a kind of amphitheatrical performance for the act of quelling the rebellion. It is as if the very structures of containment usually deployed for symbolic control (arenas, scaffolds, jousting fields) had been pressed into the service of quelling an all-too-real threat to civic power.[15]

Something similar is going on in London two years after the Smithfield tournament. In early 1392, the corporation of the city had refused a loan to Richard; the King had retaliated by stripping the mayor, sheriffs, and aldermen of office, and removing his court from London to York. The London merchants called the King's bluff, and in a show of public reconciliation, Richard returned to the city in great triumph on August 21, though precisely who had triumphed here remains a question of historical debate. The spectacles prepared for the King's entry put into practice the dynastic impulses of Ricardian classicism. In Richard Maydistone's Latin poem celebrating the event, London is repeatedly referred to as a new Troy: *Troynovant*, *Nova Troja*, and *Troja novella*. Richard himself is likened in his beauty and his bearing to the young Troilus ("Iste velud Troylus . . . decorus")[16], and Queen Anne comes off, together with her ladies, as Amazons tamed before the decorum of this new Troy:

> Anna sibi nomen – re sit et Anna precor!
> Pulchra quidem pulchris stat circumcincta puellis,
> Vincit Amazonibus Troia novella sub hiis.   (121–23)
>
> [Anne is her name – may she be Anna indeed, I pray. Very beautiful herself, she stands surrounded by beautiful maidens; the New Troy conquers under these Amazons.] (Smith, p. 179)

---

[13] Dobson, *Peasants' Revolt*, p. 167.

[14] Dobson, *Peasants' Revolt*, p. 196. The remarks of Margaret Aston come from "Corpus Christ and Corpus Regni: Heresy and the Peasants' Revolt," *Past and Present* 143 (1994): 3–47, this quotation from p. 15. See, too, Ralph Hanna's account of the theatrics of Wat's tauntings in "Pilate's Voice / Shirley's Case," *South Atlantic Quarterly* 91 (1992): 793–812, esp. 802–3.

[15] See Lindenbaum, "Smithfield Tournament," p. 13.

[16] I quote from the text and translation in Charles Roger Smith, "'Concordia: Facta Inter Regem Riccardum II et Civitatem Londonie' per Fratrum Riccardum Maydiston, Carmelitam, Sacre Theologie," Ph.D. Dissertation, Princeton University, 1972. This quotation from line 113 of the poem, pp. 178–79. Further citations will be in the text. I have discussed elsewhere the possible relationships of Maydistone's poem to the presentations of Chaucer and his audience in the Frontispiece to the Corpus Christi College, Cambridge, MS 61 manuscript of *Troilus and Criseyde*. See *Chaucer and His Readers: Imagining the Author in Late-Medieval England* (Princeton: Princeton University Press, 1993), pp. 22–23, 54–56.

Now, it is not the common ground of Smithfield but the very streets of London and its central monuments (St. Paul's, Westminster, Temple Bar) that are the stages of state theater. Now, it is not the pattern of chivalric contest but the legacy of ancient literature that writes the script for royal display. The King and Queen are, in the terms of Maydistone's poem, translated (in all senses of that word) into the characters of classical story: renamed, recostumed, and restored.

There are, of course, some obvious links between these accounts of Ricardian spectacle and the classical and political impulses of the *Knight's Tale*. The stagy pageantry of Richard's entries, with their figurations of classical gods and heroes sitting atop scaffolds on the processional way, recalls the arrangement of the *Knight's Tale*'s own idols to whom the protagonists pray; and the elaborate civic decorations for the King's procession – such that, in Maydistone's words, "it seemed that art had painted a new heaven" – resonate with the Knight's hyperbole that "swich a place / Was noon in erthe, as in so litel space" (A 1895–96).[17] Recently, Paul Strohm has argued for the specific relevance of Richard's entry to the *Knight's Tale*, and he reviewed some of these verbal resonances between Maydistone's and Chaucer's poems to define the Queen's role as an intercessor, both in public life and in its fictional representations.[18] Strohm shows how Queen Anne's intercessory manoeuvres during the summer of 1392 had a profound effect on Richard's ultimate reconciliation with the city of London. In the Westminster chronicler's account of these intercessions, as well as in Maydistone's poem on the entry, Anne appears prostrate before Richard. Indeed, the city is itself prostrate (*provoluti*) before the King, while Anne herself drops to her knees as the procession ends at Westminster. Strohm rightly calls attention to the reminiscences of such abjection when Hippolyta and Emily, together with their ladies, beg Duke Theseus to spare the lives of Palamon and Arcite:

> And on hir bare knees adoun they falle
> And wolde have kist his feet ther as he stood. (A. 1758–59)

Yet, Strohm misses the explicit Amazonian equation of Queen Anne in Maydistone's poem. What is at stake in both texts is the conquering of female power and the righting of relations in domestic power: relations not simply figured between King and Queen but between King and city. The *Knight's Tale*'s opening account of Theseus taming the Amazon Hyppolita and "al the regne of Femenye" announces metaphorically the Knight's own

---

[17] Here, and throughout this paper, quotations from the *Canterbury Tales* are from Larry D. Benson, ed., *The Riverside Chaucer* (Boston: Houghton Mifflin, 1987), cited by fragment letter and line numbers.
[18] Paul Strohm, *Hochon's Arrow: The Social Imagination of Fourteenth-Century Texts* (Princeton: Princeton University Press, 1992), pp. 107–12.

taming synthesis of reason and passion[19] and dovetails precisely with the Ricardian propaganda of courtly marital control and civic harmony defined in Maydistone's poem. For, by depicting Anne as an Amazon surrounded by her maidens, Maydistone equates Richard with the triumphant Theseus. In turn, the city he has entered stands as a submissive female, one that may be taken yet by force:

> Non laceret, non dilaniet pulcherrima regni
> Menia, nam sua sunt, quicquid et exstat in hiis. (145–46)

> [Let not the most beautiful walls in the kingdom be rent or torn, for they are the king's own and whatever is within them]. (Smith, p. 181)

Such imagery, while providing the reader of the *Knight's Tale* with a topical allusion for the "glorie and greet solempnytee" (A 870) that greets Theseus's return from the land of "Femeneye," also enhances the pervasive sense of late medieval London as the King's "chamber": the locus for his intimate relations, the place where he enacts his masculine control over a potentially recalcitrant city. London is something of the King's bride here, and the elaborate classical allusions that inform both Maydistone's and Chaucer's poems show us a political theatrics that restores not just the "social body" of the corporation but the bodies of the King and Queen to civic life.

But more than local allusion or resonance, the point of contact between Ricardian and Thesean spectacle lies in the *idea* of the theater as the medium of political consensus making. It is not so much that the theater is the vehicle for royal power crassly or intimidatingly displayed. Rather, it is that theater becomes the rhetorical device, the official venue, for consolidating potentially divisive and dividing social groups. It may, of course, matter more to us (or to Chaucer) that the social synthesis attempted by Richard's entries was hardly effective, or that the *ordo* imposed by Theseus on his sparring lovers and his half-unwilling step-niece is a patchwork of polemic and only half-believed maxims, saws, and commonplaces. What matters, in the end, is the ethos of political theatricality: the sense not just of what Charles Pythian-Adams has called the preservation and enhancement of the "wholeness of the social order" or of what Mervyn James has reconsidered as the integrity of the "social body" of the civic corporation, but of the bodily relations among ruler and ruled.[20] Chaucer, like Maydistone, deploys the stagecraft of political spectacle to make something truly comic out of

---

[19] See Patterson, *Chaucer and the Subject of History*, p. 198.

[20] Charles Phythian-Adams, "Ceremony and the Citizen: The Communal Year at Coventry 1450–1550," in Peter Clark and Paul Slack, eds., *Crisis and Order in English Towns* (London: Routledge, 1972), p. 69; Mervyn James, "Ritual, Drama and Social Body in the Late Medieval English Town," *Past and Present* 98 (1983): 3–29, reprinted in his *Society, Politics and Culture* (Cambridge: Cambridge University Press, 1986), pp. 16–47 (from which future references are drawn).

conquest and return: comic, in that both narratives center on rituals of fealty and marriage; comic in that both represent the power of that stagecraft to effect a union that cannot otherwise be managed by mere power play.

Relations between literary form and political action similarly motivate the theatrics of the following *Miller's Tale*, where both the Miller himself and his dramaturgically inclined protagonist, the clerk Nicholas, vie for control over the space of fiction in a world of social facts. The Miller's opening appearance speaking "In Pilates voys," for example, signals that question of legal and theatrical authority explored throughout the various cycle plays in which that character appears.[21] Pilate, of course, is that great stage-manager of the trial and torturing of Christ. In the plays from York and Wakefield, he invariably opens the particular pageants that center on the Passion, calling for silence, voicing his will, and, somewhat curiously, etymologizing the meaning of his name.[22] All these are strategies of authorial self-construction, strategies taken to the extremes in the Wakefield *Scourging* play, where Pilate stands as the self-christened *mali auctoris*: not just the author of evil (and hence merely a Satanic figure) but the author of Christ's punishment: the scriptor and director of the play of pain we are about to see. "Now youre desire fulfill I shall," (220) Pilate announces in the course of managing the scourging, and the question here, I think, is just whom Pilate is addressing. Not only does he grant the *tortores* their wish to beat the savior's body, but he grants his audience that secret thrill to see, mimetically enacted, the sensational punishments of a criminal – play punishments, as I have argued elsewhere, that resonated with the lived out, legal actions of the torturings and executions witnessed on the high-street of the town.[23] So, too, the *Miller's Tale*'s rich displays of dramaturgic craft (with Nicholas's kneading tubs and ropes), special effects (the scalding of his bottom with Absolon's hot poker), and comic inversion (culminating in the carpenter's arm-breaking fall) all transpire before a townsfolk now, at the *Tale*'s conclusion, theatricalized into an audience for a play:

---

[21] "But in Pilates voys he gan to crie" (A 3124). For discussion of the allusions, and critical presuppositions about them, encoded in this line, see Hanna, "Pilates Voice / Shirley's Case."

[22] Pilate opens the Wakefield *Scourging Play*, and the following from York: *Christ before Pilate I, Christ before Pilate II, The Remorse of Judas, The Death of Christ, The Resurrection*. For Wakefield, I use David Bevington, ed., *Medieval Drama* (Boston: Houghton Mifflin, 1975), pp. 553–68; for York, I refer to the texts in Richard Beadle, ed., *The York Plays* (London: Edward Arnold, 1982).

[23] For Pilate as *mali actoris*, glossed by Bevington as "author of evil," see *Medieval Drama*, p. 554, line 13 (though it might be worth speculating that what Pilate is also saying is that he is the "actor of evil"). My speculations on the relations between dramatized and legally enacted punishments in late medieval England appear in "'Representyd now in yower syght': The Culture of Spectatorship in Late-Fifteenth-Century England," in David Wallace and Barbara Hanawalt, eds., *Intersections: History and Literature in the Fifteenth Century* (Minneapolis: University of Minnesota Press, 1995).

The folk gan laughen at his fantasye;
Into the roof they kiken and they cape,
And turned al his harm unto a jape.
. . .

And every wight gan laughen at this stryf.   (A 3840–49)

The "folk" are here the viewing folk, as their acts of "kiking" and "caping," staring and gaping, transform the carpenter's house into a stage-set, while their final laughing signals to the readership of Chaucer's *Miller's Tale* that they must, too, view this tale as staged performance and laugh, not as individuated readers, but as a community of spectators.

And yet what they – and we – see are not only fabliau characters whose foibles loosely resonate with Corpus Christi theatrics. What we may see as well is the inversion of the very set of texts that stood behind the stagecraft of the *Knight's Tale*. Maydistone had gone to great lengths to detail the workings of the stagecraft that made allegorical figures appear and disappear, that brought rich costume and rare fountains into being, and that raised castles and towers into the sky. When King and Queen walk through the street they see a great building, held up by controlling cords.

Pendula per funes est fabrica totaque turris,
Etheris et medium vendicat illa locum.
Stant et in hac turri iuvenis formosaque virgo;
Hic velud angelus est, hec coronata fuit.
Cerneret has facies quisquis, puto, non dubitaret
Nil fore sub celo quod sibi plus placeat.
Rex reginaque tunc astant, bene discucientes
Quid velit hec turris alta vel hii iuvenes.
Descendunt ab ea iuvenis simul ipsaque virgo;
Nulla fuit scala nec patuere gradus.
Nubibus inclusi veniunt et in ethere pendent.
Quo tamen ingenio nescio, crede michi!   (279–90)

[The whole structure of the tower is hung on ropes, and it rises high up into the sky. On this tower stand a youth and a beautiful maiden; the youth looks like an angel, the maiden was crowned. Whoever looked upon these forms could not doubt, I think, that anything under heaven would ever please him more. The king and queen then stand near investigating fully what this high tower and these youths signify. The youth and the maiden descend together from the tower; there was neither ladder nor stair to support them. Enclosed in clouds,they come floating down in the air – by what ingenious device, I do not know, believe me!]   (Smith, p. 197)

If these devices seem to have little to do with Theseus's amphitheatrical displays, they have a great deal to do with their humorous quiting in the following *Miller's Tale*. Here, crafty Nicholas suspends his characters in kneading tubs and cords of his devising. Here, man and woman meet, not as angel and crowned Queen – sustaining the marital allegorics of the 1392 entry – but as deceiving cuckolds. And here, the machines are not objects of audience wonder, but instead, are fabrications that elicit the cruel laughter of the populace. In the world of the Miller, the carpenter descends not artfully, by "neither ladder nor stair," but roughly through the cutting of his cords. The populace now sees him – at the *Tale*'s end – not in a tower high but in his own roof. And the "fantasye" at which they laugh is the fantasy of rustic imitation, not the imagination of royal spectacle. In short, what the *Miller's Tale* turns upside down at its conclusion (in addition, of course, to everything else) is the key moment in Ricardian theatrics that restated the King's power with the civic oligarchy. The Miller's story takes the mechanics of royal pageantry and transforms it into the rough lines of a roof and kneading tubs: it suspends its characters only to have them rudely cut down to size. In the process, it presents a rustic version of the spectacle: a provincial parody not only of the Corpus Christi dramas but of civic pageantry and London royal spectatorship itself.

II

But all of this has been, as I mentioned at this paper's opening, "at one level." Virtually all the critical responses to Chaucerian theatricality in these terms, including the capsule interpretations I have offered thus far, have proceeded on the controlling methodological assumption that the information for recovering Chaucer's critiques, interpretations, or even experience of medieval theater is all of a piece. Materials for Ricardian spectacle close to the poet's ambience stand on a par with texts from northern plays and cycles – texts for which virtually no examples survive much before the early decades of the fifteenth century. In fact, as recent research has revealed, and as Martin Stevens has made the point of his initial arguments in *Four Middle English Mystery Cycles*, what we think of today as the Corpus Christi plays themselves were most likely late fifteenth-century and even early Tudor syntheses and compilations of disparate guild and civic traditions, some of which, of course, did have their origins in the four-teenth-century celebrations of the Corpus Christi feast.[24] These methodo-logical impediments are, for example, both announced and brushed aside in Sandra Pearson Prior's study of the *Miller's Tale* as a concerted parody of the typological structures of the cycle plays. She notes, in a revealing footnote:

---

[24] Martin Stevens, *Four Middle English Mystery Cycles* (Princeton: Princeton University Press, 1987), pp. 12–13.

I hope it is clear that I am in no sense suggesting the cycles as actual sources for the Miller's Tale. For one thing, the earliest dating we can give to any surviving text is only fifteenth-century. . . . In view of these problems of dating I am therefore using as possible analogues, not sources, much of the material available in the various cycles, and further supporting these examples, whenever possible, with evidence from sources which can be dated more precisely to Chaucer's time or even slightly earlier.[25]

The point, it seems to me, is not to re-engage the positivist search for "sources and analogues" of Chaucer's works. Nor is it even, through the resources of literary criticism, to relocate the "voice" of a theatrical agent onto the characters of Chaucer's fictions – a gesture Prior nonetheless deftly manages in her argument that it is Nicholas, rather than the Miller, who should be identified as the Pilatic figure of the Tale's theatrics.[26]

The point I wish to make is that the Corpus Christi plays may well have seemed as distant or as different to Chaucer as they do to us. The motivating contrast between the theatricalizations of the Knight's and Miller's Tales is the contrast between the familiar and the alien: that is, between the personal experience and current practice of royal spectacle in London and the hearsay and the fragmentary knowledge of the civic dramas of the northern towns. In assessing Chaucer's relations to the forms of medieval theater we need, first, to separate out the documentary nature of the evidence from the textual survival of the plays or spectacles, and second, to locate this separation thematically within the Canterbury Tales. The dramatic allusions of the Miller's Tale are precisely that: allusions to a heard about, recalled, or vaguely known tradition of performance outside the ambience of court and capital. At stake is not how or even whether Chaucer knew about the Corpus Christi plays, but rather how the idea of the Corpus Christi drama functions in the authorial thematics and the literary politics of the Chaucerian project. At issue is not their incorporation into Chaucer's omnivorous purview, but rather their resistance to that incorporation: their intractable otherness. It is their undocumented, non-textual, popular or provincial status in the fourteenth century that concerns both Chaucer and us. Like the poet, all we can do is construct from local chronicle, town record, or traveller's journal what such plays may have looked like; only for the later fifteenth century can we actually read them. It is the Corpus Christi plays' status as a form of literary expression, then, alien to court and city, that makes them appropriate grist for the Miller's narrative mill.

It is, therefore, not so much a question of the Miller's Tale parodying a living literary form (as, say, the way Sir Thopas parodies the tail-rhyme

[25] Prior, "Parodying Typology," p. 58, n. 4.
[26] Prior, p. 71.

romance)[27] as it is a question of incorporating, piecemeal, an alien literature along with an alien notion of literary patronage. For this is really what distinguishes the drama of the northern towns from any literary form – theatrical or otherwise – of late fourteenth-century London. As Mervyn James puts it:

> London was a town in which there was no serious challenge to the dominance of a self-coopting elite. . . . Significantly, in such towns, the celebration of Corpus Christi never acquired a public and civic status, and play cycles of the Corpus Christi type never developed. London had its great cycle plays; but the London cycle was performed by professional actors, and had no connection either with Corpus Christi or the city guilds, being probably the responsibility of the rich merchants of the Skinner's Company.[28]

James goes on to remark that the development of Corpus Christi guild drama necessitated "a specific kind of community – one in which there existed a certain tension and free play of political and social forces, and in which order and unity needed therefore to be continually affirmed in terms of shared rite and shared ritual."[29] Such communities existed in the mercantile societies of York and Wakefield, Lincoln and Coventry, Chester and Norwich, and others, and the broader point behind James's analysis (and those which he has influenced) is the presupposition that dramatic form and social practice interacted in an almost causal way. James's thesis about medieval English theatricality thus concerns the primacy of social function over literary effect. It is a thesis about public rituals and public life, not (in contrast to other, more "literary" arguments about the rise of medieval drama associated with the work of O. B. Hardison, Jerome Taylor, and V. A. Kolve) a thesis about liturgical theatrics, spiritual education, or typological structure.[30] If James is right, then, we might

---

[27] But compare Ganim's remarks: "I should like to suggest that Chaucer's allusions to the mystery plays (and I think some such case could be made for *Sir Thopas*) comprise an acknowledgement of his own difficult relation to popular literary forms, a relation not merely of disdain" (*Chaucerian Theatricality*, p. 39); and, again, "In both cases [i.e., the *Miller's Tale* and *Sir Thopas*] the parodic note is not only a criticism of the other form . . . it is also an indication of awareness of the aesthetic possibilities and dangers, for the sophisticated poet, of these naive forms" (p. 41).

[28] James, "Ritual, Drama and Social Body," pp. 41–42.

[29] James, p. 42.

[30] While I am appropriating James's work selectively here, I am aware of a growing critical response to both his methodology and central thesis. On the one hand, Lindenbaum's work challenges the notion of the "wholeness" James sees as effected in the rituals of Corpus Christi celebration, and she enhances James's distinctions between London and the northern towns. On the other hand, the recent work of Sarah Beckwith and Miri Rubin challenges James's notion of ritual itself and its eliding of an active tradition of dissent – if not upheaval – in late medieval communities (see, for example, Sarah Beckwith, "Ritual, Church and Theatre: Medieval Dramas of the

argue that the pattern of allusions to the Corpus Christi plays that pepper Chaucer's *Miller's Tale* has as its purpose not clerical parody or character definition, but instead a broader, political argument about the place of vernacular performance in civic communities.

The Miller's theatrics define a mode of medieval spectacle that not only differs from but, in the view of an England of the last decades of the fourteenth century, sought to subvert the controlling structures of the London civic corporation and the royal court. The Rising of 1381 began on May 30th of that year and reached its climax on the days immediately following Corpus Christi (June 13) – as Stephen Justice aphorizes it, "the season of festivity."[31] Both Justice and Margaret Aston have illustrated in great detail how Corpus Christi was a kind of natural occasion for popular revolt – feast time marked by the the natural theatricalities of processional and congregation. "In these celebrations," Justice puts it, "we can catch rural communities in the act of self-description," and as Aston avers: "On major feast days not only were working people at liberty to move about, but the crowds gathered for church celebrations could provide useful cover for passing information or holding meetings of a suspect kind."[32] Indeed as Aston and Justice recognize, such "information" often took the form of sustained literary discourses: of poems, chronicles, and sermons that, in their rhetorical control and their self-consciousness of allegorical narration, constituted what Justice has called the "rural idiom" in the making of vernacular authority. What arises amidst the Rising, then, are not just people but texts: rich vernacular narratives, poems, songs, and personal histories. Political activity is generated, then, not just out of economic discontent but verbal pressure. The Rising becomes a moment of profound class and individual articulation: a birthing, as it were, of literary subjects as well as of political actors.

That we know many of the names of its actors may well be testimony to this birth of literary subjectivity. And yet, what we have, it is important to note, are not so much "real" names as self-allegorizing *nomes de guerre*. Figures such as Jack Trewman, Jack Miller, Jack Carter, Jack Straw may seem hard to distinguish from their fictional counterparts in, say, the cycle and morality plays, or for that matter, William Langland's *Piers Plowman* (indeed, one chronicle of the Rising places Langland's Piers at the center of

Sacramental Body," in David Aers, ed., *Culture and History 1350–1600* [Detroit: Wayne State University Press, 1992], pp. 65–90; Miri Rubin, "The Eucharist and the Construction of Medieval Identities," in Ibid., pp. 43–64). Steven Justice, *Writing and Rebellion: England in 1381* (Berkeley and Los Angeles: University of California Press, 1994), attempts to answer "the question that Mervyn James's classic essay never puts – why did *this* feast become a popular, almost universal, expression of corporate identity" (p. 160).

[31] Justice, *Writing and Rebellion*, p. 156.

[32] Justice, *Writing and Rebellion*, p. 157; Aston, "Corpus Christi and Corpus Regni," p. 10

the historical action, effacing the boundaries between the self-conscious actions of the rebels and the self-conscious allegories of the poet).[33] These are, as Aston notes, "generic types, more proverbial than actual, though of course actors in real-life drama might choose to wear such richly resonant protective aliases. Even contemporaries might find it difficult to distinguish face from mask."[34] But this is, it seems to me, precisely the point. The decentering theatricalities of the Rising are deliberately designed to confuse face and mask. For unlike royal tournament and spectacle – where armored jousters may be recognized by signifying banners or coats of arms, or where local celebrants may stand in as transparent allegorical personae – the Millers, Carters, and Truemen, the various yet curiously interchangeable "Johns" and "Jacks," are simultaneously "real-life" people and literary types. They revel in their ambiguities, in a self-defining theater of revolt that, in the hands of chroniclers and poets, will present a challenge to the celebration of community and civic honor defined by Corpus Christi drama, and moreover, threaten London and the royal court with an insurgent, vernacular authority.

The threats of Chaucer's Miller have recently been read as those of a profoundly violent and decentering rural idiom: a rejection of the courtly world not in aesthetic or communal terms, but as an articulate challenge to the politics of regnal self-presentation and royal service.[35] This recent critical location of the pilgrim and his *Tale* in both the imagery and ideology of the Rising of 1381 grants us a powerfully politicized Chaucer: a Chaucer occupied not simply with presenting the contours of everyday existence in dramatic detail, but one more profoundly concerned with the relationships of class and power, and in turn, how literary forms may define and, perhaps, engender those relationships. As Patterson as shown, the placement of the *Miller's Tale* defines the *Canterbury Tales* as self-generating. Its principle of structure will be response and reinterpretation, rather than an *ordo* governed by external hierarchies (as in the Host's initial attempt to get the Monk to follow the Knight).[36] Its principles of allusion will thus be similarly political: texts chosen for quotation or for reference that are already charged with a social connotation as, for example, the story of Noah had been charged with the meaning of maistrye in the Corpus Christi cycles and in the polemics surrounding peasant consciousness in the late fourteenth and early fifteenth centuries.[37]

---

[33] Aston, "Corpus Christi and Corpus Regni," pp. 23–27, and for bibliography, p. 26 n. 61. See, too, Justice's remarks in *Writing and Rebellion*, p. 223, on some of what he calls the "wacky testimony" of the chronicles as to Piers Plowman's status in the Rising.

[34] Aston, p. 25.

[35] Patterson, *Chaucer and the Subject of History*, pp. 244–79.

[36] Patterson, p. 244.

[37] See Patterson, p. 262 and n. 50 and pp. 266–70.

What I would add to this ongoing critical discussion is the notion that the Miller's threats are of a violent and decentering *theatricality*: one that too easily can spill from pageant wagon on to public square, one that can use the strategies of civic celebration against themselves and, in the process, undermine both the communal values that the Corpus Christi dramas were designed to celebrate and the courtly values that Ricardian theatrics were designed to affirm. The Miller's "Pilate's voys" now breaks into the stately tournamentrics of the *Knight's Tale* to recall not only the provincialisms of the cycle drama, but to frame them in allusions to the cosmopolitan theatrics of royal power: from the rebellions of the peasant to, a decade later, the triumphal entries of a King. Though it may remain a testimony to the power of the rustic and the voice of the people, the *Miller's Tale* is very much the product of the city imagination. Indeed, if there is any "fantasye" at work here, it is the London fantasy of rural life, the cosmopolitan imagination of what cycle drama must have been like. As I suggested earlier, the last word on the theatrics of the *Tale* may be that of Richard's royal entry: a parody not of provincial theater but of London spectacle.

III

In the end, then, the Chaucerian critique of theatricality is a critique of the relations between literary form and political action, and the last word on this for the poet of the *Canterbury Tales* may be found, I think, not in the blunt, prose sermonizing of the Parson at the poem's close, but in the silences of characters announced at the beginning of the pilgrimage. In the *General Prologue*, Chaucer offers up the familiar representatives of social estates and professions, and among them are the five Guildsmen (A 360–78). These five Guildsmen, with their clothing tied to their "greet fraternitee," or local guild, with their silver knives and their displays of burgerly wealth, their guildhall bearing, – these five Guildsmen tell no tales on the Canterbury pilgrimage. Now, of course, it is true that several of the characters introduced in the *General Prologue* are not assigned tales (e.g., the Yeoman, the Plowman), and some of them (notably the Shipman and the Wife of Bath) seem to have had their stories switched around in what has been reconstructed as the formative process of the making of the poem. But I think what distinguishes the literary silence of the Guildsmen is, more than authorial neglect or narrative incompletion, their silence as a class. By introducing them as such a class – denying them the individuality of trade or character exposed in nearly all the other pilgrim portraits – and then by silencing them, Chaucer denies the civic, guild aegis for vernacular literary performance.

These Guildsmen are not indiscriminately chosen from among the ranks of the 40 or so recognized late medieval possibilities. They are specifically the representatives of making, costuming, and weaving – guildsmen whose fellows would have played a central role in the staging and preparation of the civic dramas of the Northern towns, but – and I think more importantly – guildsmen who are themselves presented as theatricalized creatures. They come accoutered with their "newe . . . geere apiked" (365), with their shining knives, decorated belts and purses. These are, in effect, actors on a stage play of the burghal: actors given costume, stage position (sitting on a dais, itself a kind of raised stage platform, 370), script (though, in this case, it is only the one word, "madame" in which their wives are to be addressed, 376), and occasion: "And goon to vigilies al bifore, / And have a mantel roialliche ybore" (377–78). These are, as I propose, not simply figures limned according to the contours of estates satire but theatricalized creatures of the pilgrim stage: representatives of an alternative vernacular literary project that, in themselves, embody the excesses of guild display and, in the process, become creatures of costume and stage-prop. They may be taken, in these terms, as something of a group metonymy for Corpus Christi drama, and their silencing may thus share in the broader and more complex critique of public theatricality envisioned in the *Knight's* and *Miller's Tales*.

And yet, this silencing of guild performers – or at the very least, this redirection of guild sponsorship away from public theater and towards privatized, yet mute, display – is not, I think, unique to Chaucer's project. In the larger narrative of Maydistone's *Concordia*, the guilds function in the theater of Ricardian control: figures arrayed and costumed in the spectacle of royal consolidation. A thousand guildsmen parade in their livery before the King. Each stands, denoted by their "secta," their representative garb, and Maydistone catalogues them all, from the silversmiths and fishmongers, through the weavers, dyers, and haberdashers, to the glovers, innkeepers and cooks. And yet, these are not guildsmen in their professional role; nor are they figures shaping the performances of guild-plays. Rather, these are guildsmen as soldiers: professional men as fighters, protectors of King and nation.

> Cerneret has turmas quisquis, puto, non dubitaret
>   Cernere se formas ordinis angelici.
> Tam valido solet auxilio, qui Marcius exstat,
>   Prelia suffultus nulla timere pugil:
> Quelibet ut proprias est ars sortita phalangas. (97–101)

> [Whoever should witness these squadrons, I think, would not doubt that he was seeing the forms of an angelic order. Accompanied by such a mighty force, the Martian soldier is wont to fear no battles, for each guild is arranged like an individual phalanx.] (Smith, p.177)

These guildsmen serve as phalanx to the king, as they prepare the way for Richard and his nobles to be brought before the populace. There is a staging of the civic, here – a performance of King controlling, yet surrounded, by his city troops. Indeed, when Richard does appear, he is, as Maydistone states, "encircled by the nobles of the kingdom as was proper" ("Nobilibus regni cignitur, ut decuit," 120). Queen Anne, too, is encircled ("circumcincta," 123) by her ladies, and these images of royal encirclement resonate, I think, with the chronicle accounts of Wat Tyler's encirclement a decade earlier. The hemming in of Wat, "environed . . . all about" by the King's forces, now stands against the royal and civic patterns of containment that define the nature of the alliance reforged in the 1392 entry and, as well, the proper nature of theatrical spectacle for the maintenance of public power. Chaucer's Guildsmen are transformed from a subversive or a threatening force into a silent clutch of men, while Maydistone's stand as a supportive regiment of soldiers.

What I propose in closing, then, is that the Chaucerian critique of medieval theatricality remains precisely that: not a criticism as such, but an ongoing query, almost a setting up on trial, of competing forms and structures of public drama operating in the last decades of fourteenth-century England. That he may find these forms wanting, yet at the same time may deploy them with a knowledge of their detail, is, of course, fully in keeping with what modern readers have come to appreciate as Chaucer's voracious experimentalism in his work – his almost uncanny ability to ventriloquize voices of alternative literatures. Yet, as I have suggested here, what distinguishes the forms of drama in his day is their place in the politics of social consolidation or revolt. Ricardian spectacle, guild play, and rural rebellious theatrics define the backdrops against which Chaucer stages his own authorial self construction – one continually striving to adjudicate between the patron and the reader, the historically immanent and the transhistorically literary. Chaucer's search for authorial autonomy takes him away from the theatrics of the court, the high street, or the field and grounds his project in a vision of a world without patrons or rebels, guildsmen or townsfolk: a world where spectators become true readers, and the performances of the stage or platform become the fictions on the pages of the Canterbury book.[38]

---

[38] This essay was originally prepared in 1994. Earlier versions of its arguments were presented at Stanford University and the University of Pennsylvania. It is my special pleasure to record my thanks to the editors of this volume for the invitation to present this paper in honor of Martin Stevens, and to acknowledge, too, Professor Stevens's enthusiasm for this, as well as other projects of mine.

The Experience of Modernity in Late Medieval Literature: Urbanism, Experience and Rhetoric in Some Early Descriptions of London

John M. Ganim

This essay is indebted to two aspects of Martin Stevens' own research: his interest in civic culture and in the complicated ways in which literary forms can represent civil ideals. My subject is the experience of the city in a few key prose descriptions of medieval and early modern London. I will begin with William Fitz Stephen's description of twelfth-century London at one historical and perceptual pole, and John Stow's famous late sixteenth-century *Survey of London* at the other.[1] I am particularly interested in how these writers negotiate their experience of the city through the rhetorical and narrative means they have available to describe that experience. For some of the most interesting and revealing passages in their descriptions occur when what they seek to describe conflicts with the means they have to describe it, when the idea of the city implicit in certain, largely spatial conventions of urban description conflicts with temporal change and momentary subjective experience. In these passages, we can locate anxieties surrounding the identification of the city with modernity and national identity which these larger descriptions seek to assert. These early descriptions of London are part of, as well as an account of, the symbolic formation of the city which the postmodern Metropolis and postmodern urban discourse has unraveled.[2] Yet some of the anxieties and inconsistencies in

---

[1] My citations below will be to John Stow, *A Survey of London*, ed. Charles L. Kingsford, 2 vols. (Oxford: Clarendon, 1908), which includes Fitz Stephen's *Descriptio* in Volume II, 223–229. The original Latin, quoted selectively in my notes to give a sample of Fitz Stephen's rhetoric, are from Kingsford's edition, although I have modernized obsolete spelling conventions. Translations of Fitz Stephen cited are from William Fitz Stephen, *Norman London*, intro. F. Donald Logan (New York: Italica Press, 1990). Although the title page does not acknowledge it, the actual translation is reprinted from that by H. E. Butler (London: Historical Association, 1934).

[2] The issues of the modern and postmodern, schematically clear in architectural theory, are problematized in actual discussions of urban space. The visionary plans of high modern architecture, typified in Le Corbusier's "Radiant City," with its skyscraper

these descriptions suggest that they have a significance beyond their usual status as eyewitness accounts or propaganda for the medieval or early modern city.

The model of the city and its bourgeois citizen as the engines of progress has come under severe interrogation. As Raymond Williams' memorable description of *The Country and the City* argued, the opposition of city and country itself obscures powerful forces at work in both.[3] The "Brenner thesis," captured most clearly in the title of Robert Brenner's article, "The Agrarian Roots of European Capitalism," has propounded the agricultural countryside, not the city, as the continually dynamic force in the English economy through the eighteenth century.[4] And yet the medieval city

elevated above a garden site, are in fact examples of what Paul de Man located, in *Blindness and Insight: Essays in the Rhetoric of Contemporary Criticism* (New York: Oxford University Press, 1971), as the paradigmatically modern desire to obliterate the historical and to renew the present by starting out from a fantasized, or literally created, point of origin. But the analysis of urbanism in theory and the criticism of its practice has in fact predicted the "postmodern" experience of dislocation caused by the grand renovative plans that mark nineteenth-century as well as twentieth-century planning. Where "modernism" is usually used as a historically limited concept rooted largely in cultural and aesthetic formulations, "modernity" is used to indicate the large-scale social and economic experiences that attend to rapid urbanization. The experience of modernity is one that has been defined by early twentieth-century social thinkers, especially George Simmel, Walter Benjamin and Siegfried Kracauer, as an analysis of the shock, dislocation and disorientation occasioned by unprecedented urbanization, development and modernization in the nineteenth century. See, for instance, Georg Simmel, "The Metropolis and Mental Life," in *The Sociology of Georg Simmel*, ed. Kurt Wolff (Glencoe, Ill.: Free Press, 1950); David Frisby, *Fragments of Modernity: Theories of Modernity in the Work of Simmel, Kracauer, and Benjamin* (Cambridge, Mass.: MIT Press, 1986); and Marshal Berman, *All That Is Solid Melts Into Air: The Experience of Modernity* (New York: Simon and Shuster, 1981). In Walter Benjamin's now virtually definitive definition of the experience of the city, both in his massive "Arcades Project" and in his spectacular brief essays on Baudelaire, and on "Paris, Capital of the Nineteenth Century," in *Reflections* (New York: Harcourt Brace, 1979), the subject who perceives the newly created surroundings of Paris, and who is in some sense a creation of these surroundings, is the "flâneur." Benjamin suggests that this apparent casualness has an ideological purpose, for the flâneur renders an illusion of coherence and unity to the otherwise threatening transformations the city is undergoing. The decentering of the city itself in the late twentieth century, the subject of postmodern urban theory, is treated in Frederic Jameson, *Postmodernism, or the Cultural Logic of Late Capitalism* (Durham, N.C.: Duke University Press, 1991), especially its influential title essay; Edward Soja, *Postmodern Geographies* (London: Verso, 1990); and David Harvey, *The Condition of Postmodernity* (Oxford: Basil Blackwell, 1989). See also Michel de Certeau, *The Practice of Everyday Life* (Berkeley: University of California Press, 1984); and Henri Lefebvre, *The Production of Space* (Oxford: Basil Blackwell, 1991).

[3] Raymond Williams, *The Country and the City* (London: Chatto and Windus, 1973)

[4] Reprinted and discussed in T. H. Aston and C. H. E. Philpin, eds., *The Brenner Debate: Agrarian Class Structure and Economic Development in Pre-Industrial Europe* (Cambridge: Cambridge Uuniversity Press, 1985).

continues, and continued, to function in some fashion as an emblem of modernity. Louise Fradenburg, in her important study of the ways in which Edinburgh and its ruler imagined themselves as mutually defining, is careful to distance herself from the celebration of the city as the source of dynamism and change, but allows that in fact change, and the mark of human construction and will, is nevertheless always more obvious in the city:

> the city poses the problem of change – of the changes giving rise to the city as well as the changes for which the city is often held responsible (sophistication, alienation, the devaluing of rural and familial experience, the making of money from money, the making of new things). Change brings newness into being; the imagination is as much at work in our economic life as in our poetry. For this reason, the city – not exclusively, but with a particular kind of power – poses the problem of how human beings construct their world. The artisanal or fictive economic activities pursued within the city are figured in the very construction of the cityscape itself. It is possible – though still a profound misrecognition – to forget the extent to which nature, the country outside the city walls, has been constructed by human curiosity, presumption, intervention, labor. It seems to be more difficult to forget the fact of the city's construction, a fact which implies human creativity and a decentered human responsibility for the shape of the world. Indeed, forgetting this fact will often require, in one historical form or another, the fantasy of a city plan that reinscribes the superreal in the form of royal or divine creativity.[5]

Fradenburg's powerful formulation in fact describes the heroic plans not only of absolutism, but of the modern city, as the epic transformations of Haussman or Robert Moses, or even of a dual figure like Peter the Great, attest.

Even one of the earliest descriptions of London we have, dating from sometime around 1180, William Fitz Stephen's *Descriptio*, celebrates its subject as both old and new, as related to and distinct from the countryside. London, for Fitz Stephen, is one of the most famous cities in the world, its wealth, commerce and general grandeur elevating it above all other cities. Its climate is mild, and this climate has seeped into the character of its citizens, enhancing their kindness and generosity. The religious importance of the city is marked not only by St. Paul's, but by the number of churches, which William counts as numbering 13 large churches in and around London, and 113 lesser parochial churches. London is defended from the east by the Palatine tower, "the mortar used in the building being tempered with the blood of beasts" (49) and two castles defend the west. The Thames, "abounding in fish" (49), has washed away what used to be fortifications on the south. Already London had developed suburbs, and William notes the

---

[5] Louise Fradenburg, *City, Marriage, Tournament: Arts of Rule in Late Medieval Scotland* (Madison: University of Wisconsin Press, 1991), 9.

beautiful gardens that surround the houses in the suburbs. The northern suburbs are the site of fields for pasture, merging into meadows that are crossed by streams, some of which drive mills. Next to these the forest still stands, abundant with game. William contrasts the gravelly soils of other regions with the fertility of London-area soil, "rich Asian plains" (50). The northern suburbs are also the site of wells of sweet water, which on summer evenings are frequented by the youth of the city. William's population figures are not clear, but he does note that in the reign of King Stephen, London provided 20,000 calvary and 60,000 infantry, though presumably these need not be inhabitants. Apparently, Fitz Stephen's London was an intellectual center rivaling what would become Oxford and Cambridge, and on festival days masters would arrange debates and other performances by their students. Fitz Stephen's description is also famous for three striking images of medieval London life: the public cook shops, the games and sports of the young men of the city, and the horse market.

The *Descriptio* was originally a preface to his biography of Thomas Becket, and Fitz Stephen, onetime colleague of Becket and a witness at his assassination, links Canterbury and London in an association, which, however determined by rhetoric and metaphor, echoes through to the *Canterbury Tales*. In language which implies the possible portability of the See from Canterbury to London, William pitches the virtues of the latter: "But since St. Thomas has adorned both these cities, London by his rising and Canterbury by his setting, each city has, in respect of the Saint himself, something further that it may urge, not without justice, one against the other" (49). Pictured as a sun-god, in language which links space and time in a way that predicts the *General Prologue*, St. Thomas traces the path between the two cities. This classicizing gesture obscures the profoundly medieval quality of the description of London, in that saint's lives were often prefaced with a description of the place of origin of the saint, especially important as canonization often had economic implications for churches and their towns.

The reader familiar with modern London or even with the archaeology of most medieval cities might be in for a surprise upon reading William's description of London:

> Among the noble cities of the world that are celebrated by Fame, the City of London, seat of the Monarchy of England, is one that spreads its fame wider, sends its wealth and wares further and lifts its head higher than all the others. It is blest in the wholesomeness of its air, in its reverence for the Christian faith, in the strength of its bulwarks, the nature of its situation, the honour of its citizens and the chastity of its matrons. It is likewise most merry in its sports and fruitful of noble men. (48)[6]

---

[6] Inter nobiles urbes orbis, quas fama celebrat, civitas Londonia, regni Anglorum sedes, una est quae famam sui latius diffundit, opes et merces longius transmittit, caput altius

William's hyperbolic praise of London's fame and wealth might conceivably be applicable to that London which would be, to paraphrase Benjamin, the capital of the eighteenth century. But in the twelfth century, London, despite its relative status among the cities of Britain, was, compared to Paris, the cities of northern Italy, especially Venice, and certainly in comparison to the metropolises of the Middle and Far East, provincial in almost every way. William must, nevertheless, make these claims rhetorically, for there is no point in describing a city unless it is or has been the greatest city on the face of the earth. William Fitz Stephen's *Descriptio* is well within the tradition of *encomium civitas*, the rhetoric of praise for the city as place, a tradition that continues into modern self-advertisements for cities (as sites for conventions, fairs, sports events), sometimes against all evidence. Even given the possibility of a major climactic shift, however, it is relatively unlikely that a riparian city of London's elevation could ever have had the lovely atmosphere that William praises (though I am reminded that early descriptions of the region I am now writing this in praised its rosy-tinged sunsets, a blush that was in fact symptomatic of its present, slowly improving, atmospheric pollution). Like the red lips and gray eyes of the romance heroine or the armor and bearing of the romance hero, the discourse William calls upon demands precisely the atmosphere of the *locus amoenus*. The language of urban description in the Middle Ages is equivalent in visual terms to a conscious squint, a soft, but blurry focus.

In his *European Literature and the Latin Middle Ages*, Curtius argues that the legacy of Hellenistic rhetoric for medieval literature lies partly in a stress on epideictic eloquence, the rhetoric of praise or blame.[7] "The influence of epideictic oratory on medieval literature," writes Curtius, "was very great," and he stresses especially the "elaborate 'delineation' (ekphrasis . . . descriptio) of people, places, buildings, works of art" (69). The challenge of this rhetorical aesthetic generally is articulated clearly by Curtius himself: "Merely from the rhetorical character of medieval poetry, it follows that, in interpreting a poem, we must ask, not on what 'experience' it was based, but what theme the poet set himself to treat. This is especially distasteful to the modern critic when he has to criticize poems on spring or nightingales or swallows" (158), all the topics, Curtius points out, prescribed by medieval rhetorical exercises.

Curtius cites an eighth-century poetic description of Milan as prototypical, and enumerates the points on which it is praised:

extollit. Felix est aeris salubritate, Christiana religione, firmitate munitionum, natura situs, honore civium, pudicitia matronali. Ludis etiam quam iocunda, et nobilium est fecunda virorum. (219)

[7] Ernst Robert Curtius, *European Literature and the Latin Middle Ages*, trans. Willard Trask (New York: Harper, 1963).

1. Its site on a fruitful plain; 2. walls, towers, and gates; 3. forum, paved streets, baths; 4. churches; 5. the piety of the inhabitants; 6. saints' tombs; 7. Ambrose and later Bishops; 8. cultivation of science, art, and liturgy; 9. wealth and charity of the citizens; 10. the rule of King Liutprand (d. 744); 11. Archbishop Theodore II (d. 735); 12. achievements of the citizens in the war against infidelity. (157)

Curtius reports that such descriptions accord with few revisions with the rules for eulogies of cities developed in late antique rhetorical theory:

> The site had first to be treated, then the other excellences of the city, and not least its significance in respect to the cultivation of the arts and sciences. In the Middle Ages this last typos is given an ecclesiastical turn. The greatest glory of a city now lies in its martyrs (and their relics), its saints, princes of the church, and theologians. (157)[8]

Curtius' acknowledgement of the conventional nature of medieval style and subject has been part of the basis of our newly recovered awareness over the past half-century of the sophistication and self-consciousness of medieval writing. At the same time, Curtius' appeal to convention (which for him was not merely a synchronic structural device but a powerful expression of the diachronic continuity of classical culture as one of the constituents of Europe itself) renders problematic the nature of medieval writings as evidence or witness. It is all very well to read a description of a swallow as a rhetorical exercise, rather than as an Audubon-like portrait, in that we can always look at our own swallows or look them up in Audubon. But what happens when the description of cities and buildings that we rely on for evidence of what was there turns out to be just rhetoric? This question is a familiar one in the wake of post-structuralist theory, with its emphasis on how apparently subjective and objective perspectives are in fact mediated by previous discourses and on how these discourses bear some relation to political status. But how then do we approach the problematic of representation in descriptions that after all still taunt us with their status as evidence, especially since the object of their description is long ago obliterated?

We can now turn to William Fitz Stephen's description of London in the time of Henry II with an awareness of the enormous significance of what his editor describes as

> a clear, vigorous and highly rhetorical Latin. If his rhetoric is at times apt to cause amusement to a modern reader, it must on the other hand be remembered that he was merely following the precepts of the Schools in employing a style descended from the flamboyant 'Asiatic' rhetoric of the

---

[8] See also Theodore C. Burgess, *Epideictic Literature* (Chicago: University of Chicago Press, 1902), pp. 110. The most complete catalogue is J. K. Hyde, "Medieval Descriptions of Cities," *Bulletin of the John Rylands Library* 48 (1966): 308–40.

first and second centuries A.D., and still clearly recognizable, despite changes of outlook, idiom and grammar. (61)

Whatever apology for William's rhetorical style might be appropriate, the fact of the matter is that the very structure of his description, perhaps what he "sees" as a narrator and hence what we see in his description, is profoundly mediated, even determined, by the prior discourse of the idea of a city. William's themes are not apparently implausible and one might argue that he is adjusting the traditional rhetorical categories of *encomium civitas* to allow for the actuality of the London he observes and experiences and to some extent – the games and entertainments and the marvelous descriptions of the public cookshop and the horse market – this is partly true. But the details of his description of the grander London he portrays suggest other sources than everyday reality:

> Moreover, there is in London upon the river's bank, amid the wine that is sold from ships and wine-cellars, a public cookshop. There daily, according to the season, you may find viands, dishes roast, fried and boiled, fish great and small, the coarser flesh for the poor, the more delicate for the rich, such as venison and birds both big and little. If friends, weary from travel, should of a sudden come to any of the citizens, and it is not their pleasure to wait fasting till fresh food is bought and cooked and "till servants bring water for hands and bread," they hasten to the river bank and there all things desireable are ready to their hand. . . . Now this is a public cookshop, appropriate to a city and pertaining to the art of civic life. (52)[9]

Even later observers such as Stow take this description of the cookshop as accurate reportage and contrast it with the uneven quality of cooked foodstuffs offered in their own time, but behind Fitz Stephen's advertisement for gentrification probably lie utopian fantasies of freely available food and wine, some of which find themselves parodied in the early thirteenth-century *The Land of Cockaigne*, with its geese flying through the air already spit-roasted. Equally striking is Fitz Stephen's picture of the Smithfield horse market:

> Thither come all the Earls, Barons and Knights who are in the City, and with them many of the citizens, whether to look on or buy. It is a joy to

---

[9] Praeterea est in Londonia, super ripam fluminis, inter vina et navibus et cellis vinariis vinalia, publica coquina. Ibi quotidie, pro tempore, est invenire cibaria, fercula, assa, frixa, elixa, pisces, pisciculos, carnes grossiores pauperibus, delicatores divitioribus, venationum, avium, avicularum. Si subito veniant ad aliquem civium amici fatigati ex itenere, nec libeat ieiunis expectare, ut novi cibi emantur et coquantur,
'Dent famuli manibus lymphas panesque'
interim ad ripam curritur; ibi praesto sunt omnia
desiderabilia . . . Haec coquinam publica coquina est, et civitati plurimum expediens, et ad civilitatum pertinens. (222–223)

see the ambling palfreys, their skin full of juice, their coats a-glisten, as they pace softly, in alternation raising and putting down the feet on one side together; next to see the horses that best befit Esquires, moving more roughly, yet nimbly, as they raise and set down their opposite feet, fore and hind, first on one side and then on the other; then the younger colts of high breeding . . . and after them the costly destriers of graceful form and goodly stature. . . . When a race between such trampling steeds is about to begin, or perchance between others which are likewise, after their kind, strong to carry, swift to run, a shout is raised, and horses of the baser kind are bidden to turn aside. Three boys riding these fleet-foot steeds, or at times two as may be agreed, prepare themselves for the contest. Skilled to command their horses, they "curb their untamed mouths with jagged bits," and their chief anxiety is that their rival shall not gain the lead. (54)

This is sports writing of the highest order, breathlessly eroticizing its subject. Underneath the action, however, is an order as deliberate as the most carefully planned city procession, for the horses are grouped virtually according to caste, and precedence and nobility are implicitly connected. Interestingly, the horse market is marked, as all of Fitz Stephen's ludic scenes are marked, by its exclusively male character (in contrast to what seems to be a largely homosocial city, women are accorded one sentence: "The matrons of the city are perfect Sabines" [50]), but nearby, the "country-folk" are described in images of fertility and therefore femininity:

In another place apart stand the wares of the country-folk, instruments of agriculture, long-flanked swine, cows with swollen udders, and "wooly flocks and bodies huge of kine." Mares stand there, meet for ploughs, sledges and two-horsed carts; the bellies of some are big with young; round others move their offspring, new-born, sprightly foals, inseparable followers. (54)

Here again, the underlying structure of Fitz Stephen's description is so obviously coded as to suggest that rhetoric as much as actuality directs his attention. If the horse-market is registered as aristocratic, as equivalent to the tournament and the court, the cattle market is marked as pastoral. But beyond these categories lies the tradition of classical rhetoric in which descriptions of horses was a commonly and widely treated theme.

This thematic appropriateness is also true of the famous description of games and entertainment in London. In place of a stage, London has "holier plays wherein are shown forth the miracles wrought by Holy Confessors or the sufferings which glorified the constancy of Martyrs" (56). At Carnival time, boys are allowed to bring fighting cocks to school, "and the whole forenoon is given to boyish sport" (56), and "after dinner all the youth of the city goes out into the fields to a much-frequented game of ball" (56). Teams seem to have been sponsored by different schools and various guilds.

Older and wealthy men come on horseback to watch, "and after their fashion are young again with the young; and it seems that the motion of their natural heat is kindled by the contemplation of such violent motion and by their partaking in the joys of untrammelled youth" (56–7). Every Sunday in Lent, young men carry on mock battles on horseback, joined by courtiers and sometimes by squires. At Easter these battles become mock naval battles: a young man standing at the prow of a rowboat aims his lance at a shield anchored in the middle of a stream. On summer feast days, more routine sports such as "leaping," archery, wrestling, stone-putting and javelin throwing become common. Winter feast days are celebrated with bull, boar or bear baiting. And Fitz Stephen concludes with his spectacular picture of ice-skating and games:

> When the great marsh that washes the Northern walls of the City is frozen, dense throngs of youths go forth to disport themselves on the ice. Some gathering speed by a run, glide sidelong, with feet set well apart, over a vast space of ice. Others make themselves seats of ice like millstones and are dragged along by a number who run before them holding hands. Sometimes they slip owing to the greatness of their speed and fall, every one of them, upon their faces. Others there are, more skilled to sport upon the ice, who fit to their feet the shinbones of beasts, lashing them beneath their ankles, and with iron-shod poles in their hands they strike ever and anon against the ice and are borne along swift as a bird in flight or a bolt shot from a mangonel. (58)

The description of sports and games is also one of the prescribed themes for the description of cities, but also one of the exercises of rhetoric instruction. Fitz Stephen's striking images, apparently drawn from life, are subsumed to a highly patterned seasonal formula, and only those striking images which have no rhetorical analogies can be comfortably regarded as documentary evidence. Aside from these details, however, something else distinguishes Fitz Stephen's London from the description of other medieval cities, and which seems to mark other descriptions of London – his sense of the pulse of street life, of crowds and their random patterns, of a city enlivened by its smaller rather than its grandest designs. Indeed, it will be this sense of London defined by people moving through it that marks the most interesting portrayals of London from Fitz Stephen through at least the eighteenth century, including such works as *London Lickpenny* and Langland's images of London in *Piers Plowman*. This sense of energetic circulation may derive from London's casual relation to its suburbs and its indifference to the strong relation between city center and city walls so characteristic of continental city plans.[10]

The rhetorically formulaic medieval description of the city limits its use as

---

[10] On the development and character of London throughout its history, the classic study is by Steen Rasmussen, *London: The Unique City*, revised edition (Cambridge, MA: MIT Press, 1982). The 1934 edition is also worth consulting for its pre-Blitz perspective.

quasi-photographic evidence. But the rhetoric reveals, even constitutes, the political and symbolic perception of the city by the writer and his audience, or more accurately, by the writer for his audience. In *City, Marriage, Tournament: Arts of Rule in Late Medieval Scotland*, Fradenburg compares the utopic and dystopic poems by poets such as Dunbar, and discusses how their images of Edinburgh reveal the complex, subjected relation between nation, town and crown. The poems Fradenburg cites are in fact consistent with the *encomium civitas* formulae in the positive version of the city and an inversion of those formulae in the negative version of the city. For the language of the city in early medieval tradition began and ended with apocalyptic discourse, with the binary poles of Babylon and Jerusalem. The human city in medieval literature was always being filtered through the ways in which the City of God was visualized. But the clear theological distinction between the earthly Jerusalem and the heavenly Jerusalem tended to break down in the phenomenological discourse of the city. The earthly Jerusalem became not only a figure for, but a figure of, the Heavenly City, and the ideology of the Crusades (as opposed to the historical experience of the Crusades when Jerusalem was reached) helped blur the distinction even more. This blurring of figuration and mimesis is everywhere in Fitz Stephen's description of London.

Such an apocalyptic framework for the city accounts at least partly for the affective rhetoric of urban descriptions, particularly the combination of awe and wonder which the approach to the city engenders. Norman Cohn describes the relation between the Jerusalem figured in theology and the apocalyptic urges behind the late Crusades, resulting in a generalization to all possible vehicles of meaning:

> Even for theologians Jerusalem was also a "figure" or symbol of the heavenly city "like unto a stone most precious" which according to the Book of Revelation was to replace it at the end of time. No wonder that – as contemporaries noted – in the minds of simple folk the idea of the earthly Jerusalem became so confused with and transfused by that of the Heavenly Jerusalem that the Palestinian city seemed itself a miraculous realm, abounding both in spiritual and material blessings. And no wonder that when the masses of the poor set off on their long pilgrimage the children cried out at every town and castle: "Is that Jerusalem?" – while high in the heavens there was seen a mysterious city with vast multitudes hurrying towards it.[11]

If one version of Christian historiography imagined its paradisaical past as a garden, it imagined its millenial future as a city. Indeed, millenial urbanism envisioned both the demonic and angelic futures in terms of the city. The perspective on the city common to much medieval literature and visual arts is one from outside the city, so that the walls, the moats, gates,

[11] Norman Cohn, *The Pursuit of the Millenium* (New York: Harper, 1961), pp. 44–45.

the river or other natural or manmade borders between the city and its surroundings are emphasized. The crossing, or failure to cross, this border is often an important feature of the narrative. Whatever its origin in the actual siting and planning of medieval cities and towns, the view from afar of the resplendent city rhetorically replicates the vision of the city in apocalyptic discourse. For all the pride implicit in the descriptions of medieval cities, the subject position which observes them remains at a certain distance, as if a visitor or a pilgrim.[12]

Behind the apocalyptic image of the city as the end and goal of history lies a geographic rather than a temporal image, for the city at the end of time tended to be imagined in terms of the most up-to-date and highly developed urban technologies, much like utopian science fiction. For the Middle Ages there was an immediate and obvious correlative – the great cities of the (sometimes fictionalized) East. Fitz Stephen describes his London at the same time that reports of the great cities of the Orient begin to filter back from the Crusades and from newly active trade routes.[13] The sense of wonder that informs Fitz Stephen's description of his own city derives partly from these prior models, and the result is a peculiar subjective perspective: the city is described as if the narrating subject were a foreigner or a visitor to his own land, and is privileged to recount what he has seen. This apocalyptic and orientalized city is a very different one from the London found in another famous description, one that nevertheless depends on Fitz Stephen – John Stow's *Survey of London*.

Most readers are now familiar with Fitz Stephen's *Descriptio* because of its inclusion in one of the chief records of London before the Great Fire, John Stow's *Survey of London*, which Lewis Mumford called "one of the great classics in urban historiography."[14]

[12] On this trope, see the wonderful essay by Gerhart Ladner, "*Homo Viator*: Medieval Ideas of Alienation and Order," *Speculum* 42 (1967): 233–259.
[13] Especially marked in the great number of guidebooks to Jerusalem. See, for instance, "Description of Jerusalem and the Holy Land," trans. J. R. McPherson, *Library of the Palestine Pilgrims' Text Society* 5 (1897).
[14] Lewis Mumford, *The Culture of Cities* (New York: Harcourt Brace, 1938), p. 546. Stow's survey and even Fitz Stephen's *Descriptio* are still cited as eyewitness sources with some frequency, but the *Survey* has been subject to surprisingly little critical or analytic scrutiny, perhaps because of the thoroughness of Kingsford's edition and his additional notes. Using the arsenal of poststructuralist analysis of historical discourse, William Keith Hall, "A Topography of Time: Historical Narration in John Stow's *Survey of London*," *Studies in Philology* 88 (1991): 1–15, interestingly describes some of the inevitable distortions when history is organized by means of a "cartographic" perspective. The most important scholarship on Stow since Kingsford's edition is almost certainly M. J. Power's "John Stow and His London," *Journal of Historical Geography* (1985): 1–20. Power suggests that Stow's interest in recent building, and particularly in fine edifices related to elite projects and areas of the city, results in a somewhat distorted topographical picture of London. Stow focuses on the City to the exclusion of the increasingly populous suburbs, and obscures the increasing class

Stow is in awe of Fitz Stephen's description of London. He is usually skeptical about, even critical of his sources, but Fitz Stephen's status as an eyewitness disarms his critical faculty. Fitz Stephen's descriptions of superb cookshops and thriving merchants, of splendid private houses and thoughtfully planned public works, all these Stow reads these as factual statement. What in Fitz Stephen seems so clearly hyperbolic to us seems entirely straightforward to Stow. Indeed, Stow follows Fitz Stephen in some part in terms of the order of his description, apparently unaware that this order is dictated by the strictures of Fitz Stephen's rhetorical formulae. But Stow needs Fitz Stephen for his own rhetorical purposes, not only because he is an eyewitness to a vanished past. For Stow, the London of Fitz Stephen is a paradise lost, that can yet be regained by renewed civic determination. Fitz Stephen's London is Stow's model of Utopia. Fitz Stephen's wonderfully functioning urban model is one that Stow seems to realize is impossible to create and he by no means represents all change as decline. Indeed, everywhere throughout Stow's description is an awareness of change and of human capacity to reshape the present condition of both people and places. Stow's sense of history tends, because of the spatial categories he relies on, to be vertical rather than horizontal, but within those vertical vectors change and transformation, sometimes slow, sometimes sudden, are always implicitly captured. It is this sense of human intervention that Stow seems always on the verge of imploring. For above and beyond the antiquarian's urge to recall the past is an equally powerful civic urge to improve and maintain that which has been recalled. Stow can ignore Fitz Stephen's hyperbole because he has his own rhetorical agenda that Fitz Stephen can be appropriated to.

The human ability to write the city as if it were a text, and even to rewrite the past, leaving only traces to be deciphered, is a constant theme in Stow's survey. This textual, even linguistic metaphor is only partly implicit, and I am making it explicit not only as a function of our own fashion.[15] Stow's city is a city of words as much as a city of places, or, perhaps more accurately, a city of places superimposed upon a city of words. Not only Fitz Stephen's account, but chronicles, legal record and other documents

---

segregation of the City, with the movement of elites to the West End and Westminster, and the growth of poorer housing and the practice of humbler trades in the East End and Southwark. For a brilliant, brief reading of the *Survey*, see Dana Brand, *The Spectator and the City in Nineteenth Century American Literature* (Cambridge: Cambridge University Press, 1991), pp. 16–17: "Implicit in Stow's description is a conception of the primacy of the city, as a feature of society subordinate to nothing else." See also the fine introduction by Lawrence Manley, ed., *London in the Age of Shakespeare* (London: Croom and Helm, 1986), pp. 1–29, which places Stow in the context of Renaissance city descriptions.

[15] See Hall, "A Topography of Time" on this aspect of Stow.

provide him with access to the cities which lie beneath the city in front of him. Stow's prosaic reminders of the importance of maintenance disguises a more poetic understanding of the city as a collection of Memory Places.[16] Each place, each crossroads, each building, releases, upon meditation, a past which floats up vertically as if exorcized. For Stow, the city's aspect is not the horizontal skyline, but an archaeology of memory constituted by the relative relation of this or that place. The relation of the city to memory, and to the medieval and Renaissance tradition of memory training, with its spatial and architectural techniques is apparent in both Fitz Stephen's and Stow's descriptions of London. Tombs, monuments, churches, even fields where famous events have occurred, constitute a city of memory in both writers. This connection, almost axiomatic to medieval and Renaissance descriptions of cities, is obscured for us by the triumph of Romanticism and by the explosion of the Metropolis in the nineteenth century. For Wordsworth, for instance, memory was inspired by Nature, and even occasional positive contemplations of urban scenes are rendered as pastoral (although Wordsworth inveighs against the uniformity and consequent seeking of sensation in the city in terms akin to Simmel's). In the nineteenth century, the development of the metropolis resulted in the association of the city with the obliteration of memory. Haussman's boulevards literally wiped out huge sections of the architectural past of Paris and the flood of migrants to the city, while they may have carried with them traditions and values connected to the countryside, had to recall them, as if in memory. Even the anonymity of the city was registered in the obliteration of a personal past, a trope familiar in American urban literature.

At times, Stow's London is as much a city of accounts and financial numbers as it is a city of words. Stow reveals his class values, and perhaps his personal financial situation, in the surprisingly frequent observations about currency, price controls and inflation. Throughout the *Survey* are anecdotes of how attempts to control prices inevitably lead to inflation, and Stow is obsessively detailed about the costs of goods, usually foodstuffs, at various points in London's history. His concern with inflation and rising prices is also reflected in his detailed account of the minting of coins and their relative content of precious metals, and, interestingly, their tensile strength. He seems to approve of attempts to control and ensure the quality of goods, but is skeptical about the control of prices. He also approves of general levies to improve London's infrastructure, particularly its walls and its water supply, but narrates in a critical tone taxation by the crown for its own purposes unrelated to the obvious well-being of the commonweal, and particularly the city. But Stow reserves his praise and his most obvious admiration for private citizens who donate public improvements or whose

[16] On memory places, see Francis Yates, *The Art of Memory* (Chicago: University of Chicago Press, 1966).

private renovations or buildings improve the face of the city. Charity, for Stow, is a crucial and even the best part of public endowment. His specific listing of names and titles and offices is partly the scrupulousness of the annalist, but partly also the rhetoric of the memorialist, praising those who have improved the city. Against the constant pressures of change with its necessity for innovation, and the decay and deterioration attendant upon time and use, Stow envisions a constantly but selectively improved material environment, one that not only functions but also announces civic pride and urban values. If one regards his description of the physical material of the city as imagery rather than factual description, one finds a poem celebrating the replacement of temporary wooden structures and buildings with those of permanent stone. Stow admires permanence and understandably seems almost to fetishize any construction in stone.

Stow's careful descriptions of the various buildings or building types that have stood on this or that site have been justifiably praised for their contribution to the historical record. In the context of the human shaping of the city and the economic interests involved, Stow also provides us with another dimension to the city, its creation and often its destruction or radical reshaping by what we would now regard as "development." Stow's London had a population of about 150,000 in 1595. But the expansion which he observes (as well as that which he obscures or ignores) is relatively slight compared to what was to come. By 1632, the population had more than doubled. While such a growth rate is not as dramatic as the growth of cities in the nineteenth century as a consequence of industrialization nor of the explosive expansion of cities such as São Paolo or Mexico City in recent decades, it was enormous by the standards of the time and in terms of the perception of its inhabitants. Descriptions of London after the fire attest to the awareness of and fear of this enormous growth and the terrible strains it put on the resources of the city, and one might regard Stow's picture of London as the "before" picture in the then and now genre of historical photography. But Stow's description, particularly if we take into account his relative minimization of the suburbs and the development which was occurring all around the city, in fact predicts this explosion, and reveals many of the pressures and attempts to contain those pressures that London's authorities undertook. He is attuned to the city recycling its own materials into new shapes, like an organism. Most often, however, these changes are described as forms of decline and bad faith. One description captures some of the tensions between private and public interests that mark our own cityscapes. In the survey of Aldgate, Sir Thomas Audley (later Lord Chancellor)

> offered the great Church of this priorie, with a ring of nine Bels well tuned, whereof foure the greatest were since solde to the parish of *Stebunhith*, and the five lesser to the parish of Saint *Stephen* in Colemans

streete, to the parishioners of Saint *Katherine Christ Church*, in exchaunge for their small parish church, minding to haue pulled it downe, and to haue builded there towards the street: But the parishioners hauing doubts in their heades of afterclappes, refused the offer. Then was the priorie church and steeple proffered to whomsoeuer would take it down, and carrie it from the ground, but no man would vndertake the offer, whereupon Sir *Thomas Audley* was faine to bee at more charges, then could be made of the stones, timber, leade, yron, &c. For the workemen with great labour beginning at the toppe, loosed stone from stone, and threw them downe, whereby the most part of them were broken, and few remained whole, and those were sold verie cheape, for all the buildings then made about the Citie were of Bricke and Timber. (I, 142)

Stow's position is clear without being stated here, underneath the objective description. He pits the stubborn skepticism of the parishioners against the ambition of Sir Thomas Audley. He also implicitly laments the destruction of the priory church and seems to defend the "small parish church" because it is there. In any case, Audley's personality unpleasantly seeps through the account.

One of Stow's most striking examples of development and change is of "Houndes ditch":

for that in olde time when the same lay open, much filth (conveyed forth of the Citie) especially dead Dogges were there layd or cast: wherefore of latter time a mudde wall was made inclosing the ditch . . .on the other side of the streete, was a fair fielde . . .this fielde (as all other aboute the citie) was inclosed. . . .Towards the street were some small cottages, of two stories high, and little garden plottes backewarde, for poore bedred people, for in that streete dwelt none other. . . .In my youth, I remember, deuout people as well men as women of this Citie, were accustomed oftentimes, especially on Frydayes weekeley to walke that way purposedly there to bestow their charitable almes, euerie poore man or woman lying in their bed within their window, which was towards the streete open so low that euery man might see them, a clean linnen cloth lying in ther window, and a payre of Beades to shew that there lay a bedred body, vnable but to pray onely. . . .About the latter raigne of *Henrie* the eight, three brethren that were Gunfounders surnamed *Owens*, gate ground there to build vpon, and to inclose for casting of Brasse Ordinance. These occupied a good part of the streete on the field side, and in short time diuerse other also builded there, so that the poore bedred people were worne out, and in place of their homely Cottages, such houses builded, as doe rather want roome then rent, which houses be for the most part possessed by Brokers, sellers of olde apparell, and such like. The residue of the fielde was for the most part made into a Garden, by a Gardener named *Cawsway*, one that served the Markets with Hearbes and Rootes: and in the last yeare of King *Edwarde* the sixt, the same parceled into Gardens, wherein are now many fayre houses of pleasure builded. (I, 128–9)

Stow's history of Houndsditch, from moat to sewer to field to hospice to cartoucherie to specialty farmland to garden suburb is as close as he comes to suggesting change and dynamism. But it is a dynamism that his apparently objective narration actually reproaches. Moreover, it is significant that this extraordinary transformation occurs outside the city gates and walls: here Stow can register change without having it conflict with his virtually cartographic perspective. The pattern of land use in this passage (which takes up only about a page of text) is interestingly varied – from empty land to polluted land to charitable use to military industry to shabby and marginal district – and would have been much rarer within the city walls. Stow's apparently artless pictures of the pious poor and the aggressively determined munitions manufacturers are, however, informed by his conservative humanism.

Stow understandably and obviously associates maintenance with stability of both houses and neighborhoods, for decline invites "strangers" to move in. This attitude we now associate with anti-urban, suburban mentality, since after the nineteenth century we equate the city with strangers. But of course the burgher's attitude is always one of suspicion towards those not citizens. In another one of those spiraling biographies of buildings, Stow describes the house of Robert de Vere, the Earl of Oxford:

> but in the processe of time the landes of the Earle fell to femals, amongest the which one being married to *Wingfield* of Suffolke, this house with the appurtenances fell to his lot, and was by his heire Sir *Robert Wingfield* sold to M. *Edward Cooke*, at this time the Queenes Atturney Generall. This house being greatly ruinated of late time, for the most part hath been letten out to Powlters, for stabling of horses and stowage of Poultrie, but now lately builded into a number of small tenements, letten out to strangers, and other meane people. (I, 163)

Aside from the architectural interest of these "chicken coop" apartments, Stow's narration is interesting because of the way the lives of buildings take over from the lives of families and individuals, and in some fashion become more real, or at any rate more important, than their inhabitants and owners.

Stow's definition of what it means to be a Londoner and the responsibilities of citizenry runs like an allegory through his most famous descriptions. He recites Hall's account of the enclosure of the suburban common fields, frustrating the young men of London who were used to practicing archery and other games in these fields, as if it were their right. The result was something like a radical ecological action – a huge number of the citizens of London assembled, shouting "Shovels and spades! Shovels and spades" and marched into the fields, where they uprooted the hedges and filled in the ditches. In response to protest by the surrounding towns, the city government responded with the equivalent of a slap on the wrist. But this carnivalesque populism, which Stow despite himself enjoys recounting, has been for nought:

but now wee see the thing in worse case than euer, by meanes of inclosure for Gardens, wherein are builded many fayre summer houses, and as in other places of the Suburbes, some of them like Midsommer Pageantes, with Towers, Turrets, and Chimney tops, not so much for vse or profite, as for shewe and pleasure, bewraying the vanity of mens mindes, much vnlike to the disposition of the ancient Cittizens, who delighted in the building of Hospitals, and Almes houses for the poore, and therin both employed their wits, and spent their wealthes in preferment of the common commoditie of this our Citie. (II, 78)

Behind the city-dweller's perennial disdain for the bad taste of the suburbs lies an older, medieval sense of charity, and behind that the underlying communal value of the "common commoditie" of London. Where medieval political philosophy as it emerged in the late Middle Ages could think of a functioning society in terms of the co-ordinated responsibility of estates, for Stow the commitment of the citizen must be expressed in bricks and mortar (or fountains and sewers as necessary). His "commoditie" can be translated as "profit," akin to the medieval sense of "common profit," but has a more material connotation.

Where Fitz Stephen can always and everywhere present London virtues as the summit of their type, for Stow, crucial aspects of civic life are in decline, and need, like buildings, to be repaired. The charity of citizens may well have been a rhetorical theme, but for Stow it was more than that; it was what corrected the excesses of the social order, and like the fulfillment of long standing agreements, was necessary for maintaining the common good. After a long list of charitable bequests to the Guildhall, for instance (which Stow describes in the same way as he would a church, with its list of benefactors and memorials), he complains: "*Nicholas Alwyn* Mercer, Mayor 1499. deceased 1505. gave by his Testament for a hanging of a Tapestrie to serue for principall dayes in the Guild hall 73.li. 6.s. 8.d. How this gift was performed I haue not heard, for Executors of our time hauing no conscience, (I speake of my own knowledge) proue more testaments then they performe" (I, 273).

When Stowe leaves his actual chronicling of London places and speaks "theoretically" about cities in general and London in specific, he begins to sound more like Fitz Stephen. London becomes not an objective place to describe, but a paragon of cities. Even here, however, he is careful to explain exactly why London should be and has been so important. It is placed, he says, on a major river, and its location allows riparian access but access difficult enough to provide defense against invasion. Its general location in the southeast allows it to face the economic potential and potential power of the Low Countries and of France. For Fitz Stephen, the idea of London is more important than London itself. For Stow, the London that has been made and transformed is responsible for London's ideal qualities. Nevertheless, this defense of London is not without its ideological dimensions, not only in terms of Stow's class and urban identity, but also in terms of his biography. Stow found himself charged with possessing seditious, specifically "Popish" writings, and though exonerated, was in some suspicion of unreformed beliefs for some part of his later life. Stow's defense of the political importance of London, and its fidelity to the crown, is in some sense a defense of himself. London, he says, has frequently supported the monarchy in crisis, and when it has found itself in conflict with monarchical expropriation, it has usually followed the lead of the aristocracy. Stow rarely interrupts his house by house account in the body of the survey, but when he does and when his digressions have any political dimension, it is to narrate an unjust legal proceeding on the one hand or the just punishment of insurrection on the other. The number of times, about six, that he mentions Walworth's defense of Richard II (almost as if to overshadow Richard's deposition) is striking and revelatory.

Stow's admirably bourgeois perspective, with its inextricable link of charity and public pride with shrewd calculation, seems to have only partially succeeded in his private life. A member of the tailor's guild, he seems to have supported himself in that trade for most of his life, but seems also to have spent most of his savings on books and on research for his *Annals* and his *Survey*. Towards the end of his life, he apparently depended on pensions and gifts to make ends meet. Despite his chronic impecuniousness, or perhaps related to it, he was part and parcel of the city's intellectual and literary community and friends with many of the leading writers of his day. The harsh accusations leveled against him during periods of political suspicion seem to have derived from his scholarly activity, particularly his harboring of "old Popish books." One can read, then, in his account of London, a defense of his own life, representing the public and political sacrifices and patronage of individuals throughout the history of the city as a form of heroism. Neither Stow nor Fitz Stephen, despite their occasional political difficulties, can be said to be major actors in the political arena. Nevertheless, both portraits of London can be seen to manifest profound political dimensions. They imagine a civil society and explain the virtues and requirements necessary to allow such a society to function. They perceive the city from a very specific class position, so that they present to us a particular perspective that highlights some things and obscures others. Their descriptions also function as political allegories, offering an apology and justification for their authors' own lives.

This political dimension to the apparently celebratory description of the city has understandably sinister overtones in Stow. One of Stow's most well known anecdotes is of an execution he witnesses:

Soone after was there a Commotion of the Commons in Norfolke, Suffolke, Essex, and other shires, by meanes whereof streight orders being taken for the suppression of rumors, diuerse persons were

94

apprehended and executed by Marshall Law, amongst the which the Baylife of Romfort in Essex was one, a man verie well beloued: he was early in the Morning of *Marie Magdalens* day, then kept holy day, brought by the shiriffes of London, and the knight Marshall, to the Well within Aldgate, there to be executed vpon a Jebet set vp that Morning, where being on the Ladder, he had words to this effect: Good people I am come hither to die, but know not for what offence except for words by me spoken yester night to Sir *Stephen*, Curate and Preacher of this parish, which were these: He asked me what newes in the Countrey, I answered, heauie newes: why quoth he? it is sayde, quoth I, that many men be vp in Essex, but thanks be to God al is in good quiet about vs: and this was all as God be my Iudge, &c. Vppon these wordes of the prisoner, sir *Stephen* to auoyde reproach of the people, left the Cittie, and was neuer heard of since amongst them to my knowledge. I heard the wordes of the prisoner, for he was executed vpon the pauement of my doore where I then kept house. (I, 144–145)

Here we find a collocation of two dimensions of medieval and early modern urban life. Throughout Stow's narrative, we find hearsay and gossip functioning as they do in village and town life, carrying with it their own values and perspectives, not necessarily those of official culture. This Bakhtinian city, which we are likely to romanticize, is in contrast with another city, something like a Foucauldian city, a city of surveillance and regulation and punishment. Such a division, however, has more to do with our own categories than with the actualities of medieval civil life. For all its touted freedoms, the great medieval cities, particularly but not only those of Italy, were highly regulated and policed. The network of gossip, which we tend to identify with folk culture, with the pre-modern, even with a positive *gemeinschaft*, is here revealed in its negative aspects, as rumor piles on rumor and the crowd becomes a mob, and as with Shakespearean or Chaucerian crowds, changes its sentiments either too easily or too late.

Fitz Stephen's description of London is not without its awareness of modernity. As I have tried to suggest, however, its utopianism, conditioned by millenial visions of the City and by a sense of wonder related to occidental perceptions of the medieval orient, renders that modernity out of time and history. London is "modern" to the degree that it resembles a future place and faraway legends. Fitz Stephen's own organization of the city not only by walls and monuments but by seasons and celebrations creates a rhythm of the city that is closer to the rhythms of agricultural life, of seasonality, on the one hand, and to the rhythms of the monastery, another utopian time scheme, on the other. In Stow, for the first time, we find an awareness of modernity as outrage and as change that simultaneously destroys and creates, sometimes in the same action. For Stow describes not just signature buildings by magnates, but the process of development and the interests of developers. The change wrought by development becomes clear to him when his conservative perspective is shocked by alterations, that is, when his almost medieval guild values of piety and charity are outraged by development. In Stow's descriptions of monastic depredations, however objective the tone he seeks to maintain, is an elegaic note, perhaps related to the official suspicion he was sometimes under. What is striking in Stow's picture of London, once we pay attention to the way he draws that picture, to its outlines and rhythms and structures, is how much like a modern city sixteenth-century London already is. Stow's account of groups and elites and trades and other groups, and the physical configurations they create, the tensions and solidarities among and between them, is an account of an enormous complexity, one that disturbs easy distinctions between modern and pre-modern, between community and group. Stow's modernity consists not just of his outcry against changes motivated by greed, but by the fact that he holds at the same time the values that motivate both the changes themselves and the places that are destroyed by change.

Noah's Wife's Flood*

Alfred David

And all flesh died that moved upon the earth, both of fowl, and of cattle, and of beast, and of every creeping thing that creepeth upon the earth, and every man: All in whose nostrils was the breath of life, of all that was in the dry land, died.

The solemnity of Genesis 7.21–22 is appropriate to the greatest catastrophe ever to overtake the earth. The drowning people and corpses of humans and beasts in medieval illustrations of the flood show that its horrors were vividly imagined. Medieval exegetes saw in the flood the type of the Last Judgment and the final destruction of the world, and in the ark, the type of the Church as the vessel of human salvation. Yet the story of Noah's ark has also had a comic side that goes far back in Christian and Islamic tradition and continues in modern times. The figure of Noah's wife plays a key role in this tradition, especially in English medieval drama where her defiance of her husband and her recalcitrance about boarding the ark are dimly remembered by John, the sely carpenter in Chaucer's *Miller's Tale*, when Nicholas reminds him of "The sorwe of Noe with his felaweshipe, / Er that he myghte gete his wyf to shipe" (I.3539–40).[1]

Whereas Chaucer exploits the trouble about Noah's wife for comedy, modern scholars of the English mystery plays have sought an explanation for her rebellious behavior in biblical typology. Although there is plenty of authority for the Flood as a type of Doomsday, the ark as a type of the Cross or the Church, and Noah as a type of Christ, when it comes to Noah's wife, there is little on which to base an exegetical reading because all she ever does in the Book of Genesis is to enter and leave the ark. Somewhat desperately medieval exegetes occasionally made her a type of the Virgin, an interpretation that is clearly inappropriate for the character in the York, Wakefield, and Chester cycles. It seems natural, therefore, if one is thinking typologically, to see in Noah's wife a type of Eve who, in the words of Rosemary Woolf, "initially repeats the pattern of the Fall" – "initially," of

---

* This essay is affectionately dedicated to Martin Stevens, a fellow survivor of the ark.

[1] *The Riverside Chaucer*, ed. Larry D. Benson (Boston: Houghton Mifflin, 1987).

course, because the story of the flood, as it turns out at least for Noah and his family, anticipates the pattern of the Redemption.[2]

The latter-day exegetes may have reason, especially in the case of the Wakefield Master, to suppose that the playwrights were extrapolating from received typology when they contrived a comic subplot with the intention of reinforcing the main plot. Noah's wife's obstreperousness outside the ark illustrates the parlous condition of a world turned "up-so-doun," whereas her co-operation once she comes aboard the ark is an instance of the grace represented by that saving vessel. In the Wakefield play the redemption of Noah's wife may be signified in her lines, "I se on the firmament, / Me thynk, the seven starnes" (422–23), the seven planets, which Noah, as the rain starts to pour down, observes, "left has thare stall" (345).[3] Thus the Wakefield Master would seem to be trying to bring harmony out of discord on the domestic as well as on the cosmic level. "Bot, husband," asks Noah's wife, "What grownd may this be?" "The hyllys of Armonye" (464–66) answers Noah. Armenia, the home of Mt. Ararat, thus becomes the ground of harmony in the new world order and in Noah's family.

This scholarly "glosyng" that, in the end, God's in his heaven and all's right with the world, does not, to my mind, fully account for or justify the dramatic effect of the argument between Noah and his wife. To be sure, in all the plays she has to be dragged aboard the ark, after which she has little to say in York and Chester, and in Wakefield she becomes an active collaborator with the scheme of salvation. But the questions her rebellion raises never receive a satisfactory answer, certainly not in the Flood plays, nor perhaps even in the Corpus Christi cycle as a whole. How well does the story of the flood, as it is presented in these plays, justify God's ways to man – and, we might add, to woman? What right does God have to destroy the entire human race except for one family, and all the animals except for one couple of each species? The theologians' justification, as usual, is sin, and all the cycle plays devote their openings to making this point in lengthy speeches by God or by Noah. The very fact that the authors protest so much might arouse suspicion that the case is not water-tight. If God, as he freely admits in the Bible and in the plays, repents of having created humankind, why did he botch the job so badly, especially if his providence told him all along how it was bound to turn out? The Great Flood is the event posing the most severe test of the doctrine of the *felix culpa*.

Noah's wife does not challenge the Almighty directly like the blustering Cain, Pharaoh, or Herod. Instead she vents her frustration, anger, and disbelief upon her husband, God's patriarchal deputy, although in these

[2] Rosemary Woolf, *The English Mystery Plays* (Berkeley: University of California Press, 1982), p. 133.
[3] *The Wakefield Pageants in the Towneley Cycle*, ed. A. C. Cawley (Manchester: Manchester University Press, 1958).

exchanges the husband appears only too fallibly human. When they laughed at these scenes, did medieval audiences truly sympathize *only* with sely Noah and regard his wife's behavior as a reprehensible subversion of the divinely ordained hierarchy in this best of all possible created worlds?

To answer these questions we need to look at a matrix of apocryphal stories about the flood, which fill in gaps in the biblical story, most of which expand the character of Noah's wife.[4] In the Gnostic Book of Noria she is allied with the powers of darkness that seek to foil God's plan by destroying the ark. By repeatedly setting the ark on fire, Noah's wife succeeds in delaying its completion. In the Koran the people are punished for mocking Noah for building his ship far from the water. Although Noah's wife is not named among the scoffers, she is denounced elsewhere in the Quran:

> Allah sets forth for those who disbelieve the example of the wife of Noah and the wife of Lot. They were under two righteous servants of Ours, but they acted unfaithfully towards them. So they availed them naught against Allah, and it was said to them, 'Enter the Fire, ye twain, along with those who enter.'[5]

These serious accounts set off the goodness and obedience of Noah against the radical evil of infidels, including a member of his own family, and thus seek to justify divine vengeance.

But there is also a mass of popular stories concerning the flood, the seriousness of which is questionable. One of these concerns a cunning trick of the devil to gain admission to the ark. Tabari, who wrote the first Arabic history of the world in the first half of the tenth century, tells the tale in this way:

> When the ass wished to enter the ark, Eblis seized hold of its tail with his hand and drew it back. At last Noah said to the ass: Accursed one, come in. When Noah saw Eblis, he said to him: O accursed one, who has allowed thee to enter the ark? Eblis answered: O Noah, I came in by thy command; for I had seized the ass's tail and was hindering him from entering; when you said, O accursed one, come in, I came into the ark, for I am the accursed one.[6]

Another widespread version of this tale substitutes Noah's wife for the ass. Noah has been going off by himself to build the ark in secret, and the devil arouses his wife's curiosity about where her husband disappears to every day. He gives her the recipe for a potion to make Noah drunk, and when his wife gets the secret out of him, the devil destroys the ark. But God gives

---

[4] The stories mentioned below and others have been gathered by Anna J. Mill, "Noah's Wife Again," *PMLA* 56 (1941): 613–26.

[5] *The Holy Quran with English Translation and Commentary*, 5 vols. (Tilford, Surrey: Islam International Publications, 1988), 5.2653.

[6] Translated by Mill, pp. 615–16.

Figure 1. *Queen Mary's Psalter*, Plate 10, folio 6r.

Noah a second chance to build the ark. When it is completed, the devil persuades the wife to stay back, until the exasperated Noah calls out, "Devil, come in." This clearly contains the germ of the motif in which Noah's wife refuses to board the ark.

That the story of Noah's wife's collaboration with the devil was known in England is shown by the illustrations in the early-fourteenth-century illustrated Bible known as *Queen Mary's Psalter* (after Mary I, who owned the codex in the sixteenth century).[7] The French caption Figure 1 (Plate 10, folio 6r) reads

> How the devil came in form of a man to Noah's wife and asked where her husband was, and she said she knew not where. "He is gone to betray thee and all the world. Take these grains and make a potion and give it him to drink, and he will tell thee all"; and she did accordingly.

Figure 2 (Plate 11, folio 6v) illustrates Noah boarding his family; the French caption reads:

> How Noah lades his ship, and carries his sons and his wife into the ship by a ladder, and of each thing male and female, as the angel of God had commanded him, in order to save the world.

---

[7] *Queen Mary's Psalter; miniatures and drawings by an English artist of the 14th century, reproduced from Royal ms. 2 B.VII in the British Museum* (London: Printed for the Trustees, 1912). The French captions are translated in the introduction, p. 57.

Figure 2. *Queen Mary's Psalter*, Plate 11, folio 6v.

Figure 3. The devil shown simultaneously preparing
to board the ark and exiting below the water line;
compare figure 4. Pierpont Morgan Library, New
York, Manuscript 302, folio 1v (detail).

The *Psalter* doesn't show the devil boarding the ark through the naming
trick, but we see him, concealed from Noah, riding piggy-back on Noah's
wife in Figure 3 from a fourteenth-century psalter, manuscript 302 (folio 1v)
in the Pierpont Morgan Library. We know that the devil *was* aboard the ark
from Figure 4 (Plate 12, folio 7r) in *Queen Mary's Psalter* because it
portrays his exit; the French caption reads:

How Noah sends a raven and a dove to learn if they find any land. The
raven has found a horse's head, where it stops. And the dove has
returned, and brings a branch in its beak in token that it has found

Figure 4. *Queen Mary's Psalter*, Plate 12, folio 7r.

land. And Noah at its entering the ship cries "Benedicite," where he sits at the helm. And the devil flees through the bottom of the ship, and the serpent thrusts his tail into the hole.

The identical story is acted out in a fragment of a fifteenth-century non-cycle play, the *Newcastle Shipwrights' Play*. After God has stated his plans to destroy the sinful world and his angel has given Noah the specifications of the ark, *Deabolus intrat*, saying:[8]

> Out, out, harro, and welaway.
> That ever I uprose this day!
>   So may I smile and say,
> I wene there has been none alive,
> Man, beast, child nor wife,
>   But my servants were they.
>
> All this I have heard say,
>   A ship that made should be,
> For to save withowten nay,
>   Noah and his meenye.
>
> Yet trow I they shall dee–.
> Therto I make a vow:
> If they be never so slee,
>   To taynt them yet I trow.
>
> To Noah's wife will I wynd,
>   Gare her believe in me;
> In faith she is my friend.   (95–111)

The devil then involves Noah's wife in the plot to make her husband drunk to confirm the fact that he is building an ark. The manuscript breaks off just before the beginning of the flood. Noah exits to fetch his household and blesses the audience. The last speech is Satan's:

> All that is gathered in this stead
>   That will not believe in me,
> I pray to Dolphin, prince of dead,
> Scald you all in his lead,
>   That never a one of you thrive nor thee.   (202–6)

Compared to the extant cycle plays, the Newcastle play is crude stuff. Its devil is a buffoon like the vice-characters in the morality plays, and the text, even were it complete, would hardly support a serious typological reading. If they knew it, the other playwrights ignored the story of Noah's wife's

---

[8] *Non-Cycle Plays and Fragments*, ed. Norman Davis, Early English Text Society, s.s. 1 (London and New York: Oxford University Press, 1970).

complicity with the devil, but the comic spirit, which informs the legends and the illustrations in *Queen Mary's Psalter* as well as the Newcastle play, survives in the motif of her stubborn refusal to come aboard the ark. This comic spirit, I want to argue, far from supporting the exegetical readings of the Flood, undermines them, and with them salvation history and the epistemology of biblical exegesis on which it is based.

The human imagination cannot easily contemplate the horrors of a universal holocaust or the horrors of eternal punishment, even or perhaps *especially* at a time when these remain matters of unquestioned belief. The tendency is to turn the awe-inspiring priestly accounts of the great flood in the Bible and the Quran back into the mythology and legend from which they arose originally, to surround them with apocryphal tales perhaps even older than the canonical ones, thereby disarming them of some of their terror. God does not speak to Noah's wife any more than he does to Sarah to tell her that her husband must sacrifice their only-begotten son. The audience can sympathize with the Brome Isaac when he says to Abraham, "Good fader, tell ye my moder no-thyng, / Sey þat I am in another cuntré dwellyng" (205–6).[9] Isaac's request not only elicits compassion, but innocently brings out the monstrousness of God's command.

Noah's wife's intransigent adherence to merely human relationships inspires affectionate sympathy as well as laughter. Neither God or Noah exhibits any regrets over the sinful humanity that must perish. Noah's wife in the York cycle wants to take her gossips and cousins along, and she laments, "My frendis þat I fra yoode / Are ouere flowen with floode" (151–52). She asks her husband, "But Noye, wher are nowe all oure kynne / And companye we knwe before?" He cold-bloodedly replies, "Dame, all ar drowned, late be thy dyne" (269–71).[10]

In the Chester Play of Noah's Flood, the gossips actually appear to drink a farewell pot with Noah's wife. Together they sing:[11]

> The fludd comes fleetinge in full faste,
> one everye syde that spredeth full farre.
> For fere of drowninge I am agaste;
> good gossippe, lett us drawe nere.
>
> And lett us drinke or wee departe,
> for ofte tymes wee have done soe.
> For at one draught thou drinke a quarte,
> and soe will I doe or I goe.

[9] *Non-Cycle Plays and Fragments.*

[10] *The York Plays*, ed. Richard Beadle (London: Edward Arnold, 1982).

[11] *The Chester Mystery Cycle*, ed. R. M. Lumiansky and David Mills, 2 vols., Early English Text Society, s.s. 3 (London and New York: Oxford University Press, 1974).

Here is a pottell of malnesay good and stronge,
yt will rejoyse both harte and tonge.
Thogh Noe thinke us never soe longe,
yett wee wyll drinke atyte. (225–36)

Concerning the protestations of the Wakefield and Chester wives, Rosemary Woolf remarks, "These excuses are on a par with those in the parable
made by the guests invited to the marriage feast, and it is important to
interpret them in this way, as otherwise the attachment of Noah's wife to
her friends might be taken as a sympathetic sign of human feeling, which
the authors manifestly do not intend."[12] If they do not (something I doubt),
then they have manifestly failed in their purpose, at least with the lewed
members of the audience.

Woolf makes an interesting point about what she calls "the much-praised
realism in the portrayal of Noah's wife." That style, she argues, only *seems*
real in the context of the religious drama when in fact it is a style of comic
exaggeration. "To see Noah's wife as a realistic character sketch is to distort
the pattern of the cycles, for the more her irascible disobedience is
dramatically exaggerated the more incomplete she seems."[13] I do not
think there is real danger that modern or medieval audiences might perceive
Noah's wife as "a realistic character sketch," yet her exaggerated earthiness
(a term I prefer to realism) and her pragmatism, in all their comic simplicity,
also expose the truly fantastic character of a deluge that covers the earth
and an ark stocked with pairs of each kind of animal. In its way, the
rebellion of Noah's wife mocks the abstract and fanciful nature of typology
itself as a means of understanding our history and our future here on earth
and in whatever world to come.

To say so is not to dismiss the ultimate comedy, in Dante's sense,
celebrated by typology and by the Corpus Christi plays, nor is it to
substitute the comic subplot of Noah's Wife's Flood for the main plot of
Noah's Flood. Rather it is to maintain that those plots co-exist and appeal
to different and divided elements in medieval audiences and in modern
audiences notwithstanding the alterity that separates them. Noah's wife and
her quondam alliance with the devil clearly belong to an antifeminist
tradition that reaches back from the Middle Ages to antiquity, but that
tradition, too, is by no means monolithic. It allows sympathy for the devil
and even for woman. Another case in point is the alewife scene that forms a
coda to the Chester Harrowing of Hell. *Mulier* was "Sometyme . . . a
tavener, / a gentle gossippe and a tapster" (285–86), damned for adulterat-
ing her brew. She is welcomed at hellgate by a trinity of fiends in lines
parodying the Song of Songs: "Welcome, dere daughter, to us all three"
(325), "Welcome, sweete ladye! I will thee wedd" (329), "Welcome, deare

---

[12] Woolf, 140.
[13] Woolf, 144.

"Woman, are you mad?"

Figure 5. "Woman, are you mad?" Drawing by Oldden; © 1968,
The New Yorker Magazine, Inc.

darlinge, to endles bale" (333). The irony does not cancel the endearing
effect of "dere daughter," "sweete ladye," and "deare darlinge," and, to
that extent, undercuts the terror of the "endles bale" portrayed so vividly in
the Inferno and scenes of the Last Judgment in Books of Hours and the
western facades of cathedrals as well as in the plays of the Judgment.

In an age of growing religious controversy and nonconformity – the period
leading up to and following the Reformation – the mixed style of works like
the *Canterbury Tales* and the late Corpus Christi plays does not always
produce the concord in which some twentieth-century "historicizing" critics

Figure 6. "You mean it hasn't even started yet?" Drawing by Chas. Addams; © 1961, 1990 *The New Yorker Magazine*, Inc.

believe. Rather these works often throw into humorous focus the perpetual tension between the human and the divine, between the biblical letter and its mystical interpretation, between Noah and his wife. No story in the Bible is more subject to that tension than the tale of Noah's ark, which in our time is remembered mainly through children's books and toys and an endless succession of cartoons.

I want to conclude with two cartoons that seem to me to continue the comic tradition of Chaucer and the authors of the English mystery plays, which makes "game" out of the "ernest" of the Great Flood. In Figure 5 Noah's wife is blissfully watering her garden provoking her husband to exclaim furiously, "Woman, are you mad?" If we disregard Noah's insider information and hindsight, which one of this pair seems insane? In Figure 6 (one of many Charles Addams Noah's ark cartoons), a wearily put-upon wife stands in a cavernous ark at the foot of a ladder, holding her iconic broom, while high above her on the ladder, Noah extends an upraised palm through a porthole. "You mean to say it hasn't even started yet?" In these images and in the English flood plays, Noah's wife both comically and touchingly expresses our secret hope that doomsday is an idle threat made up by the patriarchal god, his prophets, and his clerks to keep us in our places.

Textual Pleasure in the *Miller's Tale**

Richard Daniels

> Ces analyses oublient . . . le formidable envers de l'écriture: la
> jouissance: jouissance qui peut exploser, à travers des siècles,
> hors de certains textes . . .
>
> Roland Barthes, *Le Plaisir du Texte*

In the *Miller's Tale* Chaucer took a contemporary story, rooted in
European folklore, which was little more than a bawdy joke and artistically
flawed even in its best versions, and gave it the complexity and integrity that
mark pleasing narrative art. He also set it in a series of relations to the
Knight's Tale and to other tales and perhaps groups of tales within the
Canterbury Tales, in part by making it one of those potentially anarchic
texts, in Roland Barthes' terms, out of which "bliss" (*jouissance*) "can
erupt, across the centuries."[1] The word *jouissance* refers, roughly, to fleeting
intense, disruptive pleasure, such as one may feel, and most certainly wish
to feel, in the moment of climax during sexual intercourse. A recent article
argues that it is "the word for the pleasure of orgasm even when it is not
organ-specific and does not look like what patriarchy calls orgasm;
whatever it is that comes when it comes. It is a sexuality that, because it
is before the phallus is also *beyond* the phallus."[2] Here, I want to study some
of the erotic sites of the *Miller's Tale*, passages where a reader might feel
such bliss – and along the way I hope to suggest, too, some notes towards a
materialist reading of Chaucer's text, indeed of the poetic and narrative
structures of which it is a part and which make up the *Canterbury Tales* as a
whole.[3]

---

* My thanks to Professor William E. Bettridge of the University of Maryland, Baltimore
County, for reading an earlier version of this paper and generously offering insights and
information about the folkloric background of Chaucer's tale.

[1] Roland Barthes, *The Pleasure of the Text*, trans. Richard Miller (New York: Hill and
Wang, 1975), 65. Hereafter cited as *PT*.
[2] H. Marshall Leicester, Jr., "Newer Currents in Psychoanalytic Criticism, and the
Difference "IT" Makes: Gender and Desire in the *Miller's Tale*," *ELH* 61 (1994): 489.
[3] Barthes writes that "the text itself, a diagrammatic and not an imitative structure, can

But the *Miller's Tale* is my subject. The tale involved is (of course) the type called "The Flood," and it combines three motifs: The Flood, The Misdirected Kiss, and The Branding.[4] In its less developed versions the tale shows the somewhat simpleminded inadequacy that usually marks "dirty jokes."[5] A number of the analogues contain only one of the jests, usually the Misdirected Kiss. In others, the ligatures between the two jests are painfully apparent. There are too many characters, and the desire for concealment does not seem justified by the situation. As Larry D. Benson and Theodore M. Andersson have pointed out, "the literary gap between 'The Miller's

reveal itself in the form of a body, split into fetish objects, into erotic sites. All these movements attest to a *figure* of the text . . ." (*PT*, p. 56). I won't pretend to delineate that body or figure (for the *Miller's Tale* or the *Canterbury Tales*), but do explore some of its erotic sites. A few pages later Barthes notes that "what we are seeking to establish in various ways is a theory of the materialist subject" (*PT*, p. 61). I'm in a sense turning that around and as an ongoing project trying to do a materialist as opposed to an ideological (religious, political, academic) reading of Chaucer's text(s). What I mean by "materialist" is indicated in Yirmayahu Yovel's study (especially volume 2) of Spinoza and his continuing influence. The following quotation from the end of vol. 2 (p. 186) suggests the nature of a materialist view, and is close in some ways to the skeptical, limiting, mostly comic spirit of Chaucer's work: "in recognizing finitude – and finite rationality – as the foremost human mark, we assume both its potential and limitations, its promise and burden, as specifically *ours*. We accept finite rationality as the overall context of immanence, from which nothing can lift or 'save' us, but within which human life can give structure and meaning to itself, always prone to transcendent illusion and self-deception, and constantly in need of restraining mementos" (*Spinoza and Other Heretics*. Vol. I, *The Marrano of Reason*; Vol. 2, *The Adventures of Immanence*. Princeton: Princeton University Press, 1989). The *Miller's Tale* is perhaps the first place in the *Canterbury Tales* where the problem of "transcendent illusion and self-deception," for example, becomes an issue (in the vision of a second deluge that Nicholas presents to Old John, which refers at least obliquely to Theseus's Chain of Love speech in the *Knight's Tale*), and this becomes critical to interpretation in the dialectics of corrupt present and idealized past and of fraudulent versus fruitful work and teaching, for instance, in Fragment VIII, and then in the Parson's concluding meditation on sin and penance – always assuming that one considers the parts of the whole work in their complex relations with each other.

[4] The Tale Type is ATT 1361. The motif numbers are: The Flood, K1522; The Misdirected Kiss, K 1225; The Branding, K 1577 – this and other information is found in W. F. Bryan and Germaine Dempster, *Sources and Analogues of Chaucer's Canterbury Tales* (Chicago: University of Chicago Press, 1941), pp. 106–23. Hermann Varnhagen showed long ago that the tale is a combination of two originally separate jests, the story of the flood (K 1522) and the affair of the misdirected kiss (K 1225 and K 1577) – see "Zu Chaucers Erzählung des Müllers," *Anglia* 7 (1884): 81. (The versions of the tale used here are later than Chaucer's, but in this study, as often in the study of folktales, the logical and narrative relations among the analogues are more important than the chronological. It is no part of my purpose to speculate about questions of source and influence.)

[5] "What we call dirty jokes," Leicester says, are "what medievalists call fabliau – the sort of dirty joke the *Miller's Tale* is . . ." ("Newer Currents," p. 480). My analysis shows that the tale both is, and is a great deal more and other than, this sort of "dirty joke."

Tale' and [its analogues] is indeed very great, and nowhere in the analogues will the reader find the same ingenious management of the story."[6] Or, as V. A. Kolve says of the analogues, "they do not charm."[7]

The nature and extent of the changes Chaucer made (his creation of erotic sites) can best be seen by comparing the *Miller's Tale* with five of the versions closest to it: the seventeenth-century German *Lyrum Larum Ser Nugae Venales Ioco Seriae*;[8] a Flemish tale of about 1400; a German version of 1559, in Valentin Schumann, *Nachtbülein*, No. 2; a German version of 1537, Hans Sachs, *Der schmit im Pachdrog*; and a mid-sixteenth-century Latin poem, also of German origin, by Caspar Cropacius.[9] Like Chaucer's narrative, three of these versions represent the story in its most highly developed form. (These tales are all readily accessible, but brief summaries of them may prove useful and are included in the notes.)[10]

What did Chaucer do to make his version art, where other versions remained the very stuff of dirty jokes? Comparison and contrast of corresponding aspects of the five analogues used here and the *Miller's Tale* reveal

---

[6] *The Literary Context of Chaucer's Fabliaux: Texts and Translations* (New York: Bobbs-Merrill, 1971), p. 4.

[7] *Chaucer and The Imagery of Narrative: The First Five Canterbury Tales* (Stanford: Stanford University Press, 1984), p. 190.

[8] Reinhold Köhler, "Nochmals Zu Chaucer's The Milleres Tale," *Anglia* 2 (1879): 135–36.

[9] Text and translation of the Flemish tale appear in *Sources and Analogues*, pp. 112–18. Texts and translations of the Schumann, Sachs, and Cropacius tales appear in *Literary Context*, pp. 64–7, 60–3, 72–7.

[10] In the *Lyrum Larum* the young wife of an old farmer has two lovers, a pastor and a blacksmith. To gain easy access to the girl, the pastor predicts a flood and urges the husband to stay in a dough trough tied to the gable. When the pastor is with the girl, the smith arrives, is made to kiss the pastor's rump, returns with a hot iron, and burns his rival. The pastor cries for water, and the farmer, fearing the flood, cuts the ropes and falls. In the Flemish tale, Heile of Bersele promises love to a miller, a priest, and a smith – all in one night. When the priest arrives, the miller hides in a tub hanging conveniently from the rafters. The priest, once satisfied, predicts the flood (for no apparent reason). The smith arrives, kisses the priest's behind; angry, he brands the priest with a hot iron: "Water!" The miller cuts the rope with his knife, breaks an arm and a leg in the fall. The priest tumbles into a latrine; the smith has his revenge. The Schumann tale has a priest and a smith as lovers of the young wife of a rich merchant. In this version, the husband hears the prediction of the flood in church, but the prophet is apparently not his wife's lover, and there is no deliberate attempt to deceive. Again, the smith comes to the house (to the window) when the priest is with the wife, and the rest of the events follow as before. In Sachs's *Der Schmit im Pachdrog* the flood is predicted by the wife's priest-lover in order to deceive the husband, a smith. Here, however, the wife is unaware of her husband's presence in the suspended bread trough, and the smith's servant is the second lover. The rest of the tale is the same. The Cropacius version is like the *Lyrum Larum* and Sachs versions in that the flood prediction is a deliberate trick on the part of the priest-lover to evade the farmer-husband. Except that the second lover is not identified, the events of the tale are the same.

several plot elements Chaucer has borrowed and suggest ways he has changed or expanded them to create sites of bliss.[11] Careful analysis of the analogues, which contain both the Flood and Misdirected Kiss motifs, reveals a common sequence of events: (1) prediction of the Flood by the favored lover; (2) husband or lover concealed in a tub hung from the ceiling or the roof; (3) the adulterous meeting; (4) second or vying lover comes to the window; (5) the Misdirected Kiss; (6) the Branding; (7) the one branded screams for water, and the man in the tub cuts loose and is injured in the fall.[12]

This, in broad outline, is the exact sequence of these events in the *Miller's Tale* as well and indicates that Chaucer's artistry lies in his purposeful, detailed development of event, scene, and character rather than in their invention. In each analogue, for example, the kiss takes place at a window which is never mentioned until the plot requires it, and then it is described no more than is absolutely necessary. In the *Miller's Tale*, however, Absolon makes a dry run to the fateful window some 330 lines before the plot requires it (line 3695): "And dressed hym up by a shot-wyndowe / That was upon the carpenteris wal" (3358-9).[13] The observation that it is a "shot-wyndowe," a window which works by a hinge or bolt, is already more detail than any of the analogues ever give about their windows. Later in the poem, but still almost forty lines before Absolon's unfortunate kiss occurs, Chaucer tells us that Absolon "stant under the shot-wyndowe– / Unto his brest it raughte, it was so lowe" (3695-6).[14] Furthermore, Chaucer makes a point of having Alisoun open the window for the kiss (3727) and then close it when the deed is done (3740). And Nicholas, much to his grief, opens it once again a bit later (3801). All in all, the window is mentioned or described ten times in the course of the tale – Chaucer brings us into a kind of intimacy with it.[15] More than this, it is a detail *invested* in, in a way

---

[11] Best to keep in mind here Leicester's warning that "no pleasure of the sort under discussion is dependably *transmitted* by the text." And he further states that "like all other signifying relations, that between bliss and language is a relation of *différance*: language does not *convey* bliss, it only ambiguously marks its traces, where it has been." See *The Disenchanted Self: Representing the Subject in the* Canterbury Tales (Berkeley: University of California Press, 1990), pp. 207–8.

[12] This analysis is based on the one that appears in *Sources and Analogues*, pp. 106–7.

[13] All quotations from Chaucer's narrative are taken from *The Riverside Chaucer*, ed. Larry D. Benson, 3rd ed. (Boston: Houghton Mifflin Co., 1987). Paul A. Olson ("Poetic Justice in the *Miller's Tale*," *MLQ* 24 [1963]: 228) has pointed out that "Absolon's wake outside Alysoun's window (I, 3353–69) looks to the scenes in the main action where he twice more stands beneath the window to pay homage to his fair favorite (I, 3657–3741; I, 3783–3810)."

[14] Kolve says that "Chaucer had to invent for the carpenter's house a street window very low indeed" (*Imagery of Narrative*, p. 194), which is, strictly speaking, a misuse of the word "invent" since the poet is working with and elaborating a received element.

[15] The window is referred to in lines 3358–9, 3676–7, 3695–6, 3708, 3723–4, 3727, 3732, 3740, 3789, 3801.

no details in a dirty joke are: it becomes a center of implicit resonance, whose bliss is released, tapped, at the climactic moment of Chaucer's tale.[16] By the time Nicholas is branded, the shot-window is a familiar scene, and its tactility and lowness have been so much emphasized that the delighted reader sees the exact relationship in which Absolon stands to it during the climax.

Another example of Chaucer's close attention to detail is the ax with which John cuts the ropes when he hears Nicholas cry for water. Since the tubs are suspended from the ceiling inside the house, the three adventurers must have a way to get out through the roof, else they would drown in their vessels. It is to Nicholas' credit that he foresees the need for an ax rather than a knife, for John, being a carpenter, would have seen immediately that a knife could not get them out of the house. This detail of the ax is an instance in which Chaucer has altered and then expanded a borrowed plot element in order to suit his own unique purpose. The analogues solve the problem of getting out of the house in various ways, but none involves the use of an ax. In the Flemish narrative, for example, the problem seems not to have been considered, for William the miller cuts his trough away from the ceiling with a convenient knife he finds in the tub. In the Sachs version, a cutting tool is not specified. In the *Lyrum Larum*, Schumann, and Cropacius analogues, however, the problem is solved when the husbands tie their "boats" to the roof outside (thus disallowing the dialectic of inside/outside that is so pleasing in Chaucer's version). In the *Miller's Tale*, Nicholas goes to great lengths to explain the double purpose of the ax to old John:

> And whan thou thus hast doon as I have seyd,
> And hast oure vitaille faire in hem yleyd,
> And eek an ax to smyte the corde atwo,
> Whan that the water comth, that we may go
> And breke an hole an heigh, upon the gable,
> Unto the gardyn-ward, over the stable,
> That we may frely passen forth oure way,
> Whan that the grete shour is goon away,
> Thanne shaltou swymme as myrie, I undertake,
> As dooth the white doke after hire drake.
> Thanne wol I clepe, 'How, Alison! How, John!
> Be myrie, for the flood wol passe anon.'
> And thou wolt seyn, 'Hayl, maister Nicholay!

---

[16] I must note with Barthes that "bliss is unspeakable, inter-dicted" (*PT*, p. 21). Also, as he truly says, one can "only *circle* such a subject . . ." (p. 34). Still, something can be said about this "bliss." It is, in a sense, a particular kind of pleasure which distinguishes "euphoria, fulfillment, comfort (the feeling of repletion when culture penetrates freely), from shock, disturbance, even loss, which are proper to ecstasy, to bliss" (p. 19). The text's moments of bliss are also "like a sudden obliteration of the warrior *value*" (p. 30).

Good morwe, I se thee wel, for it is day.'
And thanne shul we be lordes al oure lyf
Of al the world, as Noe and his wyf.[17]   (3567–82)

Nicholas has here elaborated upon that one detail, the necessity for an ax,
until he has painted for John a very tempting picture of their escape from
the house and their utopian destiny once the flood has abated. Indeed, this
vision which Nicholas presents to John (even though seen through a hole
chopped in the roof) is the only instance in the poem that anyone's
perspective transcends the homely reality of John's house and the object
of the males' desire that it contains.[18] Part of Nicholas' deception of John,
the vision is stated in exactly the right terms to appeal to the old man's
avarice: Nicholas offers him Alisoun and the world, with no competition.
But John is so intent upon his vision of lordship of world and wife that he
does not notice the inaccuracy of the comparison: Noah and his wife were
two; John, Nicholas, and Alisoun are three. It would be a brave new world
indeed that started off with a *ménage à trois*. (To the extent that the reader
engages with the two happy young people we have, of course, a different
kind of love triangle.) Thus we see that this grand but deceptive vision, in
which John sees himself in secure possession of the entire world and (what is
more) of his Alisoun, has grown from the simple necessity for an ax. What
gives the detail of the ax resonance – what makes it into a promise (of bliss)
– is its use here as a catalyst of the learned young Nicholas' extended
fantasy of the second flood. After such a moment and such a usage, the ax
has to reappear: its bliss has to be released.[19]

[17] The duck and drake image in 3576 is interesting for the reversal of roles it ironically
points up: among humans the husband will trail after the wife (John after Alisoun), thus
upsetting the proper medieval hierarchy; while among the ducks and drakes the female
naturally follows the male. Here once again we see Chaucer's pervasive habit of
reinforcing his theme in even the smallest of details. (This is not to say that Chaucer
never nods. John and Robin knock down Nicholas' door to find him gaping [3468–71],
but a few minutes later the young scholar is able to push that door firmly shut [3499].)
[18] Leicester does very well what I have no space to do: show the ways Chaucer has
developed Alison's character, allowing her (among other things) to escape being a
merely stereotypical object of male desire ("Newer Currents," pp. 488 ff.). Jacqueline
Rose writes that "The woman is implicated, of necessity, in phallic sexuality, but at the
same time it is 'elsewhere that she upholds the question of her own *jouissance*,' that is,
the question of her status as desiring subject . . . – what escapes or is left over from the
phallic function, and exceeds it. Woman is, therefore, placed *beyond* (beyond the
phallus). That 'beyond' refers at once to her almost total mystification as absolute
Other (and hence nothing other than other), and to a *question*, the question of her own
jouissance, of her greater or lesser access to the residue of the dialectic to which she is
constantly subjected" (*Feminine Sexuality: Jacques Lacan and the École Freudienne*, eds.
Juliet Mitchell and Jacqueline Rose [New York: Norton, 1982], p. 51; quoted in *The
Disenchanted Self*, p. 206).
[19] As of course it will be. One of the most perceptive of Chaucer's critics has written that

There are other details worth noting in the above quotation where the witty Nicholas presents John a bogus vision of a second deluge. First, there is the poet Chaucer's intentional silence, the lack of even a hint of his attitude toward the vision of John. Second, the passage shows the illiterate old John's ignorance of the biblical account (Gen. 9.11–15), where God explicitly promises that there will never be another deluge.[20] Third, Nicholas' spirited evocation of the flood excludes the moral dimension of the Noah story: in legend, Noah spent his life after the flood preaching the word of God, establishing religious schools, even planting vines and discovering fermentation, but not fondling a dazzling young wife.[21] The omission emphasizes the selfishness and shallowness of *sely* old John, as well as *hende* Nicholas' powers of selection.

Chaucer's artistry in the development of character, as seen in the *Miller's Tale*, is best illustrated by comparing his treatment of Absolon (the second or vying lover) to that of the corresponding characters in the analogues. In the *Lyrum Larum* version, there is no vying lover to correspond to Absolon: the branding is done by the smith, who is a manly, decisive fellow. In the Schumann tale, also, there is only the priest and the smith who brands him. In the Flemish tale there is a vying lover whose role in the plot corresponds to Absolon's, but that is the only significant similarity. In the Sachs analogue the vying lover is the smith's (husband's) servant boy, and it is possible that Chaucer found such a smith-servant relationship in his source and then changed it to the Absolon-Daun Gerveys utilitarian friendship of the *Miller's Tale*. But beyond this slim conjecture little or nothing in this

---

"the breathtaking effect of the poem's climax surely owes much to this process [recurrence resulting in psychological consequence]. The focal images – the flood, the carpenter in his tub, the axe and the cord – are suddenly brought to our conscious attention, not from nowhere (with an effect of mere surprise and chance), but from the semi-conscious storage of previous acceptance, unanticipated, perhaps, but inevitable" (Charles Muscatine, *Chaucer and the French Tradition: A Study in Style and Meaning* [Berkeley: University of California Press, 1957], pp. 225–6).

[20] John's ignorance of the biblical account and the way Nicholas gleefullly takes advantage of it is another aspect of town–gown conflict in the *Miller's Tale*, a conflict that crops up again at the end when all the clerks gather to attest to John's madness (3845–48), thus in a sense ironically fulfilling a part of Nicholas's earlier prophecy (3506–07). It also sets the stage, of course, for the town/gown conflict of the *Reeve's Tale*.

[21] Don Cameron Allen, *The Legend of Noah: Renaissance Realism in Art, Science, and Letters* (Urbana: University of Illinois Press, 1963), pp. 115–16. See also Francis Lee Utley, "The One Hundred and Three Names of Noah's Wife," *Speculum* 16 (1941): 431–35. Perhaps the most extensive treatment of the amoral nature of Nicholas' use of the Noah legend is found in Kolve, *Imagery of Narrative*, pp. 197–216. Kolve also offers in these pages a very interesting argument for the possible relevance of the Noah plays of the mystery cycles to the *Miller's Tale*, a subject taken up as well by Lee Patterson in *Chaucer and the Subject of History* (Madison: University of Wisconsin Press, 1991), pp. 262 ff.

analogue, besides the role of vying lover, suggests the character of Chaucer's Absolon. The Cropacius analogue mentions only "another lover" as the character who plays the role of vying lover, and very little detail is given about him. However, the fact that "another lover" returns to the window with a pair of red-hot "serrated tongs" to do the branding might indicate some kinship between him and Absolon, for they are the only branders who choose specific (and terrifying) instruments for their task (Absolon of course uses a "kultour" – the blade of a plow; the others use simply a hot iron).

We see, then, that the role Absolon plays in the *Miller's Tale* is common to three of the five versions of the story here discussed, and that these versions do suggest a few general aspects of Absolon's character and function in Chaucer's tale. But Chaucer's Absolon, unlike those shadowy figures who correspond to him in the analogues, is more than a necessary element to engender the preordained action of a set plot; for as the action of the *Miller's Tale* unfolds, Absolon is individualized.[22] And by the end of the tale the action has caused a significant (though still comical) change in his attitude and character. A change in character often indicates that there is some sort of didactic purpose, however slight, in the work at hand. The fabliau genre is traditionally both humorous and "lightly didactic."[23]

---

[22] The change in Absolon's character is also discussed in Cornelius Novelli's "Absolon's 'Freend So Deere': A Pivotal Point in *The Miller's Tale*," *Neophilologus* 52 (1968): 65–9. Joseph A. Dane suggests that Absolon "is, in a sense, reborn" ("The Mechanics of Comedy in Chaucer's *Miller's Tale*," *Chaucer Review* 14 (1980): 219. Beryl Rowland has noted that the fabliaux usually exploit "stock types and [keep] the attention focused on action rather than character by employing certain conventions of behavior which the audience can readily anticipate and accept" and that fabliau characters as types "are not elaborated" ("What Chaucer Did to the Fabliau," *Studia Neophilologica* 51 [1979]: 205, 209). Chaucer generally follows this scheme in the *Miller's Tale*, although at moments our attention suddenly, artfully is focused on a change or development of character, an elaboration, as is the case with Absolon, and at such moments he utterly transcends the given "stock types" of the fabliau genre. V. A. Kolve (*Imagery of Narrative*, p. 193), in an analysis to which I will return, writes that Chaucer "is interested in Absolon not merely as the recipient of an insult, but as someone who creates the occasion for its delivery." Leicester argues in part that Absolon is feminized and is punished for acting "too much like a woman" ("New Currents," p. 490).

[23] Charles Muscatine, *Chaucer and the French Tradition*, p. 58. Beryl Rowland notes that Chaucer "also uses the occasional didacticism that may occur in the fabliau" ("What Chaucer Did to the Fabliau," p. 206). R. E. Kaske has argued that the *Miller's Tale* is in part a parody of the *Canticum Canticorum* and that it is thus in certain ways profoundly didactic ("The *Canticum Canticorum* in the *Miller's Tale*," *SP* 59 [1962]: 479–500). When Kaske says that the tale is "perhaps . . . part of a governing moral theme in the *Canterbury Tales*" (p. 500), I would not necessarily disagree. But I do understand "didactic" to mean that which is explicitly intended to teach, a narrower meaning than Kaske intends. There is no doubt that Absolon's "wooing speech" parodies the *Canticum* (Kolve, *Imagery of Narrative*, pp. 188, 440). Patterson argues that Absolon's (mis-)use of the Song of Songs points to a "tradition of interpretation . . .

Chaucer's short and funny verse tale is humorous throughout, certainly, and the achievement of this complex humor is the tale's proper end. But there is in addition a certain light didacticism, found mainly in the bitter lesson old John learns (that doddering old men ought not to marry winsome and frisky young women). Also lightly didactic, however, is the sudden change of character Absolon undergoes.

Chaucer's initial description of Absolon's curly blond hair, "peaches-and-cream complexion," grey eyes, and vain dress (3312–25) is too well-known to need rehearsing here.[24] Also familiar is the description of Absolon's very high singing voice, his finesse at dancing and guitar playing, and his tavern habits (3326–38). Immediately following these twenty-seven lines of exquisite, detailed description, Chaucer sums up the character of his parish clerk with two words when he calls him "jolif . . . and gay" (3339). Indeed, he is "joly Absolon" (or "jolif") six times in the course of the poem.[25] And to go back a step, we see that he is also "somdeel squaymous / Of fartyng, and of speche daungerous" (3337–8). Moreover, while Nicholas,

in which is visible the coercive manipulation inherent in the institution of biblical exegesis per se" (*Subject of History*, p. 261; the idea suggests connections with the *Wife of Bath's Prologue* and certain other prologues and tales). But the tale of the Miller echoes other biblical passages. Nicholas, Alisoun, and Absolon are not remembering their Creator in their youth, and certainly not "while the sun, or the light, or the moon, or the stars, be not darkened, nor the clouds return after the rain: In the days when the keepers of the house shall tremble . . . and those that look out of the windows be darkened, And the doors shall be shut in the streets, when the sound of the grinding is low, and he shall rise up at the voice of the bird, and all the daughters of music shall be brought low . . ." (Eccles. 12: 1–4). The tone and theme of these verses of Ecclesiastes surely seem at least as Chaucerian and as readily appropriate to the *Miller's Tale* as do those of the Song of Songs – if one must have biblical echoes.

[24] E. Talbot Donaldson interprets the word "rode" as meaning a "peaches-and-cream complexion" ("Idiom of Popular Poetry in the Miller's Tale," in *Speaking of Chaucer* [1970; rpt. New York: Norton Library, 1972], p. 21). Kolve glosses the description of Absolon in *Imagery of Narrative*, p. 164.

[25] Paul E. Beichner notes this in "Characterization in *The Miller's Tale*," in *Chaucer Criticism: The Canterbury Tales*, eds. Richard J. Schoeck and Jerome Taylor (Notre Dame, IN: University of Notre Dame Press, 1960), pp. 122, 128 (note 16). Absolon is "Joly" or "Jolif" in lines 3339, 3348, 3355, 3371, 3671, 3688. In addition, line 3316 informs us that the part in his hair is "joly" as well. Of the epithet "joly," E. Talbot Donaldson says that it is "generally in the mouths of bourgeois characters and that in the senses 'handsome' and 'pretty' it modifies men or women with equal frequency. But it is, perhaps, the secret of Absolon's ill-success that all his jollification makes rather for prettiness than for masculine effectiveness" ("Idiom of Popular Poetry," p. 20). My argument is that we see a change in Absolon from effeminate "prettiness" as well as appearance, to a kind of "masculine effectiveness." Thus, Thomas D. Cooke's reference to the "transformation of the crude and virile blacksmith of the analogues into the fastidious and ineffectual Absolon" tells only half the story (*The Old French and Chaucerian Fabliaux: A Study of Their Comic Climax* [Columbia: University of Missouri Press, 1978], p. 176).

the energetic and successful lover, is at the beginning of the poem "allone, withouten any compaignye" (3204), Absolon, "that is for love alwey so wo bigon" (3658), is on the fateful Monday "at Oseneye / With compaignye, hym to disporte and pleye" (3659–60). But Absolon's playfulness, amorousness, and delicacy all disappear the moment he hears Nicholas mock his reaction to his unfortunate kiss:

> "A berd! A berd!" quod hende Nicholas,
> "By Goddes corpus, this goth faire and weel."
> This sely Absolon herde every deel,
> And on his lippe he gan for anger byte,
> And to hymself he seyde, "I shal thee quyte."[26]   (3742–6)

He is no longer "joly" but "sely" (wretched) Absolon. The word "sely" occurs five times before this in the poem, but always in reference to old John the carpenter.[27] Thus, Absolon is subtly equated with old John at this point: both have been victimized by Alisoun and "hende" Nicholas, who have taken quick advantage of their venality. But Absolon, unlike John, is "sely" only briefly; for the instant he hears the mockery of Nicholas he goes into a rage (3744–6). And the upshot of Absolon's ire leads, finally, to the downfall of Nicholas and John.

Furthermore, this Absolon, who was once "of speche daungerous" (3338), after the unfortunate kiss can say:

> "My soule bitake I unto Sathanas,
> But me were levere than al this toun," quod he,
> "Of this despit awroken for to be.
> Allas," quod he, "allas, I ne hadde ybleynt!"   (3750–3)

There is no fastidiousness of speech here. And Absolon earlier that day had been (as we have seen) with company, amusing himself and playing; but when in the company of the smith Gerveys, who tries playfully to joke

---

[26] The referent of the pronoun "thee" (1346) is unclear: it could be Alisoun (assuming he knows it is her *ers* he has kissed) or Nicholas (whose mockery he has just heard). Edward C. Schweitzer notes that in "all the analogues of the *Miller's Tale*, wherever the cast of characters includes two rival lovers, Absolon's counterparts kiss the successful lover's rump, not the woman's" – "The Misdirected Kiss and the Lover's Malady in Chaucer's *Miller's Tale*," in *Chaucer in the Eighties*, eds. Julian N. Wasserman and Robert J. Blanch (Syracuse: Syracuse University Press, 1986), pp. 226–7.

[27] At lines 3404, 3423, 3509, 3601, 3614. Chaucer might be punning on the word as well. "Sely" also means "innocent," which is probably the meaning he mostly intends in reference to John. Thus, calling Absolon "sely" here is also a commentary on John's erstwhile innocence. The word's older meaning is "blessed," which could apply at this point only obliquely, if at all; and "sely" is the forerunner of our word (and sense) "silly." Here we see another example of Chaucer's uncanny talent for capturing a word's changing meanings – gathering up the past and looking into the future.

about the fair sex, Absolon "ne roghte nat a bene / Of al his pley; no word agayn he yaf" (3772–3). Before the kiss, moreover, Absolon is "amorous Absolon, / That is for love alwey so wo bigon" (3657–8); but after the kiss we find his attitude much changed:

> His hoote love was coold and al yqueynt;
> For fro that tyme that he hadde kist hir ers,
> Of paramours he sette nat a kers,
> For he was heeled of his maladie. (3754–7)

After the kiss, then, Absolon is no longer "jolif," "amorous," and "of speche daungerous"; instead, he becomes a man dedicated to the single end of avenging the great wrong done to him. The sudden disappearance of Absolon's prissiness is understandable and pleases the reader, leading to a feeling of empathy for the developing character. And Chaucer emphasizes the change in Absolon in one other important way. Before the kiss, Absolon is "somdeel squaymous of fartyng"; but after the kiss this has altered, for Nicholas' final insult does not stay Absolon from his decided course of action:

> And therwith spak this clerk, this Absolon,
> "Spek, sweete bryd, I noot nat where thou art."
> This Nicholas anon leet fle a fart
> As greet as it had been a thonder-dent,
> That with the strook he was almoost yblent;
> And he was redy with his iren hoot,
> And Nicholas amydde the ers he smoot. (3804–10)

Nicholas' last insult (the rumble of thunder that precedes the flood) and Absolon's firm reaction to it (his redemption from squeamishness) might be seen as a kind of objective correlative for the moral quality of the change in Absolon's attitude and character; and this indicates exactly how light the didacticism of the *Miller's Tale* really is. One critic has argued that the fart is "Chaucer's means of underlining a serious theme, the inappropriateness of behavior like Absolon's, especially in religious officials."[28] But this seems too serious, if not puritanical. Surely the honest reader (perhaps the dishonest one as well) prefers (and preferred) the manly brander to the squeamish clerk. Besides, revenge is sweet.

In this paper I do not try to draw conclusions about the relation of the *Miller's Tale* to its folklore analogues. Rather, by contrasting Chaucer's tale with selected analogues I try to determine points at which he was no longer working with borrowed material but was beginning to create an original and pleasing work of art, one that is also a text of bliss, a figure formed by

---

[28] Peter G. Beidler, "Art and Scatology in the *Miller's Tale*," *Chaucer Review* 12 (1977): 99.

its erotic sites. The window is mentioned in the analogues only when needed to advance the plot. Under Chaucer's influence the window not only serves its essential function in the plot; it also becomes a particular kind of window and thus is used to foreshadow future action and to make that action seem more realistic when it occurs. Chaucer uses the action of the plot to develop a highly individualized Absolon just as much as he uses Absolon as a means of furthering the plot. The detail of the fart – like others in the narrative – follows an obverse trajectory. When the idea of it is first encountered (3337–8) it doesn't seem to mean much; we don't necessarily see promise in it or *expect* to return to it. So our pleasure here stems from the delightful surprise we feel when this detail unexpectedly reveals a hidden promise at the moment when it (as it were) releases its charge. The knife which is used only for cutting the ropes in the analogues becomes in the *Miller's Tale* an ax, which serves the essential function better than a knife. And that ax, with the help of Nicholas' fancy and deceit, allows the old carpenter in imagination to chop his way through the roof which encloses his homely and painful fabliau world to gain a brief and absurdly grandiose vision of himself as God's chosen servant and lord of all the earth.

The *Miller's Tale* pleases all but prudes, yet scholars and critics constantly seek in it meanings that, in effect, make it respectable and give serious students reasons (excuses?) to study it. But allusive or allegorical qualities are not what make us remember the narrative. One critic has claimed that "morality is simply not at issue. The resolution of the tale is aesthetic and results from a highly stylized plot designed to achieve its maximum effect in the moment of denouement."[29] This, although it rings partly true, is austere and abstract, seems too cold, a modern version of Cato's voice. Chaucer's art may be more anarchic, more devoted to giving pleasure, than most of its professional students have wanted to admit. Roland Barthes has argued that, in attaining the pleasure of the text, "what is overcome, split, is the *moral unity* that society demands of every human product." He states further that bliss can make the text into "that uninhibited person who shows his behind to the *Political Father*," a term that suggests the nature of the relations of the *Miller's Tale* to the *Knight's Tale*, and perhaps of the Miller to the Knight, in the relations of their stories. The more general idea of pleasure is culture-laden, while bliss, one particular kind of pleasure, is "non-cultural." The pleasure that is called bliss is, moreover, a "trivial, unworthy name" that can "embarrass the text's return to morality, to truth: it is an oblique, a drag anchor . . . without which the theory of the text would revert to a centered system, a philosophy of meaning."[30] And this helps explain not only the function of the flatus, for

---

[29] Joseph A. Dane, "The Mechanics of Comedy in Chaucer's *Miller's Tale*," *Chaucer Review* 14 (1980): 223.
[30] *PT*, pp. 53, 62, 64.

instance, in the *Miller's Tale* (and in that tale's relations with the *Knight's Tale*), but also of the fabliaux within the *Canterbury Tales* taken as a whole.[31] Perhaps it helps explain, too, why successful generalizations about the whole work are so very rare.

Chaucer, we can be sure, was neither prude nor policeman. Morality is in a way a concern of the *Miller's Tale*, for the poem is a space where the "moral unity" society demands (and critics often supply) is, however briefly, both split and overcome. In the moments of climax, of *jouissance*, readers across the centuries have been and continue to be moved beyond words – for the greater part they laugh and play – and herein lies the pleasure of Chaucer's text.

---

[31] Patterson observes that the Miller's interruption of the Host to tell his own tale is "a subversion of form. The principle of hierarchy derived from the three orders is set aside in favor of an internally generated and self-sustaining principle of 'quiting.' The tale-telling game . . . becomes itself a fabliau and is . . . to be governed by the fabliau principle . . ." (*Subject of History*, p. 245). This is, of course, a new articulation of an interesting, useful older idea; but it is not the same argument I am suggesting here.

Petrarch, Chaucer and the Making of the Clerk

Warren Ginsberg

When Harry Bailly calls on the Clerk to tell a tale, he attempts to construct the identity of the man from a variety of discourses which can be associated with him:

> "Sire Clerk of Oxenford," oure Hooste sayde,
> "Ye ryde as coy and stille as dooth a mayde
> Were newe spoused, sittynge at the bord;
> This day ne herde I of youre tonge a word.
> I trowe ye studie aboute som sophyme;
> But Salomon seith 'every thyng hath tyme.'"[1]

Uppermost in the Host's mind, it seems, is his desire to have the clerk be a character out of literature. Certainly the pilgrim's reserve has made Harry think of the demeanor of ladies in courtly romance, even as the terms he uses remind us of the Knight, whose comportment makes him "as meeke as is a mayde" (A. 69). But the Host also knows that Oxford clerks are schoolmen, given to philosophy and its language, both of which Harry apparently prefers less than the "solas" of fiction. By urging the scholar to remember that everything has its time, he calls the Clerk to the present moment with its concrete demands and preoccupations. He suggests the time is out of joint for the "sophyme" he imagines the Clerk has silently contemplated all day; its abstruseness distances the man who ponders it as far from his fellow wayfarers as the rarified fancies of romance remove its personages from the real world. In any case, by quoting Ecclesiastes to induce his cleric to tell his tale, the Host signals as well his knowledge that clerks preached, which Harry wants to forestall most of all: no lengthy, lenten sermon, if he can help it.

Even before he says a word, then, literary, philosophical, and spiritual discourses compete to define the subjectivity of the Clerk. Each comes already marked by contexts that will enter into dialogue with the meanings

---

[1] All quotations are from *The Riverside Chaucer*, gen. ed. L. Benson (Boston: Houghton Mifflin, 1987).

and intentions the Clerk will bring to his utterances. Yet the way Chaucer has represented these discourses – as expressions of his pilgrims' tendency to construct others according to their own motives and desires – shows that no one can be defined in isolation from the others. When Harry sees the Clerk as a maid newly married sitting at the board, he has positioned him between two worlds. With its evocations of virginal chasteness and demure obedience, the scene has an out-of-time delicacy which arrests it against our knowledge of its impending loss. The idealized sublimations of courtly romance will end with the consummation of the marriage, which is imminent. Innkeeper that he is, Harry is very aware of this in his own, earthy way. He knows "every thyng," even this wedding tableau, "hath tyme," that after the board there is the bed, after mirth, a reckoning that must be paid. Against the Clerk's detachment from the other pilgrims, which has suggested a solitude the Host knows he must counteract, Harry sets a clerk of his own invention, one who will leave behind fancies of the intellect for the work-a-day demands of ordinary life. Yet however much Harry patterns this cleric after his vision of himself, the Clerk he conjures up is equally an extension and fulfillment of his own fantasies. Perhaps the Clerk's attendance at Oxford causes Harry to remember Nicholas, the handy Oxford prognosticator of the *Miller's Tale*. The attitude that prompts Harry's simile has much in common with the Miller's reaction to the Knight's high romance; if he thinks this Clerk should be more like his fabliau counterpart, Harry may well think he himself should be too. But the reversal of sexual roles in Harry's figure also suggests that he might fancy another clerkly surrogate for himself in his own post-nuptial life, not Nicholas, but Jankyn, the Wife of Bath's fifth husband, another Oxford man, who like Harry has learned the "wo that is in mariage." Jankyn may have suffered a fate similar to Nicholas' when Alice knocked him into their hearth-fire, but unlike Goodelief's spouse, he struck back.

For Chaucer's Clerk, however, the sexual innuendoes of the Host's gentle raillery, together with its implied alternatives of and confusion between not so gentle masculine self-assertiveness and womanly submission, are translated into a set of choices conditioned more by historical institutions than by the conventions of literary genres. On emerging from the world of thought where he seems suspended, the Clerk will either redirect the impulse toward abstraction into the abstinence of actual clerks who, if at University, were in orders, and would remain celibate when they became priests. Or he will join the secular world, a world so many clerks did in fact enter as scribes. But whether he becomes a "lerned . . . clerk" like the Parson, or a clerk of the king's works like Chaucer, the social realm in which he will define himself will be overwritten by colliding discourses that have already laid claim to him. The Clerk certainly shall bring to this world a dialectics to master and control the instabilities of time and death and meaning, all of which he refers to repeatedly in his response to Harry. But he will have already heard enough to know that neither time nor death submits to one language alone. In this world, widowhood has given the Wife of Bath the opportunity to assume prerogatives reserved for men and clerks, which she has used to turn gender identity topsy-turvy by arguing it is as much contested by experience as it is defined by authority. Once this cleric hears he rides "as coy and stille as dooth a mayde," he cannot present the simultaneous commitments to the ideal and the actual he represents except as a response to the Wife's sexual politics. But as a man who "unto logik hadde longe ygo," the Clerk would find his sense of self threatened less by the preacherly discourse of Alice's "Prologue" than by her recourse to what Louise Fradenburg has emphasized as the "pastness" of her romance.[2] Though meant to neutralize the disruptions and reversals she has practiced in life by consigning them to a fairy-tale world whose time has passed, the Wife is fully aware that her tale is an anachronism. By opening an irreparable disjunction between then and now, Alice locates herself in history; her "joly body" threatens to make authority, which derives its strength by claiming it transcends historical difference, nothing more than a spectral abstraction, a remote "sophyme."[3] Little wonder then that the Clerk chooses to oppose the Wife rather than, say, the Miller's depiction of Nicholas or Absolon. In answering her, the Clerk will argue that ideas and principles exert as much bodily force in the material world as arms and legs.

This proliferation of intersecting discourses suggests Bakhtin's dialogism; like his tale, the Clerk himself may be read as a compound of style, the artistic image of various social languages which he speaks and is spoken by.[4] In this the Clerk is not unlike many other pilgrims. More than other pilgrims, however, the Clerk affords us an opportunity to view the discourses that fashion him historically. For whatever else he is, the Clerk is the product of Chaucer's intellectual encounter with Petrarch, a poet like himself, but a man whose ideological and literary allegiances were decidedly different. By looking to the Canterbury pilgrim, we can gain a sense of what

---

[2] See Louise Fradenburg, "The Wife of Bath's Passing Fancy," *SAC* 8 (1986): 31–58.

[3] See Lee Patterson, "'For the Wyves Love of Bathe': Feminine Rhetoric and Poetic Resolution in the *Roman de la Rose* and the *Canterbury Tales*," *Speculum* 58 (1983): 656–95.

[4] Recently, a number of critics have read the "Clerk's Tale" in light of Bakhtin. John Ganim has stressed the carnivalesque elements of the "Envoy" in "Carnival Voices and the Envoy to the *Clerk's Tale*," *Chaucer Review* 22 (1987): 112–27; Lars Engle, "Chaucer, Bakhtin, and Griselda," *Exemplaria*, 1.2 (1989): 429–59, and William McClellan, "Bakhtin's Theory of Dialogic Discourse, Medieval Rhetorical Theory, and the Multi-voiced Structure of the Clerk's Tale," *Exemplaria* 1.2 (1989): 460–88, have stressed the dialogism of the tale. I see the Clerk's character as being similarly structured. Other studies, without explicitly invoking Bakhtin, approach the tale in not incompatible ways. I have found especially useful Judith Ferster, *Chaucer on Interpretation* (Cambridge: Cambridge University Press, 1985), 94–121, and Peggy Knapp, "Knowing the Tropes: Literary Exegesis and Chaucer's Clerk," *Criticism* 27 (1985): 331–45.

Chaucer understood of Petrarch's story of Griselda, what he could not have understood, and how he translated what he did and did not comprehend. In this essay in honour of Martin Stevens, with whom I first studied the Clerk some twenty-five years ago, I therefore propose to discuss Chaucer as reader of his own trans-cultural experience. Even though I will concentrate almost entirely on Petrarch, I offer these thoughts as a prolegomenon to Chaucer's making of a character, for it is in the figure of the Clerk, I think, maybe even more than in the story he tells, that we see the English poet as a "grant translateur."

In the last decade, Anne Middleton, Charlotte Morse, and especially David Wallace have written about the ideological suppositions and political commitments that underwrite Petrarch's translation of Griselda and the subsequent reception of it.[5] Each of these important studies breaks new ground; each in its way theorizes the Clerk's tale by locating it in the contestatory space which translation inevitably opens. In this space, as Rita Copeland has shown, the mastery and authority of a source is paradoxically affirmed by another text whose different language both displaces that of the original and makes it subject to cultural appropriation.[6] The differing ends this act of appropriation serves, of course, effectively constitute the historicity of the translation. In Petrarch's case, these ends cannot be separated either from the elitism of his humanist project or from the tyrannical political regimes that supported it. As Wallace has shown, Petrarch was seduced by the Viscontis of Milan precisely because they could free him from what he calls his hatred of the vulgarities of the forum. The "vita solitaria," the "otium," which for Petrarch were preconditions for the higher "studia" of poet and philosopher, far from removing the scholar from the petty affairs of the day, proved in fact to be rhetorical shibboleths for the political power that secured them, a power that reproduced itself in the masculine, learned cliques, whose members were arbiters of judgment, which Petrarch's writings called into being.

Wallace's critique of Petrarch seems to me convincing. Very possibly Chaucer did gain enough knowledge on his visits to Italy to understand the political implications of Petrarch's Griselda; Chaucer's version of the tale certainly shows that such implications were of interest to him. I want to enter into dialogue both with Wallace's reading and with the other studies I

---

[5] Anne Middleton, "The Clerk and His Tale: Some Literary Contexts," *SAC* 2 (1980): 121–50; Charlotte Morse, "The Exemplary Griselda," *SAC* 7 (1985): 51–86; David Wallace, "Whan She Translated Was": A Chaucerian Critique of the Petrarchan Academy," in *Literary Practice and Social Change in England 1380–1530*, ed. Lee Patterson (Berkeley: University of California Press, 1990), 156–215. Morse is concerned pre-eminently with the reception of the Griselda, Wallace with its ideology. Middleton discusses both.

[6] Rita Copeland, *Rhetoric, Hermeneutics, and Translation in the Middle Ages* (Cambridge: Cambridge University Press, 1991).

mentioned, however, not so much because I disagree with them, but because I think they do not pay enough attention to how Petrarch represents his allegiances. Everything Petrarch wrote he wrote about himself: if any claim can be called Petrarchan, it is his insistence that the unique virtue of literature was its capacity to spur the formation of the autonomous, moral self. The process by which this self was created, however, was highly complex, a double act of burial and disinterment, of rupture with the past so that the present might be made continuous with it. For Petrarch, the Griselda is an exemplary case of what Thomas Greene has called the humanist hermeneutic of history, a meditation on the role of imitation in the ontology of the self, a critique of the social world and the place of the individual seeking truth in it.[7] Epistemological issues, deep concern for moral and spiritual values, the effects of time and death on the progress of the soul: these matters, even more than the politics of the tale, I think, were what interested Chaucer. The question I raise here is how Chaucer translated the philosophical declaration of the role of the self in Petrarch's tale, its sense of the moral purpose of imitation, and its re-definition of exemplary literature, into terms he, and his audience, might understand.

The impediments to Chaucer's understanding of the Griselda were in fact substantial, mostly because the tale is part of an on-going discussion Petrarch conducted with Boccaccio about the nature and purpose of literature. In its most immediate context, the Griselda is a counter-example to the *Decameron*, which Petrarch both faults and defends in the first part of the letter that contains his translation.[8] Its proximate context, however, is the previous letter of the *Epistolae Seniles*, in which Petrarch had vigorously rejected Boccaccio's request that he put aside his exhausting literary pursuits in deference to his age; it is his writing, Petrarch responds, that gives his age its virtue and its meaning. If Chaucer did not have access to this letter, or indeed to the other two letters, also addressed to Boccaccio, that comprise the seventeenth book of the *Seniles*, he could not have seen that the exemplary tale occupies a crucial position in its overall argument: it

---

[7] Thomas Greene, "Petrarch and the Humanist Hermeneutic," in *Italian Literature: Roots and Branches*, eds. G. Rimanelli and K. J. Atchity (New Haven: Yale University Press, 1976), 201–24; expanded in *The Light in Troy* (New Haven: Yale University Press, 1982), 81–146. Unless otherwise noted, I quote from *Light in Troy*.

[8] For the Latin letter to Boccaccio, I follow the text established by J. Burke Severs, *The Literary Relationships of Chaucer's 'Clerkes Tale'* (1942; rpt. New Haven: Archon, 1972). No critical edition of the *Epistolae Seniles* exists; unless otherwise indicated all translations are from *Letters from Old Age*, trans. Bernardo, Levin, Bernardo, 2 vols. (Baltimore: Johns Hopkins University Press, 1992). For the Latin text of the *Familiares*, see *Le Familiari*, ed. V. Rossi, 4 vols. (Florence: Sansoni, 1933–42); all translations are from *Rerum familiarum libri*, trans. Aldo Bernardo, 3 vols. (Albany: State University of New York Press, 1975, vol. 1; Baltimore: Johns Hopkins University Press, 1982–85, vols 2–3).

demonstrates in literary form the answer Petrarch had just given rhetorically. Furthermore, as the last complete book of the *Seniles*, these letters
assume special importance as a group, comparable to that which the
Griselda occupies in Boccaccio's book, in an even larger conversation
Petrarch had begun with his friend in his previous collection of letters,
the *Familiares*. They express nothing less than Petrarch's final conviction,
which is the conviction of Renaissance humanism, that literature and
rhetoric, more than any other discourse, create not only the independent
moral self but the pious Christian soul. Indeed, Petrarch ultimately justifies
his criticisms of the *Decameron* by offering the relation that joins yet
distinguishes his two compendia of letters as a contrasting model.

These issues are encapsulated in the animadversions on the *Decameron*
which serve as Petrarch's preface to his translation of Griselda. Petrarch
says he has seen Boccaccio's book; like a hurried traveler, however, he has
only leafed through it, since it is very long and written in vernacular prose
for the common herd; moreover, Petrarch was distracted by the wars that
were breaking out in Italy in 1373. Among the things he did note with
approval, though, was Boccaccio's defense against the attacks the *Decameron* had provoked. If some parts of the *Decameron* are lewd, Boccaccio's youthfulness, as well as the literary demands of the book, its style,
idiom, subject matter, and audience, excuse them. Most of all, however,
Petrarch commends the beginning and end of the book. The description of
the plague is perfect, not least because Boccaccio magnificiently deplores
the condition of the country. And the final story of Griselda so impressed
and delighted Petrarch, he desired to memorize and translate it, "something
I would not have readily undertaken for anyone else."

With his opening sentence, Petrarch puts in motion an intricate set of
relations between his own writing and Boccaccio's. Petrarch invites his
younger correspondent to read the *Decameron*, the product of a youth long
since passed ("Librum tuum, quem . . . olim, ut oppinor, iuvenis edidisti
. . ."), from a maturer perspective, the very perspective in fact which age
gives the *Epistolae Seniles*. Perhaps Petrarch issues the invitation because he
recognized that the different tenor of the *Decameron*'s last tale ("et multis
precedencium longe dissimilem") gives it a sense of alterity similar to that of
the *Canzoniere*, Petrarch's own large collection of youthful lyrics in the
vernacular. He had opened this cycle of 365 poems by declaring his
estrangement from the experiences it records: in his introductory sonnet
Petrarch confesses that his hopes and griefs have proved his passion vain
and have made him "a different man from the one he was" (1.1–4). But
simply opening a rhetorical space for retrospective regret of former excesses
of desire is not what Petrarch wants his friend to undertake now. Rather he
requests that Boccaccio join in a hermeneutical revision which asks nothing
less than the active reformation of his authorial self. The Latin letter
Boccaccio has before him will provide a model for this translation: the

slack and low style of youthful indulgence will be transfigured into the exemplary rhetorical discourse of moral and religious fervency. In offering his version of Griselda to Boccaccio, Petrarch offers as well a paradigm for self-translation.

A complicated theory of reading history lies behind Petrarch's remarks, a theory whose documents include letters in the *Familiares* and *Seniles* which Petrarch had addressed to Boccaccio himself. As Greene has shown, Petrarch was acutely aware that the classical culture he so admired and desired to emulate was inescapably alien to him. Early in life, an active mind let Petrarch animate landscapes so that they might grant access to the spirit of former times which remains immanent in them. In a letter addressed to Virgil, for instance, Petrarch describes how, visiting Mantua, he sought glades, fields and streams, not for their own sake, but to question them:

> I constantly wonder ("assidue mecum volvens") by what path you were wont to seek the unfrequented glades . . . what streams to visit. . . . Such thoughts as these bring you back before my eyes ("Atque ea praesentem mihi te spectacula reddunt").[9]

Nature triumphs over change; like the "genius loci," Virgil is still part of the Mantuan countryside for a mind sufficiently invested to evoke his presence. But when one looks on the ruins of antiquity, or still more at the manuscripts in which its culture is inscribed, one is confronted not by the past but by its textuality, written with the ink of decay. This antiquity was not something one could see or summon directly, but had to read. Thus, in that crucial moment when, as Greene says, "the poet turns from landscape to the literary remains," he becomes an archeologist who "struggles to pierce their verbal surfaces to reach the living particularity of the past they bear within them" (93). But because that past was latent, or hidden, or perhaps ultimately indecipherable, because it could be constituted only as the object of historical, not experiential knowledge, a certain epistemological ghostliness attends both it and the one who attempts to recover it.

In his conversations with antiquity, Petrarch continually acknowledges the gap that exists between the factuality of classical culture and the facticity of his mental reconstruction of it. For him, knowing the past meant knowing his own temporal relation to it, the distance which the passage of centuries has placed between him and the greatness of an age that is no more. Consequently, for Petrarch the "verbum mentis," rather than a transparent expression of the essence of the object it comprehends, as it was in scholastic psychologies of understanding, makes knowledge possible by declaring its own historicity as a signifier. Where in Aristotelian epistemologies the mind's utterance had constituted the rational substance

---

[9] *Familiari*, 24.11. Quoted and discussed by Greene, *Light in Troy*, 89–90.

of particular entities by setting them in the form of a proposition, in Petrarch mental discourse defines its own nature and propriety as a sign when it registers the difference between it and the remote, far more estimable world it represents.[10]

The psychic consequences of such a hermeneutic are considerable. From Plato on, understanding had presupposed a likeness between knower and what is known: an analogy was thought to link the ways sensible, imaginative and intellectual knowing were arranged in the mind and the hierarchy of material, mathematic, rational realities they had as their objects. With Petrarch, however, the likeness between the self and the past it desires to know is constructed not by analogy but by a dialectic of mutual subordination: each subjects and is subject to the other. Antiquity, though prodigious, exists only as absence; the present, though real, is dwarfed by the magnitude of prior achievements.

Out of such an interplay of forces, one the necessary condition for the formation of the other, yet also the spectre of its dissolution, Petrarch generated the historical soul, a soul that needs to be divided for it to be a true expression of itself. Always attending to itself, it forever endeavors to make itself better than it now is by looking to disappeared models of former greatness. Confident of his own superiority because of his knowledge of the past, Petrarch continually fears to be eclipsed by the eminence and renown of writers he communed with. Forever exiled, he asserts his homeland is the autonomy and freedom of solitude; sovereign of himself, he nevertheless chooses to live under an emperor. This is the interplay between rupture and continuity that underwrites Petrarch's epistemology; as Giuseppe Mazzotta has shown, it gives his ethics, his psychology, and his politics their form as well.[11]

To understand "a voice from the depths of time," however, is one thing: to converse with it, as Greene says, Petrarch had to find an outward style to catch the inner movements of his soul. He needed a mode of writing which would fortify his own sense of selfhood, even as it acknowledged its dependence on earlier exemplars. He found this style by simultaneously imitating ancient authorities and by seeking to surpass them. By imitating them, Petrarch deferred to his models, but by emulating them, he would at the same time re-bury them.

---

[10] For further discussion of the role of the "verbum mentis" and expression as a proposition in medieval epistemology, see my "'Medium autem, et extrema sunt eiusdem generis': Boccaccio's *Filostrato* and the Shape of Writing," *Exemplaria* 5 (1993), 185–206.

[11] For a brilliant reading of Petrarch's historical self-construction, see Giuseppe Mazzotta, *The Worlds of Petrarch* (Durham: Duke University Press, 1993), especially chapters 1 and 5. The rest of Mazzotta's study convincingly demonstrates how this sense of the fragmented self underlies Petrarch's conception of rhetoric, poetry, ethics, politics, and the other "worlds" he spent his life reformulating.

Petrarch had described what we might call his elements of style in a number of earlier letters to Boccaccio. In *Familiares* 22.2, written in 1359, Petrarch discussed how his writing reflects his soul:[12]

> I much prefer that my style be my own, rude and undefined, perhaps, but made to the measure of my own mind, like a well-cut gown, rather than to use someone else's style, more elegant, ambitious, and ornamented, but suited to a greater genius than mine. . . . Certainly each of us has naturally something individual and his own in his utterance and language as in his face and gesture. It is better and more rewarding for us to develop and train this quality than to change it.[13]

Some six years later, he developed his thought further: it is incumbent, he says, that an imitator "take care that what he writes resemble the orginal without reproducing it":

> we writers must look to it that with a basis of similarity there should be many dissimilarities. And the similarity should be planted so deep that it can only be extracted by quiet meditation. The quality is to be felt rather than defined. Thus we may use another man's conceptions and the color of his style, but not his words. In the first case the resemblance is hidden deep; in the second it is glaring. The first procedure makes poets, the second makes apes. (*Familiari* 23.19)[14]

What Petrarch says here can be extended to everything he penned. Style is an act of imitation, analogous to the intellectual process which discovered it, by which antiquity gains a real presence in the world, both at the level of representation and at the level of experience. In his poems, Petrarch made Virgil, in his prose, Cicero and a host of other authorities, subtexts which, though lying beneath the surface of his own, gave them their shape. In his life, Petrarch gave the events that comprised it a style by which they too reveal a prior, authorized pattern beneath.[15]

---

[12] For dating Petrarch's letters, see Ernest H. Wilkins, *Petrarch's Correspondence* (Padua: Antenore, 1960).

[13] With this image of a well-cut gown, Petrarch virtually defines his style as a kind of translation. As Carolyn Dinshaw has shown, translation nearly became synonymous with a whole range of sartorial tropes in Rome and during the Middle Ages. The image is especially prominent in Petrarch's version of the Griselda. See *Chaucer's Sexual Poetics* (Madison: University of Wisconsin Press, 1989), 132–55 et passim. See also Kristine Gilmartin Wallace, "Array as Motif in the *Clerk's Tale*," *Rice University Studies* 62 (1976): 99–110.

[14] I follow here Greene's fine discussion of these passages in *Light in Troy*, 95–99.

[15] When Petrarch chose to stay with the despotic Viscontis in Milan, it outraged his friends in Florence, who viewed their city as the defender of liberty. However contradictory it seemed to them, however, Petrarch's decision would have seemed consistent to him: how could the poet of the *Africa*, in which Virgil lived again, not reside with a latter-day Augustus, whom he might help bring an era of peace to Italy's warring

Petrarch therefore would have fully expected Boccaccio to read his comments about the *Decameron* and his translation of the tale of Griselda poised between recognition of differences and appreciation of a fundamental continuity. Though he deprecates Boccaccio's book because it is in the vernacular, the product of his youth, and in prose, Petrarch also honors it by according its final story the same status he grants Cicero, whom he also on occasion imitated and criticized at once. Just as Virgil's spirit breathes beneath the *Africa*, so the different style ("stilo . . . alio") of Petrarch's translation will reform the spirit of Boccaccio's tale and be animated by it. Though Petrarch considers his style and the purpose it supports nobler than Boccaccio's, both men are united in their conviction that literature is exemplary.

Consider again Petrarch's approval of Boccaccio's defense of the *Decameron*: though attacked by the bites of dogs ("librum ipsum canum dentibus lacessitum"), Boccaccio repulsed them with his walking stick ("baculo") and yells ("tuaque voce"). Undoubtedly Petrarch is referring here to Boccaccio's introduction to the tales of the fourth day, where he answered critics of the first part of his book by telling the story of Filippo Balducci and his son, who continues to hanker after women even after having been told they are geese. Petrarch, however, offers a different defense. There is a class of insolent and lazy men, he explains, who are eloquent only in chastizing in others what they themselves do not want, or know, or are unable to do.

Of course Petrarch rides the hobbyhorse of his own haughtiness here.[16] Boccaccio's apology appears as much impugned as praised. His story, reduced to "sticks and shouts," is made to seem a "vulgar" thing in itself, especially when compared to the measured dignity of Petrarch's own stately reproof. Yet while he may scorn the style of the response, what Petrarch approves must be the fact that Boccaccio answered his detractors by means of a story.[17] Indeed, Boccaccio's point was that the *Decameron*, directed to "graziosissime donne," properly justifies itself by vindicating the moral innocence of natural passion. Petrarch's is that a

---

factions by means of his poetry? See further Wallace, "Whan She Translated Was", 173 ff. In one sense, I agree with Wallace that Petrarch desired to escape history entirely (p. 161); this is balanced, however, by the immersion in history that forms the basis of his hermeneutic and his politics as well. For a revealing analysis of Petrarch's conception of ambivalences of historical power, see Mazzotta, *The Worlds of Petrarch*, 111 ff. and 181–92.

[16] The prior discounting of the *Decameron* because it is in the vernacular and in prose is a good example of this haughtiness. Petrarch implies that the *Canzoniere*, though also vulgar and nugatory, at least can claim the elevation of poetry.

[17] See Glending Olson's perceptive comments about Petrarch's criticism of the *Decameron* in *Literature as Recreation in the Later Middle Ages* (Ithaca: Cornell University Press, 1982), 217–22.

story which apologizes for animal desire by claiming it is part of human nature is the apt response to the doggy rabble who missed the point because they were deaf to its style. Though their reasons differ, both would agree that literature, even prose in the mother tongue, has its place in the reformation of the soul.

It is in fact precisely the various ways different texts can reform the soul that Petrarch stresses here. While Boccaccio was reading this letter, he might well have recalled another Petrarch had sent to him ten years earlier, in which he passionately defended his own style against criticism. That epistle Petrarch had begun without greeting, by itself an indication of his indignation:

> I ought either to have said nothing or gone into hiding, or better still, not to have been born so as to avoid these barking Scyllas. To come out into the open is not a game. Strong dogs rage with their teeth, weak ones with their bark .... (*Ep. Sen.* 2.1)

The letter continues in a similar state of high dudgeon, employing all the rhetoric of invective. In retrospect, Petrarch suggests that just as Boccaccio had given a fitting answer to those curs who disparaged the natural pleasures of the senses, his emotional outbursts in Latin, the language of knowledge, properly answered those dogs who claimed his writings are ignorant and untruthful. In the preface to his translation of Griselda, however, Petrarch's censure of the hounds of criticism is dispassionate; at the end of his life, he has put invective aside in favor of moral philosophy.[18] Once again, the level and purpose of these discourses differ: together the three responses form a virtual paideia for perfecting the self and soul. Yet they all say the same thing about the role of literature in that process of amelioration: whether it is vernacular fiction that appeals to the senses, or the Latin rhetoric of emotional invective, or the dispassionate persuasions of reason, because censors blind themselves to the exemplarity of each,

---

[18] Petrarch may well have expected Boccaccio to connect and distinguish the remarks he had made in his letter with both the arguments about knowledge in his invective *On His Own Ignorance*, which inspired it, and the translation of the tale of Griselda. The barking dogs in Petrarch's letter echo the use he had made of the figure at the beginning of the invective: "I have grown deaf to the murmur of those who are barking at me, and now I have been hardened against their envious teeth" (p. 52). The prohemium to the Griselda in turn, with its emphasis on the course of the Po, which "cuts violently through Liguria with whirlpools" ("Liguriam gurgite violentus intersecat"), echoes the use Petrarch had made of the "whirling waves of the Po" as a figure for the "whirlpool of human affairs" in the *On His Ignorance* (p. 120). [Quotations are from *The Renaissance Philosophy of Man*, ed. Paul Oscar Kristeller, et al. (Chicago: University of Chicago Press, 1969)]. Limitations of space prevent me from discussing the implications of these associations fully here; I will say, however, that Chaucer's Clerk's dismissal of the prohemium as "a thyng impertinent" (E. 54) is as ironic as the fact that he's an Aristotelian logician. The specific barking dogs Petrarch heaps so much scorn on in *On His Ignorance* are Aristotelian logicians.

because they do not understand its style, they fail to be transformed by it. To underscore this point, Petrarch exemplifies it one last time in his final letter to Boccaccio (17.4): he describes how a friend from Verona remained unmoved as he read the translated Griselda because he thought it untrue. Though he did not argue with his Veronese interlocutor, Petrarch says to Boccaccio "The answer was simple." He then repeats the precept he had used to defend the *Decameron*: "there are some who consider whatever is difficult for them impossible for everyone."

The *Decameron*, in short, does cultural work; Petrarch may denigrate the culture, but he never devalues the work. We may suppose, therefore, that the act of retelling the tale of Griselda is Petrarch's own version of Boccaccio's story of Balducci's son: it too is an argument, a defense of his writing and the motives that have driven it. In the letter to Boccaccio placed before the translation (17.2), Petrarch had rejected his friend's counsel to put aside the toils of composition, now that he had surpassed the fame of Virgil and Cicero, in order to preserve his health. As we have seen, Petrarch responded that writing sustains his life because through it he exercises his virtue, which is the only reason to live. By placing his recasting of Griselda after this letter, even though he tells Boccaccio he wrote the translation first, Petrarch gives the substance of experience to what might otherwise have remained a mere bromide from the realm of authority. The tale of Griselda embodies the precepts Petrarch has given in more abstract form in the preceding letter.

In this Petrarch repeats a note he had long sounded: because rhetoric and poetry solicit the emotions and engage the will, these discourses, far more than the empty, formalistic analyses of dialecticians, provide the ground which makes the imperatives of philosophy and theology real, authentic, and knowable. As Petrarch had said earlier in the *Secretum*, when he spoke of contemplating death, to prevent one's thoughts from "flying past, and not sinking in," the entire soul needs to be engaged:

> We must picture to ourselves the effect of death on each several part of our bodily frame, the cold extremities, the breast in the sweat of fever, the side throbbing with pain. . . .[19]

The catalogue of ailments goes on and on until their specificity gives the meditation the materiality of a lived event.

This particular passage about death in fact helps us understand why Petrarch admired the description of the plague that opens the *Decameron*. It

---

[19] *Secretum*, Bk. 1, in Francesco Petrarca, *Opere*, ed. G. Ponte (Milan: Mursia, 1968), p. 460; quoted in Charles Trinkaus, *The Poet as Philosopher* (New Haven: Yale University Press: 1979), 62. I follow here two of Trinkaus' chapters, "Petrarch's Critique of Self and Society" and "Theologia Poetica and Theologia Rhetorica in Petrarch's Invectives."

corresponds to that meditation on mortality which Petrarch made one of the cardinal points of his spiritual exercises. But in addition to this, the Griselda is a valedictory on two other issues that have dominated Petrarch's thought throughout his life: the cultivation of virtue in the face of the miseries brought by fortune, and the salvation of the soul. In the *Secretum*, Petrarch's early interior dialogue with St. Augustine, the latter, speaking for piety, had proposed that these three concerns are interrelated: one should continually contemplate death, because doing so will make one realize that true happiness depends on virtue rather than on fortune's transitory goods. Since virtue is largely an act of will, striving to achieve it becomes a spiritual act, what one can do to make oneself worthy to receive the gift of grace. But the conflict between the nature of the virtues Petrarch wishes for and the manner in which they are acquired makes following such a program difficult. For Augustinus, spiritual and worldly goals are incompatible. Petrarch's pursuit of fame, love, and glory is a pursuit of illusions; qualities honored in the city of man find no place in the city of God. Yet as Augustine's own experience proves, to sequester oneself from the world avoids that engagement of the will, of the fully self-conscious mind, which makes religious devotion meaningful. One must be in the world to transcend it. This burden Petrarch takes up again in the "De otio religioso," in which he contemplates the life his brother Gherardo leads with his brother monks in a Carthusian monestary.

For Franciscus, who in the *Secretum* speaks for Petrarch's ambitions, the struggle takes a different form. He remains convinced of the worthiness of his aspirations. The palms he craves, however, are fundamentally civic virtues, yet these, like spiritual attainments, can only be won in solitude, through an intensely private inner battle to determine the constitution of the self. This thought becomes the centerpiece of Petrarch's "De vita solitaria." Out of these contradictions, Petrarch developed, in Charles Trinkaus' words, a twofold ethic:

> In one sphere of life (the external, public, social) men act according to certain necessary conventions or compulsions. There is no freedom there, and the best advice is to "submit patiently to circumstances." In the other sphere (the internal, private, spiritual and moral) men have power and freedom to change their feelings as they please, to accept divine grace when proffered or spurn it (83).

Throughout his life Petrarch sought a means which could accommodate the centrifugal impulses of this "double consciousness." The Griselda represents his maturest attempt to reconcile the paradoxes which arise from it.

At the end of the translation, Petrarch says he has told the tale "in a different style not so much to move women of his time to imitate her patience, which scarcely seems imitable to me, but to urge readers to imitate her constancy, that what she took on herself for her husband, we might dare to take on ourselves for God" (my translation). When she marries Walter, Griselda exercises her autonomy of will by choosing to bury it, once and for all. Griselda vows an obedience that is timeless; the patience which proves it collapses every situation into the all-encompassing moment of her promise. This voluntary relinquishing of will cannot serve as an example for the public or the private soul, because with her oath Griselda forfeits the freedom to choose to obey or disobey in the future. When Griselda converts contingency into necessity, her patience becomes scarcely imitable, not because it is unattainable; as his reaction to his reader from Verona shows, Petrarch allows it the possibility of occurring in the real world. It is inimitable because it is scarcely historical, for Griselda has sacrificed the power to re-enact her choice after having taken into account the shifting circumstances of time and place which make each decision a different decision, even if the conclusion reached is always the same. Because it transcends history, Griselda's submission, in its absolutism, opens itself to allegory: it can stand either for the principle of the soul's stoical resignation in the face of life's unavoidable pain, or for its total, self-subsuming surrender when it is folded forever into God's embrace.

Griselda's constancy, however, is exemplary, though she herself exemplifies it only incidentally, because constancy presupposes the historicity of choice. Her pledge freezes Griselda in the instant of its utterance, but she exists in time; the various predicaments Walter devises to test her make Griselda prove her steadfastness again and again. It is this proof over time that Petrarch urges his readers to imitate: what he finds commendable is the resolution to affirm one's choice in full recognition that changed conditions could have led one to decide otherwise.[20]

Griselda's exemplarity therefore depends on our ability to translate her patience into her constancy. Petrarch asks us to read her invariable faithfulness temporally, according to the same hermeneutic by which he has read the antiquity by which he has constructed his style and his self. But instead of emphasizing the remoteness of the past even as his text

---

[20] In this regard, compare Greene's remarks about the difference between Christian allegoresis and Petrarch's hermeneutic: "the older method presupposed a fullness of knowledge awaiting the successful interpreter":

> This method aligned author and reader in a single universe of discourse wherein no cultural distance could exist because, with the sole exception of the Christian revelation, historical change was virtually unknown. The new "archeological" hermeneutic, on the other hand, presupposed a considerable distance. . . .Instead of a relation between "veil" and "truth" that, once discovered, is easily grasped and formulated, there emerges an interplay of entities that resists total description because it operates in the elusive domain of style (p. 92).

In the Griselda, Petrarch has defined exemplarity as the temporal image of allegory. Morse, "The Exemplary Griselda," therefore makes the division between exemplariness and allegory too stark, at least insofar as Petrarch is concerned.

recovers it, Petrarch now posits and bridges the distance between this world and the next. Amid the conflicting goals that divide the soul in this transient world, constancy can urge the will to make its own fragmented existence in time an image of the unity of salvation. The power to choose becomes a palimpsest, under which Petrarch discerns the choice of absolute submission of will to God. Petrarch has aligned the dialectic whereby he has understood himself in history with an allegorical understanding of himself in eternity.

It is in this spirit that Petrarch would bid Boccaccio read his masterpiece against the two collections of letters, the *Seniles* and the *Familiares*, which are their counterparts. Like the *Decameron*, both of Petrarch's compendia begin with the plague. The *Familiares* opens with a (brief) lament to Petrarch's Socrates, Ludwig van Kempen, about the desolation the outbreak in 1348 has caused; the *Seniles* with the resolution, delivered to his Simonides, Francisco Nelli, that Petrarch will bear stoically the depredations of 1361, when the Black Death robbed him of everything the earlier eruption had left, even his Socrates. Like the *Decameron*, each collection ends with a meditation about its own style. The *Familiares* concludes with a series of letters to Horace, Virgil and Homer; the *Seniles* with the four letters to Boccaccio and the unfinished letter to posterity. Both collections are engaged in the same project of the formation of the moral soul, yet the difference, signaled by Petrarch's choice of names for the men he didicates them to, constitutes a significant transformation. The *Familiares* chronicles the formation of the moral out of the archeological excavation of the ethical authority of antiquity. The *Seniles* begins there, with its professions of stoic resignation in the face of fortune and death, and ends by aligning this soul with Christian revelation. Socrates was a philosopher; Simonides, as Petrarch notes (*Sen.* 3.1), a poet *and* priest.

What, then, could Chaucer have made of all this? As Severs shows (41–46), almost certainly Chaucer's manuscript of Griselda contained Petrarch's preface to it; even if he did know the book referred to was the *Decameron*, however, without reading the other letter Petrarch mentions (17.2), Chaucer would have to have found the critique difficult to grasp fully. Indeed, without knowing the two collections of letters, or more generally Petrarch's historical construction of the self, Chaucer would have lacked the information he needed to understand what Petrarch understood in the tale he translated. Similarly, without knowing the *De vita solitaria* and *De otio religioso*, Chaucer might have found Petrarch's equally intense abhorrence and involvement in the political affairs he mentions in the preface contradictory.

Apart from this, some aspects of Petrarch's project clearly escaped Chaucer. A Clerk who "unto logyk had longe ygo," and who was a devoted follower of "Aristotle and his philosophie" (A.295), is precisely the wrong man to make his disciple, considering the contempt Petrarch heaped on

Aristotelian dialecticians in general (especially in the *On His Ignorance*), and on the sophistic "Brittani" in particular.[21] And someone who dismisses the geographical prohemium to the tale as a "thyng impertinent" does not see in landscape what Petrarch saw.

Just as clearly, however, Chaucer did comprehend a great many of the issues Petrarch raises, not in precisely the form he raises them, which spoke to the cultural and historical conditions of Italy, but in cultural and historical forms Chaucer did know. The emphasis on time and especially on death in the "Prologue" and "Envoy" is very Petrarchan, even if the Clerk, thinking of the Wife of Bath, has his own reasons for stressing each. More importantly, a clerk educated in the nominalism of Oxford, who came of age during the period of the "Franciscan hegemony," to cite Heiko Oberman's characterization of fourteenth-century theology, would understand the rhetorical emphasis of Petrarch's humanism, and his conviction that by influencing the will literature produces the knowledge that makes a person not only self-standing but virtuous.[22] He would have felt as well the dialectical ambivalences that tug at Petrarch's Griselda, the temporal difference which at once distinguishes her constancy from her patience and establishes a relation between them. Moreover, "the idea of public poetry in the reign of Richard II," as Middleton has called it, with its pointed call for poetry to aid the establishment of peace, would have prompted Chaucer to ponder the politics of Petrarch's translation, as well as the role of the detached, retiring Clerk, as a master of language, in the common profit.[23]

Ultimately I would argue that Chaucer responded to the competing forces at play in Petrarch's construction of himself by reconfiguring them into those discourses which, by negotiating the boundaries between the secular and the ecclesiastical, worldly experience and transhistorical authority, strive to constitute the Clerk's character.[24] Appropriately enough, the Clerk embodies the problems that history poses to epistemology; how Chaucer translated what he knew, and what he could not have known,

---

[21] On Petrarch's contempt for followers of Aristotle in general, see above, note 18. For his scorn of British logicians in particular, see Trinkaus, *Poet as Philosopher*, 57, and Neil Gilbert, "Richard of Bury and the 'Quires of Yesterday's Sophisms,'" in *Philosophy and Humanism, Renaissance Essays in Honor of Paul Oskar Kristeller*, ed. E. Mahoney (New York: Columbia University Press, 1976), 228–257.

[22] Heiko Oberman, "Fourteenth-Century Religious Thought: A Premature Profile," *Speculum* 53 (1978): 80–93. See also Oberman's *The Harvest of Medieval Theology* (Cambridge, MA: Harvard University Press, 1963); Charles Trinkaus, *In Our Image and Likeness*, 2 vols. (Chicago: University of Chicago Press, 1970).

[23] See Anne Middleton, "The Idea of Public Poetry in the Reign of Richard II," *Speculum* 53 (1978): 94–114.

[24] In this I echo a position I took long ago; see "'And Speketh so Pleyn': The Clerk's Tale and its Teller," *Criticism* 20 (1978): 307–23.

form a prolegomenon to his cleric's character. Obviously I have identified here in only the most cursory of ways some elements I think would play a part in establishing how Chaucer read one aspect of his Italian journey. It seems right, though, that I offer such a preface in honor of Martin Stevens, who, like Petrarch, will only increase his knowledge in retirement. For him, from whom I have learned so much, and gladly taught what I learned, the past has always been prologue for better things to come.

The Crisis of Mediation in Chaucer's
*Troilus and Criseyde**

Robert W. Hanning

The two main nontitular characters of Chaucer's *Troilus and Criseyde* (TC) are a translator and a (more precisely, the eponymous) pander. The parallels between the narrator and Pandar have often been noticed,[1] and the text in effect links them at the end of Book One through Chaucer's borrowing of the "housebuilding" image from the beginning of Geoffroi de Vinsauf's *Poetria nova* (TC 1.1065–71; cf. *Poetria nova*, lines 43–45). The simile, applied by the earlier Geoffrey to the poet and by his namesake to the pander, suggests a metaphoric equivalency, within TC, between the narrator constructing a poem and Pandar constructing a love affair.

Another way in which the narrator and Pandar resemble each other is their common function as mediators – purveyors of desired commodities (women or love stories) to a designated recipient (Troilus; the audience assembled for the occasion).[2] In the following pages I want to examine their mediating position in terms of what the poem tells us about mediation as a cultural as well as an amorous activity. Concentrating on TC's early

---

* I am pleased to acknowledge the invaluable assistance of Dr. Suzanne Akbari in the preparation of this essay.

[1] See, e.g., John M. Fyler, *Chaucer and Ovid* (New Haven and London: Yale University Press, 1979), pp. 129–39, and note 6 on p. 194; see also Dinshaw, following note.

[2] Cf. Carolyn Dinshaw, *Chaucer's Sexual Poetics* (Madison, University of Wisconsin Press, 1989), p. 48: "both of these mediating acts, pandering and translating, are substitutes for amorous action – Pandar and the narrator are both, by their own admission, unsuccessful in love – and both activities yield vicarious pleasures"; further, p. 63: "Chaucer . . . as a bourgeois in the aristocratic court . . . like Pandarus, was responsible for its various traffics . . .: we recall that he served as messenger for Prince Lionel; as esquire, transacted Edward III's business; monitored commercial traffic in the Port of London as Controller of Customs; managed royal property as clerk of the works; even participated in negotiations regarding Richard II's marriage." Fyler, p. 131 (comparing the narrator's words at TC 1.19–21 and Pandar's at TC 1.1042–43): "The nearly identical phrasing of these generous self-denials implies that the narrator is, like Pandarus, a go-between. . . ." See also Gretchen Mieszkowski, "'Pandras' in Deschamps' Ballade for Chaucer," *ChauR* 9 (1975): 327–36.

representations of its narrator (through the Proem of Book Two), I offer preliminary comments about the dimension of the poem that problematizes mediation, erotic and textual/poetic, both in terms of the larger network (or circulation) of desire within the poem itself, but also within the context of a "crisis of mediation," centrally involving translation and translators, within late medieval English society.

That Chaucer's contemporaries would be aware, even if subliminally, of the mediating position of the translator is beyond doubt. His almost exact contemporary, John Trevisa (1340? – 1402?) – priest, fellow of Queens College, Oxford, and one of the most prolific translators of the day – wrote a *Dialogus Inter Dominum et Clericum* to accompany his translation of Ralph Higden's *Polychronicon* (completed 18 April 1387 [!]) and dedicated to his patron, Thomas, Lord Berkeley.[3] Early in the dialogue, the "Dominus," enumerating ways in which post-Babel linguistic confusion can be compensated for, explains that "som man lurneþ and knoweþ meny dyuers speches. And so, bytwene strange men of þe whiche noþer vnderstondeþ oþeres speche, such a man may be mene and telle eyþer what þoþer wol mene."[4] "Mene" is, of course, the term Pandar uses, early in Book Three, to describe his activities on Troilus's behalf: ". . . for the am I becomen, / Bitwixen game and ernest, swich a meene / As maken wommen vnto men to comen" (TC 3.253–55).[5]

Pandar's self-description is an anxious one, offered in the context of a plea to Troilus "that priuete go with vs in this cas – / That is to seyn, that thow vs neuere wreye" (TC 3.283–84). Clearly, Pandar regards his activities, if known, as subject to moral scrutiny and condemnation. Although the fact

[3] See the summary of what is known about Trevisa's life, with references to fuller studies, in Anthony S. G. Edwards, "John Trevisa," in A. S. G. Edwards, ed., *Middle English Prose: A Critical Guide to Major Authors and Genres* (New Brunswick, N.J.: Rutgers University Press, 1984), pp. 133–34. On Trevisa as a translator, see Traugott Lawler, "On the Properties of John Trevisa's Major Translations," *Viator* 14 (1983): 267–88.

[4] Quoted (with emphasis added) from Ronald Waldron, "Trevisa's Original Prefaces on Translation: A Critical Edition," in Edward Donald Kennedy, Ronald Waldron, and Joseph S. Wittig, eds., *Medieval English Studies Presented to George Kane* (Cambridge: D. S. Brewer, 1988), pp. 289–90, lines 17–20. (The pun on "mene/mene," whether or not intended, emphasizes the crucial role of mediation – personal or cultural – in the production and reception of meaning: verbal, visual, or behavioral.) A few lines later, in requesting from the "Clericus" an English translation of Higden's Latin *Polychronicon*, the "Dominus" makes it clear that such a translation will be the written equivalent of a "mene" between the "noble and gret informacion and lore" of the Latin text and English-speakers who cannot otherwise understand it: p. 290, lines 32–37.

[5] All quotations from and references to TC follow Geoffrey Chaucer, *Troilus and Criseyde: A New Edition of "The Book of Troilus*," ed. B. A. Windeatt (London and New York: Longman, 1984). The text continues, "Al sey I nought, thow wost wel what I meene" (3.256); the rhyme "meene/meene" thus duplicates the pun in Trevisa's text mentioned in the preceding note.

that Criseyde is his kinswoman aggravates his anxiety, any purveying of women to men, or otherwise facilitating non-marital sexual encounters, would be stigmatized by the poem's first audiences.[6]

Sexual go-betweens were certainly long-standing figures of obloquy in European literary texts: Ovid's famous bawd Dipsas (who, in *Amores* i.8, is actually not a pimp for his *puella* but an experienced old woman giving a younger one advice on how to attract men and take their money in return for, or anticipation of, sexual favors) served as ancestor for many subsequent characters, often knowing old women, who arrange for male wooing, seduction, or rape of younger women, or for clandestine, adulterous meetings between wives and their lovers, in return for financial and other considerations. Derivatives of Dipsas appear in the twelfth-century Latin "comedy," *Pamphilus de amore*; the second part of Gautier d'Arras's *Eracles*; Jean de Meun's *Roman de la rose*; the pseudo-Ovidian *De vetula*; Juan Ruiz's *Libro de Buen Amor*, and so forth. William Matthews once referred collectively to this group of characters as "The Wife of Bath and all her sect," and there is no doubt that their depiction, as Lee Patterson has argued, evokes male fear and dread of female (especially aged female) sexuality, garrulousness, and uncleanness, combined with a revulsion at the commercialization of sex – which was in fact primarily imposed on poor young women by rich men, but projected onto poor old women in a blatant,

---

[6] Pandar has already expressed his anxiety graphically at 2.351–57, even as he hypocritically denies that he is serving as Troilus's sexual pander: "ffor me were levere thow [Criseyde] and I and he [Troilus] / Were hanged, than I sholde ben his baude" (353–53). In the London of Chaucer and his contemporaries, "baudes" would, in most if not all cases, be the procurers, male or female, for the prostitutes whom the city authorities sought to contain in brothels located outside the city in Southwark. "It was decreed that each alderman should receive complaints in his wardmote concerning common whoremongers, common adulterers, common bawds, common courtesans, common adulteresses, common female bawds, and common scolds. . . . It was decreed that if any man were convicted in the Mayor's Court of being a common whoremonger, his head and beard were to be shaved . . . and he was to be put in the pillory for a period to be determined by the mayor and aldermen . . ." (D. W. Robertson, *Chaucer's London* [New York: John Wylie, 1968], p. 102). See also G. Salusbury-Jones, *Street Life in Medieval England* (1939; repr. Totowa, NJ: Rowman and Littlefield; Hassocks, Sussex: Harvester, 1975), pp. 152–53. For the case of a Florentine who pandered for his wife, in Florence and Pisa, over a period of several months in 1417 before being apprehended and punished by whipping and a substantial fine, see Gene Brucker, ed., *The Society of Renaissance Florence. A Documentary Study* (New York: Harper, 1971), pp. 199–201.

By contrast with panders, marriage-brokers were a recognized part of European society at many levels, and were, e.g., normally involved as go-betweens (*sensali, mezzani*) in marriage negotiations among merchant families in the Florence of Chaucer's day. See Anthony Molho, *Marriage Alliance in Late Medieval Florence* (Cambridge, Mass., and London: Harvard University Press, 1994), pp. 110n., 183n.; Christiane Klapisch-Zuber, *Women, Family, and Ritual in Renaissance Italy*, trans. Lydia G. Cochrane (Chicago: University of Chicago Press, 1985), pp. 183, 192–93.

if not uncommon, act of scapegoating. But from a Chaucerian perspective, Pandar and all his ilk would be a more apt designation.[7]

Perhaps the most prominent fictive male antecedent of Pandar known to Chaucer – aside from Boccaccio's Pandaro, his immediate model – is Galehaut, "Roy d'outre les marches," a character in the thirteenth-century French prose romance, *Lancelot*. Chaucer's knowledge of Galehaut was presumably both direct – he alludes to the *Lancelot* in the *Nun's Priest's Tale* – and mediated by Dante, in an episode of the *Commedia* (the pilgrim/ narrator's encounter with Francesca in *Inferno* 5) that stresses the equivalency between the morally dubious activities of sexual go-betweens and those of texts, especially texts containing love stories. Francesca's self-exculpating exclamation, "Galeotto fu'l libro e chi lo scrisse," describes the effect on her and her lover Paolo of reading together, in private, the account of Lancelot and Guinevere brought together in adultery through the mediation of Galehaut.[8]

Boccaccio was sufficiently impressed by this emotionally intense moment in *Inferno* 5 to appropriate it in a rivalrous manner on at least two occasions. First he gave to the *Decameron* the subtitle "Prencipe Galeotto" – thereby claiming for it, by implication and with an unascertainable component of irony, the power to purvey to its supposed primary audience of narrowly confined and bored (and lovesick?) women either vicarious erotic pleasures or, perhaps, the wiles and strategies necessary to evade their male guardians and find "real" sexual satisfaction.[9]

---

[7] William Matthews, "The Wife of Bath and All Her Sect," *Viator* 5 (1974): 413–43; Lee Patterson, "'For the Wyves Love of Bathe': Feminine Rhetoric and Poetic Resolution in the *Roman de la rose* and the Canterbury Tales," *Speculum* 58 (1983): 656–95. See further Georges Duby and Michelle Perot, gen eds., *A History of Women*: vol. 2, *Silences of the Middle Ages*, ed. Christiane Klapisch-Zuber (Cambridge, Mass.: Harvard University Press, 1992), pp. 61–62, 75–76; and on Pandarus's place in this tradition, see G. Mieszkowski, "Chaucer's Pandarus and Jean Brasdefer's Houdée," *ChauR* 20 (1985): 40–60, and Thomas Garbáty, "The *Pamphilus* Tradition in Ruiz and Chaucer," *PQ* 46 (1967): 457–70.

[8] Dante Alighieri, *The Divine Comedy*, trans. Charles S. Singleton; I: *Inferno* (Princeton: Princeton University Press, 1970), v, 73–142 (Paolo and Francesca; the quoted line is 137). For the meeting between Lancelot and Guinevere, when Galehaut convinces the Queen to kiss the lovesick knight, see Norris J. Lacy, gen. ed., *Lancelot-Grail. The Old French Arthurian Vulgate and Post-Vulgate in Translation*, vol. 2 (N.Y. and London: Garland, 1993), Part II (trans. Carleton W. Carroll), p. 146. On Chaucer and *Inferno* v, see Karla Taylor, "A Text and its Afterlife: Dante and Chaucer," *CL* 35 (1983): 1–20; and "*Inferno* 5 and *Troilus and Criseyde* Revisited," in R. A. Shoaf, ed. (with the assistance of Catherine S. Cox), *Chaucer's Troilus and Criseyde "Subgit to alle Poesye." Essays in Criticism* (Binghamton: Medieval and Renaissance Texts and Studies, 1992), pp. 239–56.

[9] For differing opinions on the implications of Boccaccio's affixing the name "Prencipe Galeotto" to the *Decameron*, see Robert Hollander, *Boccaccio's Two Venuses* (New York: Columbia University Press, 1977), pp. 102–07, 225–28; Joy Hambuechen Potter, *Five Frames for the Decameron. Communication and Social Systems in the "Cornice"*

Later, in his incomplete commentary on the *Commedia*, Boccaccio, in "explicating" *Inferno* 5, dismisses, as probably fictional, Dante's version of the circumstances surrounding the adultery and execution of Paolo and Francesca, and substitutes an equally fictive account of his own, which reads like one of the sentimentally tragic *novelle* told on the 4th day of the *Decameron*.[10] As SunHee Kim Gertz has recently noted, in Boccaccio's version the book as go-between/pander is replaced by a whole corps of human go-betweens: Paolo himself, who is betrothed to Francesca as a stand-in (*procuratore*) for his ugly brother, Gianciotto; one of Francesca's *damigelle*, who misleads her into believing that the handsome Paolo is actually to be her husband, so that she falls in love with him, only to discover the terrible truth when she wakes up in bed beside Gianciotto the morning after her wedding; the servant of Gianciotto who, discovering Francesca's passionate affair with Paolo, informs his master. Finally, when the outraged husband surprises the lovers, and attempts to kill his brother with his sword, Francesca "misesi in mezzo tra Polo e Gianciotto," and for this act of literal mediation receives her death from the blow intended for her beloved.[11]

Boccaccio's version of the Paolo-Francesca story, which highlights the analogy between various kinds of going between,[12] all risky and potentially disastrous, presents itself as a mediating term between the *Commedia* and its

(Princeton: Princeton University Press, 1982), pp. 91–93, 197; Giuseppe Mazzotta, *The World at Play in Boccaccio's "Decameron"* (Princeton: Princeton University Press, 1986), pp. 56–58; and for an elucidation of the idea of "going between" as a key to Boccaccio's vernacular poetic see Francesco Bruni, *Boccaccio: L'invenzione della letteratura mezzana* (Bologna: Il Mulino, 1990), esp. chs. 4–6.

[10] Raising the issue of how Paolo and Francesca began their affair, Boccaccio says, ". . . mai non udii dire, se non quello che l'autore [i.e., Dante] ne scrive; il che possibile è che così fosse. Ma io credo quello essere più tosto fizione formata sopra quello che era possibile ad essere avvenuto, chè io non credo che l'autore sapesse che così fosse." I quote the Boccaccian text from the *Commentary* on the Inferno by Charles Singleton (Princeton: Princeton University Press, 1970), pp. 85–86. Singleton notes (p. 84) that Boccaccio's version is "embroidered nicely to exculpate Francesca as much as possible"; her portrayal as a woman of "altiero animo" and great passion inevitably recalls Ghismonda in *Decameron* 4.1. For a comment on the difference between Dante's and Boccaccio's treatments, see Wesley Trimpi, *Muses of One Mind: The Literary Analysis of Experience and Its Continuity* (Princeton: Princeton University Press, 1983), pp. 349–52.

[11] SunHee Kim Gertz, "The Readerly Imagination: Boccaccio's Commentary on Dante's *Inferno* 5," *Romanische Forschungen* 105 (1993): 23–24. See further, on Boccaccio's version of the story of Paolo and Francesca, Jonathan Usher, "Paolo and Francesca in the *Filocolo* and the *Esposizioni*," *Lectura Dantis* 10 (1992): 22–33, and Vittorio Russo, "Nuclei e schemi narrativi nelle 'Esposizioni,'" in '*Con le muse in Parnaso': Tre studi su Boccaccio* (Naples: Bibliopolis, 1983), pp. 154–65.

[12] As Gertz puts it (24), ". . . Boccaccio's tale . . . reveals the insistent presence of eloquent or persuasive go-betweens. . . . The reference to Dante is clear. . . . Francesca's life on earth is mediated by actual go-betweens, whose acts transform her life into the material about which the literary mediators, or poets, spin their tales."

reader, with a view ostensibly to elucidating Dante, but in fact at emending and replacing him, in a clear gesture of intertextual (and inter-poetic) contest. But in so positioning himself is the commentator risking (from a literary point of view, presumably) a fate like Francesca's, i.e. condemnation for betrayal of the master-text to which he has promised fidelity in setting out to explicate it? A similar anxiety haunts the TC narrator, as we shall shortly see.

Well before either of the two instances just cited, Boccaccio had already represented the book as prospective, or willed, go-between in the framing fiction of *Il Filostrato* (ca. 1340?), his version of the story of Troilus and Criseyde. The narrator, brought close to death by the extended absence of his beloved, undertakes to plead his cause for her return (and, as he makes clear in the *proemio*, her compliance with his wishes for sexual intimacy) by sending her his poem about the Trojan lovers, and characterizing it for her (and of course for Boccaccio's audience) as the shield (*scudo*) behind which he has discreetly concealed an account of his suffering and desires – as well, we might add, as a not-so-veiled threat to consider her wanton and faithless if she does not respond favorably to it.[13] The brief ninth, and last part of *Il Filostrato*, addressed by the narrator to "canzon mia pietosa" (9.1.2), sends the poem on an "alta ambasciata" (9.8.1) to the "donna gentil della mia mente" (9.5.2), charging it, when it comes into her hands, to recount its maker's present misery and plead "quanto puoi" (9.7.4) that she either return or send back a death sentence for him.[14] (Chaucer will put this melodramatic offer of alternative outcomes, *mutatis mutandis*, in the mouth of Pandar when he first comes to Criseyde on Troilus's behalf [TC 2.316–43, 383–85, 429–46, greatly expanding the suggestion in *Filostrato* 2.64]).

At about the same time Boccaccio was composing *Il Filostrato*, Juan Ruiz, Archpriest of Hita, provided a further, striking variation on the theme of the connection between human and textual erotic mediation, in his *Libro de Buen Amor* (1330–43), which, like the other instances mentioned so far, may well have been known to Chaucer.[15] At one point in the *Libro* (st. 910f.), the narrator describes undertaking to woo a beautiful, well-born, but inaccessible young woman. To aid him (and following the advice of Andreas Capellanus), he enlists as messenger an old woman whom he

---

[13] See further R. W. Hanning, "Come In out of the Code: Interpreting the Discourse of Desire in Boccaccio's *Filostrato* and Chaucer's *Troilus and Criseyde*," in R. A. Shoaf, ed., *Chaucer's Troilus and Criseyde "Subgit to alle Poesye." Essays in Criticism* (Binghamton, N.Y.: Medieval and Renaissance Texts and Studies, 1992), pp. 127–30.

[14] All quotations from and references to *Il Filostrato* follow *Filostrato* a cura di Vittore Branca, in vol. 2 of *Tutte le opere di Giovanni Boccaccio* a cura di Vittore Branca (Milan: Mondadori, 1964).

[15] I follow the text in Juan Ruiz, *The Book of True Love*, ed. Anthony N. Zahareas, trans. Saralyn R. Daly (University Park and London: Pennsylvania State University Press, 1978).

refers to as a convent-trotter (*trotaconventos*; 912.3).[16] When he thought-lessly insults the go-between, by calling her "picaça parladera" ("chattering magpie"; 920.1) to her face, she becomes angry and, in revenge, reveals the illicit courtship to the lady's mother. After reeling off a near-endless catalogue of slang terms used for pimps and panders, the Archpriest tells how he begged his go-between's pardon, as a price for which she instructs him not to call her evil names ("nonbre malo nin de fealdat"; 932.1): "Call me True Love [*Buen Amor*] and I will give you my true loyalty, / Because a good word pleases everybody, you'll agree . . ." (932.2–3). The narrator continues, "From love of that old woman and to speak in simple truth, / I called my book *True Love* [*Buen Amor*] and her the same, I here record" (933.1–2). As a result she continues to serve him, faithfully and effectively.

The book and the go-between share the same title, and in both cases, the Archpriest implies, it is a euphemism for the potentially corrupting purveyance of desire. The *trotaconventos* is a tale-teller above all: she brings gossip (*la fabla*) to the Archpriest and to the beloved tales and songs of his passionate devotion. And in order to undo the damage she has done to his suit while she was angry at him, she feigns madness and thereby makes her former revelations about the affair seem the crazed mouthings of a "vieja loca" (935.2). All of which, by the nexus of the shared (and clearly false) name, casts doubt on the reliability of the text and on the author, who may have designs on his readers analogous to those of the Archpriest on his erotic object.

The equivocal status of the text as mediating artifact is compounded when the text in question is a translation. Much has been written recently about medieval theories and practices of translation, some of it very fine, and this is not the place to summarize it.[17] Instead I will confine myself to a few relevant comments based on texts contemporaneous with Chaucer: Trevisa's *Dialogus inter dominum et clericum* and *Epistola* to Lord Berkeley, and excerpts from an anonymous prologue to the Wycliffite translation of the Bible. At the beginning of Trevisa's *Dialogus*, the "Dominus" locates the translator's work firmly within the context of human sinfulness, specifically the sin of pride which led to the divine intervention against

---

[16] Cf. Andreas Capellanus, *De amore* i.1: " . . . when a man sees some woman fit for love and shaped according to his taste, he begins at once to lust after her in his heart. . . . Then after he has come to this complete meditation, love cannot hold the reins, but he proceeds at once to action; straightaway he strives to get a help and find an intermediary." Quoted from Andreas Capellanus, *The Art of Courtly Love*, trans. John Jay Parry (New York: Columbia University Press, 1941, repr. 1959), p. 29.

[17] Of special note is Rita Copeland, *Rhetoric, Hermeneutics, and Translation in the Middle Ages. Academic Traditions and Vernacular Texts* (Cambridge: Cambridge University Press, 1991). See also Roger Ellis, et al., eds., *The Medieval Translator: Theory and Practice of Translation in the Middle Ages* (Cambridge: D. S. Brewer, 1989).

the tower of Babel, the origin point of the diversity of languages which immensely complicates the problem of human communication: "dyuers men buþ straunge to oþer and knoweþ noȝt of here speche" (lines 2–3). The translator seeks to overcome the effects of Babel; as such, Trevisa implies, his labors are a "new creation" parallel to those of Christ (the quintessential mediator between God the Father and his fallen creation), and they will remain necessary until the end of time: the *Dialogus* concludes with "Clericus's" recapitulation of salvation history: the Genesis story of creation and paradise lost (of which Babel is both a consequence and a replay), Christ's redemption of humanity, and his return for Final Judgment, after which "al men þat buþ ywryte yn þe bok of lyf schal wende wiþ hym ynto þe blysse of heuene" where they shall "se and knowe hys godhede and manhede" forever; only then will neither God's judgments nor God's nature require mediation (lines 199–202).

But translation carries its own risks. As "Clericus" points out "ȝef a translacion were ymad þat myȝte be amended yn eny poynt, som men hyt wolde blame" (lines 154–55).[18] In chapter fifteen of the anonymous prologue to the Wycliffite Bible translation (1395–97?), the catalogue of procedures followed by the "symple creature" who has rendered the Latin into English is also a catalogue of the difficulties facing the conscientious translator mediating the authoritative Latin text for English readers: (1) finding a "trewe text" of the Latin Bible to work from; (2) choosing enough, and the best, commentators to elucidate the sense of the text to be translated; (3) obtaining assistance from grammarians in deciphering "harde wordis and harde sentencis"; (4) translating "to þe sentence" (i.e., according larger units of meaning) rather than word by word, yet not "go[ing] . . . fer fro þe lettre." And the translator devotes a passage to the need for special care "in translating of wordis equiuok, þat is þat haþ manie significacions vndur oo lettre," and in rendering prepositions.[19] To do all this, "a translatour haþ greet nede to studie wel þe sentence, boþe bifore and aftir, and loke þat suche equiuok wordis acorde wiþ þe sentence. And he haþ nede to lyve a clene lif and be ful deuout in preiers and haue not his

---

[18] Trevisa's "Dominus" ridicules this argument; but cf. the Proem to TC Book Two, as below, for Chaucer's recognition of same problem.

[19] I quote from "Prologue to Wycliffite Bible, chapter 15," in Anne Hudson, ed., *Selections from English Wycliffite Writings* (Cambridge: Cambridge University Press, 1978), pp. 67, 71. The anonymous translator also undertakes to forestall a variety of objections to his work. If it is incorrect, he says, correct it, but not from a corrupt Latin text, of which there are many. To the argument that those less holy and brilliant than Jerome should not translate Jerome's Latin he replies (p. 69) that Jerome was less holy than the apostles, even as the "seventi translatouris" (of the Hebrew Scriptures into Greek) were less holy than Moses. Against those who scorn biblical translation into English he adduces (p. 71) examples of translation into other vernaculars, as well as earlier English efforts (by Bede and Alfred).

wit ocupied aboute worldli þingis" in order that the Holy Spirit keep him from error. Successful translation is thus presented as a point of conjunction between expertise and personal piety, a characteristic it shares with preaching, another form of mediation.[20]

In general, the erotics of translation as a mediating activity need to be kept in mind: the translator is purveying the substance and accidents, the "doctrine" and the words in which it is couched, of an antecedent text to the audience which (presumably) wants, but for lack of language skills cannot otherwise have it. But at the same time he is fulfilling the original text's desire to communicate, a desire temporarily thwarted by language differences. The translator is a midpoint in a system of reciprocal desires, both of which he/she must seek to satisfy. And in so mediating, he/she runs the risk of displeasing both ends of the equation: the author of the original text (if he/she is alive and/or identifiable) or his/her surrogate, and the audience to which the translation is addressed.

The problems of mediation enumerated thus far – the text as pander/ Galeotto/fabricating Trotaconventos; the translation as inadequate, incorrect, dangerously misleading – underlie Chaucer's representation of the narrator and his task in TC. But the Chaucerian strategy for exploring these problems differs considerably, in its complexity, from any of those I have just briefly enumerated. TC begins with a version of the book-as-go-between theme adapted to the narrator's situation (in contrast with the Boccaccian narrator of *Il Filostrato*) as a non-lover. But this model is immediately complicated by the narrator's assumption of a relationship between himself and his audience based on an ecclesiastical, rather than a literary, paradigm of mediation. Shortly, a further, more problematic perspective on mediation – in this case involving the narrator and his story – enters the poem when it becomes clear that the narrator is not simply (re)telling an old love tale but translating a Latin (and therefore culturally authoritative) text.

By the beginning of Book Two (the latest point in the poem to be dealt with here), the authority the narrator has implicitly claimed for himself in setting out seems to have wilted under the pressure of anxieties associated with the translator's mediating task. The passage evoking those anxieties invites interpretation as Chaucer's comment on tensions between clerical and translational models of mediation – tensions he could have noted, or at least sensed, in the English society of his day.

---

[20] Cf. Trevisa's *Dialogus* (lines 146–51): "Also þe gospel and prophecy and þe ryȝt fey of holy churche mot be tauȝt and ypreched to Englyschmen þat conneþ no Latyn. þanne the gospel and prophecy and þe ryȝt fey of holy cherche mot be told ham an Englysch, and þat ys noȝt ydo bote by Englysch translacion. Vor such Englysch prechyng ys verrey Englysch translacion . . .".

The narrator establishes his mediating presence strongly in the opening lines of the poem – but as a storyteller, not as a translator. Mixing representations of medium and transmission here as elsewhere with strategic effect, Chaucer creates an occasion of oral narration – to an audience with whom the narrator has formed a temporary relationship, and to whom it is his "purpose" to tell the tale of Troilus, "ere that I parte fro ye" (TC 1.5) – even as he simultaneously depicts himself as writing "weeping" verses (TC 1.6–7).[21] The evocation of a temporary intersection between teller and audience in effect directs attention to the former's mediating role: without him, no story, and, in effect, no audience qua audience. (This situation is thus quite different from the one constructed at the beginning of *The Canterbury Tales*, where a group of people sharing a religious and geographical goal – pilgrimage to Canterbury-constitute themselves as a "felaweship" and agree on practical principles of self-regulation ["and made forward erly for to rise . . ."] well before anything is said about storytelling.)[22]

But the narrator, having thus established himself as mediator of story to audience, immediately evokes, and justifies, the presence of further links in a chain of mediation: he needs a muse (in this case the Fury, Thesiphone) to help him write, and would like the assistance as well of the God of Love himself, although he says his "unlikeliness" (as a lover or a storyteller?) appears to rule out his requesting it. Concurrently, he establishes his own mediating status in yet another way by describing himself as "the sorwful instrument / that helpeth lovers, as I kan, to pleyne" (TC 1.10–11). In effect, in addition to purveying stories to an audience of lovers (as they will momentarily be defined, or constructed by him), the narrator is a kind of pen or voice through whom/which the complaints of lovers can be uttered; the text leaves it unclear whether this means he is simply the voice of Troilus whose "aventures . . . in lovynge" (TC 1.3) he has announced his intention to relate, or whether the current performance is but an instance and model of a task he has performed/can perform for other lovers as well.

The presence of the latter possibility endows this statement of mediation with an air of self-advertisement, as by a scribe who commands the forms of appropriate love utterances in letters and songs and is available for hire to tongue-tied or illiterate lovers – until quite recently a not uncommon office,

---

[21] Cf. *Canterbury Tales* I.3176–77 (The "Prologue" to the *Miller's Tale*): the overall narrator, in justifying his telling ribald tales, advises his putative audience, "And therfore, whoso list it nat *yheere*, / *Turne over the leef* and chese another tale" (emphasis added). All references to the *Canterbury Tales* (CT) follow the edition in Larry Benson, gen. ed., *The Riverside Chaucer*, 3rd ed. (Boston: Houghton Mifflin, 1987).

[22] See CT 1.19–35.

at least in the Mediterranean world.[23] In fact, the narrator goes on to say, if his efforts "don gladnesse / To any louere and his cause auaille" (TC 1.19–20) – an oblique reference, perhaps, to the narratorial persona and project defined in the *proemio* to *Il Filostrato* – he is willing to do the work and let the lover take the credit, as would in fact be the case with a scribe "ghost-writing," and thus mediating, a lover's expression of desire to his beloved. (On Pandar's similar statement see n. 2, above.)

In the latter part of this prologial section (TC 1.22–56), the narrator appropriates an even more authoritative model of mediation. Exhorting that part of his audience now constructed as "loueres that bathen in gladnesse" (TC 1.22), he urges them to remember their own past woes and those of others in love, and then leads them through a series of prayers for unfortunates suffering one or another of love's miseries. As has frequently been noted, the narrator's posture is now that of a priest at Mass, preaching to his congregation and leading them in the so-called "bidding prayers." Within the post-Lateran IV institutional Church, the priesthood occupied a crucial mediating position in the Christian's quest for

---

[23] In connection with the application of rhetorical theory to written, as opposed to spoken, utterance, and the concomitant evolution (first in Italy, later in northern Europe) of formal instruction in letter writing (*ars dictaminis*), collections of model letters (*dictamina*) were widely composed during the twelfth and thirteenth centuries, mostly in connection with the requirements of political or religious institutions, but also containing, e.g., formulae for students to use in asking their parents for more money to cover expenses. (See, e.g., the description of Guido Faba's collection, *Dictamina rhetorica* [ca. 1226–27] in Charles B. Faulhaber, "The Letter-Writer's Rhetoric: The *Summa dictaminis* of Guido Faba," in James J. Murphy, ed., *Medieval Eloquence* [Berkeley, Los Angeles, and London: University of California Press, 1978], p. 89.) Boncompagno of Signa, a flamboyant *dictator* in early thirteenth-century Bologna, composed a collection of model love letters, *Rota Veneris* – more, however, as a feat of rhetorical mastery than as a practical guide. See Boncompagno da Signa, *Rota Veneris*, ed. and trans. Josef Purkart (Delmar, N.Y.: Scholars' Facsimiles and Reprints, 1975). For an elision of the "model letter" and the fictional narrative (or "epistolary novella") in Boncompagno's *Rhetorica antiqua* (bef. 1215), see Robert L. Benson, "Protohumanism and Narrative Technique in Early Thirteenth-Century Italian 'Ars Dictaminis,'" in Marga Cottino-Jones and Edward F. Tuttle, eds., *Boccaccio: Secoli di vita* (Ravenna: Longo, 1977), pp. 42–48.

John H. Fisher, in *The Importance of Chaucer* (Carbondale and Edwardsville: Southern Illinois University Press, 1991), has hypothesized that Chaucer spent several years (1360–66) living and studying in the Inns of Chancery in London, where he would have been taught "the art of composing letters and documents in appropriate forms and styles" by "writing masters . . . [,] independent entrepreneurs . . . who instructed students not only at the inns but also at Oxford and Cambridge" (p. 53), using as their texts collections of standardized letters inherited from the *ars dictaminis* (pp. 63–65).

On the perseverance of a dictaminal tradition in Elizabethan England, see Frank Whigham, *Ambition and Privilege* (Berkeley, Los Angeles, and London: University of California Press, 1984), pp. 57–60; Whigham speaks of the "ghostwriting" of the "private emotional document" and notes that "it was not uncommon for [sixteenth-century English] epistolary manuals to offer instruction in writing love letters . . ." (57).

salvation, thanks to its exclusive role in consecrating the eucharist and dispensing penance.[24] Presiding over this mediating caste, and largely the architect of its exalted status, was the Papacy, whose occupants had, during the twelfth century, appropriated to themselves (from various European secular rulers, to whom it had previously pertained) what might be called the ultimate mediator's title, Vicar of Christ.[25] And the narrator, even before establishing his credentials as a "priest of lovers," appears to set himself up as "Pope of Love" when he refers to himself as "I, that god of loues seruantz serue" (TC 1.15), an obvious parody of the papal title, *servus servorum Dei*. (In contrast to this narratorial strategy of evoking multiple mediations at work in the activity of a love poet, the narrator of *Il Filostrato* focuses all authority and inspiration in his "bella donna" (1.4.1), whom he declares to be his Jove, his Apollo, and his muse (1.2.7–8).)

When the narrator announces (TC 1.53) "now wol I go streght to my matere," he indirectly reminds us that he has in effect been neglecting, or avoiding, that "matere" ("The double sorwe of Troilus . . .") since announcing it as his subject in TC's first stanza. In fact, TC 1.6–51 constitute a massive deferral of one salient fact of the story not mentioned in that first stanza: the hero's "louynge of Criseyde, / And how that she forsook hym or she deyde" (TC 1.55–56). By putting off for so long, and through such elaborate dilatory manoeuvers, the admission that Troilus's sorrow is intimately related to Criseyde's "forsaking" him, the narrator intimates his resistance to a crucial part of his chosen story, and begins the process of rendering problematic his mediating role – a process that will accelerate considerably in the opening stanzas of the following book.[26]

---

[24] On the cultural construction and centrality of the eucharist, see Miri Rubin, *Corpus Christi: The Eucharist in Late Medieval Culture* (Cambridge: Cambridge University Press, 1991), p. 35: "sacramental power, and particularly performance of the eucharist were the basis for sacerdotal power"; p. 49: "the priesthood and its life were designed as closely as the eucharist, since like it they supported the church's claim to exclusive and universal mediation of grace, of supernatural power"; p. 50: "priests were seen as teachers but above all as ritual performers of sacramental acts, those acts which tie the Christian world to God through repeated, and reiterated procedures that only the priests could perform." See also Chapter Two, "Beyond design: teaching and reception of the eucharist." For confession, see Thomas N. Tentler, *Sin and Confession on the Eve of the Reformation* (Princeton: Princeton University Press, 1977), pp. 22–27, "The Power of the Priest's Absolution"; pp. 233–301, "Sorrow and the Keys," a section of Chapter Five, "The Working of the Sacrament of Penance."

[25] Until the twelfth century, the Pope was normally referred to as the Vicar of St. Peter, whose successor as leader of the Christian church he claimed to be. See R. W. Southern, *Western Society and the Church in the Middle Ages* (Harmondsworth: Penguin, 1970), pp. 104–05.

[26] In *Medieval to Renaissance in English Poetry* (Cambridge: Cambridge University Press, 1985), p. 77, A. C. Spearing notes "the various types of mora (or 'delay') treated by writers on rhetoric as means of amplification. . . . Chaucer's widespread and elaborate use of them marked a new departure in English poetic style, and one that

In effect, the narrator's delaying tactics place him into a hypothetical rivalry with the "received" form of his tale. That rivalry surfaces at least twice more in Book One, at points in the text that have been widely noted and discussed, but not usually as instances of "the revolt of the mediator." The first is the enamorment of Troilus. There are actually two consecutive reports of this foundational event, of which only the second (TC lines 270f.) awards priority to the Trojan prince as its proper subject. The first (TC 1.206–69), which begins in response to Troilus's scornful words about "ȝe loueres, and ȝoure lewed obseruaunces" (198), and proleptically self-condemnatory comment, "ther nys nat oon kan war by other be" (203), introduces the God of Love punishing the scorner ("for suddenly he hitte hym atte fulle" [209] with his arrows), modulates to a consideration of how human folly is punished, and turns into a homily on the advantages of meek submission to the irresistible power of love, with Troilus as negative example of vain resistance. Once again, as in the opening stanzas of the poem, we see the narrator slide easily from one mediating role – storyteller – to another – priest of love, this time to exercise his preaching function (another aspect of the priest's role as exclusive mediator of Christian doctrine to the faithful).

But while the homily is directed at the poem's audience with a view to shaping its behavior – "and therfore I ȝow rede / To folowen hym that so wel kan ȝow lede" (258–59) – it is also directed against Troilus, and implies (especially in the simile between "this fierse and proude knyght" humbled by love and a horse whipped for daring to "skippe / Out of the weye" [218–19]) a pleasure taken in seeing the hero in pain. Following suggestions by Leo Bersani and René Girard, we can, perhaps, understand this harsh treatment of Troilus as a reflection of the fact that, in Bersani's words, the narrator (and behind him the bourgeois poet?) "distrusts his alienated and ideal self [incorporated in the hero], and in fact he very often ends by having him killed,"[27] or alternatively that Troilus's enamorment begins what Girard calls a relationship of triangular or mediated desire, with the narrator and Troilus as rivals for Criseyde's affections, and Criseyde taking on some of the value she has for the narrator precisely because Troilus desires her.[28] In any case, the addition of a second, "moralized"

---

deeply impressed his successors." Of the techniques mentioned by Spearing (pp. 77–78), the passage here under discussion most closely approximates *digressio*.

[27] Leo Bersani, *Baudelaire and Freud* (Berkeley, Los Angeles, and London: University of California Press, 1977), p. 119. In fact, the narrator does "kill off" Troilus in TC Book 5; Chaucer is of course following Boccaccio's text closely at this point (cf. TC 5.1800–06 and *Fil* 8.27).

[28] See René Girard, *Deceit, Desire and the Novel. Self and Other in Literary Structure*, trans. Yvonne Freccero (Baltimore and London: The Johns Hopkins University Press, 1965; orig. French ed., 1961), esp. chs. 1–4. That the narrator also desires Criseyde has been a commonplace of TC criticism at least since E. Talbot Donaldson's influential

version of the enamorment of the hero signals a rivalrous intervention by the narrator into his received story.

Shortly after, in depicting a lovesick Troilus composing a song to his beloved, the narrator claims, "And of his song naught only the sentence, / As writ myn auctor called Lollius, / But pleinly, saue oure tonges difference, / I dar wel seyn in al that Troilus / Seyde in his song, loo, euery word right thus / As I shal seyn . . ." (TC 1.393–99). Much has recently been made of the illogicalities and deconstructive implications of this passage;[29] but it can also be argued, I believe, that the narrator is engaging simultaneously in rivalry with his *auctor*, Lollius (here named for the first time), and with his hero. To Troilus's skill in composing the song and Lollius's in recording its "sentence" (393) he matches his own skill in translating it, "euery word right thus / as I shal seyn."

The narrator's contention that he is reproducing Troilus's song as written, "saue oure tonges difference" (395), sets the stage for the fuller consideration of the trials and dangers of translation in the Proem of Book Two. Here the relationship between narrator/translator and *auctor* undergoes a sea change, as the former undertakes to mediate to his audience an established, Latin text, in the face of varying obstacles: his own lack of "sentement" (TC 2.13), the fact that "in fourme of speche is chaunge / Withinne a thousande yeer" (23–24), and so forth. (The latter concern, derived ultimately from Horace's *Ars poetica*, 69–72, also resonates with Trevisa's contemporaneous reflection on the relationship of the translator's task to the events at Babel, where divine intervention mandated analogous, if simultaneous, "chaunge" in the "fourme of speeche," as well as with the anonymous Wycliffite Bible translator's worry about the equivocality of Latin words (on which see p. 150, above)).

The narrator must deal with the constant change of customs as well as language, thanks to which many in his audience "that herkneth, as the

essay, "Criseyde and Her Narrator," repr. Donaldson, *Speaking of Chaucer* (London: Athlone Press, 1970), pp. 65–83. For a recent analysis of the critical implications of Donaldson's own (mediated) desire for Criseyde, see Dinshaw, pp. 30–31, 35–39. It would be interesting, but not relevant here, to compare the narrator's analytic, but also desirous, involvement with Criseyde in Book Two – up to and including the recounting of her erotic, violent dream – with Freud's attitude toward Dora in his famous case study of her hysteria; cf. Sigmund Freud, *Dora. [Fragment of] An Analysis of a Case of Hysteria* (1905; English translation repr. New York: Collier Books, 1963).

[29] See especially H. Marshall Leicester, Jr., "Oure tonges *différance*: Textuality and Deconstruction in Chaucer," in Laurie A. Finke and Martin B. Shichtman, eds., *Medieval Texts and Contemporary Readers* (Ithaca and London: Cornell University Press, 1987), pp. 15–26, and Dinshaw, pp. 42–43. In an interpretive move anticipating my own here, but reaching an opposite conclusion, Dinshaw argues, "the narrator's claim of historically faithful, word-for-word translation here works as a cover for his deeper involvement, his deeper substitution: it masks his identification with the lover of the woman, Criseyde" (43).

storie wol deuise, / How Troilus com to his lady grace" will respond, resistantly, to the account: "so nold I nat loue purchace" (TC 2. 31–33). In effect, by coming out of the closet as a translator in this Proem, the narrator surrenders any authority to control his audience; the translator of an old text must deal with changing sensibilities and customs over time and must recognize the inherent variousness, and thus ungeneralizable nature, of personal experience. Ironically, this insistence on variety – "Ek scarsly ben ther in this place thre / That haue in loue seid like and don in all. . . ." – recalls the insistence of confessional manuals (borrowing ultimately from classical rhetoric) that account be taken of individual "circumstances" – including the status and motivation of the sinner – in determining the sinfulness of an act.[30] But, as the Proem to Book Two demonstrates, it simultaneously takes away the power of the pulpit by subverting the idea of a lovers' community (on the model of the Christian community) sharing a general understanding of the world and of the norms of Christian behavior.

One can generalize that the representation of the mediator's authority in the opening stanzas of TC gives way to a dramatization of his anxieties in the Proem to Book Two. This anxiety is summed up in the Proem's last, and perhaps most famous, line: "myn auctor shal I folwen if I konne" (49), which appears, in its hesitancy, to offer a revisionist recollection of, and perspective on, Dante "following" Vergil, fictively and textually, through the first and second cantiche of the *Commedia*, while recalling as well the similar contingency expressed by the texted paraphrase of the opening lines of the Aeneid on the walls of the dream-temple in the first book of the "Dantesque" *House of Fame*.[31] Clearly Chaucer understands the perils of

---

[30] See D. W. Robertson, "A Note on the Classical Origin of 'Circumstances' in the Medieval Confessional," *SP* 43 (1946): 6–14; Johannes Gründel, *Die Lehre von den Umständen der menschlichen Handlung im Mittelalter* (Münster: Aschendorff, 1963), esp. pt. 2, ch. 2, "Die Lehre von den Umständen in den Bussschriften und Bussummen" (pp. 393–418). But the narrator's anxieties at this point in TC also recall the situation after God's intervention at Babel: experience is (now) so fragmented as to be uncommunicable.

[31] At the opening of his dream in *The House of Fame* (HF), the narrator is in a temple of Venus: "But as I romed up and doun, / I fond that on a wall ther was / Thus writen on a table of bras: / 'I wol now synge, yif I kan, / The armes and also the man / That first cam, thurgh his destinee, / Fugityf of Troy contree, / In Italye, with ful moche pyne / Unto the strondes of Lavyne" (140–48). Cf. the *Legend of Good Women* (LGW), 924–29, where the narrator, praising Vergil, declares, ". . . and I shal, as I can, / Folwe thy lanterne, as thow gost byforn, / How Eneas to Dido was forsworn" the image of Vergil lighting the way for the Chaucerian narrator recalls the words of Statius to Vergil in *Purgatorio* xxii: "Facesti come quei che va di notte, / che porta il lume dietro e sé non giova, / ma dopo sé fa le persone dotte. . . . (67–69). Later in this canto, as Virgil, Statius, and the Dantean narrator walk through the Purgatorial landscape, Dante uses a spatial configuration to characterize his poetic discipleship to his illustrious predecessors: "Elli givan dinanzi, e io soletto / di retro, e ascoltava i lor sermoni, / ch'a poetar mi davano intelletto" (127–29; I follow the text in Dante Alighieri, *The Divine Comedy. Purgatorio*, trans. Charles S.

translatio, not just as a technical problem of dealing with language's instability, but in the larger sense of *translatio studii*, the appropriation and domestication of authoritative texts "out of Latin in my tonge" (TC 2.14). (That he sees such poetic "following" as opportunity as well as challenge is implied in a last evocation of the metaphor at the end of TC, the famous "go litel bok" instructions that suggest the "modern" poet has successfully, if respectfully, imitated the "ancient" masters. But he couples this indirect assertion of accomplishment with a reiterated worry about the "so gret diuersite / In Englissh and in writyng of oure tonge" [TC 5.1793–94] which would worry him both as poet and as translator.)[32]

But it is worth considering from yet another perspective the "crisis of mediation" at the beginning of Book Two. As Ralph Hanna has recently, and masterfully, reminded us – and as Trevisa's *Dialogus* and the anonymous Wycliffite "Prologue" corroborate – translation as it applied to Scripture was a hot and contentious issue in the latter years of Chaucer's life and on into the fifteenth century.[33] The availability of the biblical text to all Christians in their native language was a cornerstone of the demands made on the institutional church by a broad spectrum of reform elements which we oversimplify (as did their opponents at the time) by lumping them together under the name "Lollards." The arguments against vernacular translation made by representatives of the church hierarchy stressed the

---

Singleton [Princeton: Princeton University Press, 1973]). Dante's use of the diminutive, "soletto," can perhaps be seen as an analogue, albeit one with a different resonance, to Chaucer's "if-I-kan" locutions.

[32] In HF and LGW, Chaucer demonstrates a more appropriative model of *translatio*, combining Vergilian with Ovidian versions of the Dido-Aeneas story in a manner that suggests a quite different significance for the locution "if I kan," i.e., if I can do so and still tell the story as I believe it should be told. See LGW 928–29 (the lines immediately following those quoted in preceding note): "In thyn Eneyde and Naso wol I take / The tenor, and the grete effectes make." On this passage and its implications, see further Copeland, *Rhetoric, Hermeneutics, and Translation* (note 17, above), pp. 198–201; and on the larger issue of medieval poetic authority *vis à vis* the ancients, Jacqueline T. Miller, *Poetic License. Authority and Authorship in Medieval and Renaissance Contexts* (New York and Oxford: Oxford University Press, 1986), ch. 1, "Authority and Authorship: Poetic License"; and Michelle A. Freeman, *The Poetics of "Translatio Studii" and "Conjointure:" Chrétien de Troyes's "Cligés"* (Lexington, KY: French Forum, 1979).

[33] Ralph Hanna, "The Difficulty of Ricardian Prose Translation. The Case of the Lollards," *MLQ* 50 (1990): 319–40. The greater part of Trevisa's *Dialogus* is taken up with posing, and disposing of, a series of arguments against translations from Latin into English, in the course of which the specific question of Englishing the Bible is repeatedly addressed, directly or indirectly. The most unequivocal endorsement of such translation appears at line 131f: "Also holy wryt was translated out of Hebrew ynto Gru and out of Gru into Latyn and þanne out of Latyn ynto Frensch. þanne what hap Englysch trespased þat hyt myȝt noȝt be translated into Englysch?" Cf. note 19, above, for a recapitulation of arguments against translating the Bible countered in the Wycliffite "Prologue."

dangers to the faith of having "lewed" men and women undertake to interpret the gospel message. In fact, as Hanna argues, at least as important a reason for opposing vernacular scriptures was their potential to undermine the status and authority of the priesthood, in whose care the explication and preaching of the Christian faith, along with the sacramental powers central to the eucharist and penance, were exclusively vested.[34]

It is clear from extant records that an attack on all these mediating activities of the clergy was a consistent part of reformist and "Lollard" agitation during the late fourteenth and fifteenth centuries.[35] Hence it is also clear that, from the perspective of religious orthodoxy and controversy, priestly authority and translation activity could be seen as diametrically opposed, quite incompatible forms of cultural mediation.[36] It is hard to resist the conclusion that in the opposing representations of his narrator in the first two "proems" of TC – first as priest of love, then as anxious translator of a love story – Chaucer is reflecting at some level of awareness (the precise level is both unascertainable and ultimately irrelevant) the inherent tension between these two embodiments of the mediating function in his society.[37]

---

[34] See Hanna, 324–25, summarizing the argument by the Oxford Franciscan, William Butler, made as part of "an extensive debate which went on at Oxford in 1401 over the propriety of biblical translation into English." Butler "argues against translation on the grounds that the right to read Scripture is uniquely reserved for those in clerical status . . . Clerics should experience Christian truth directly; they may then pass on to others what is proper and necessary."

Trevisa was himself a priest, but many reformers / "Lollards" were ordained clergy who protested the privileged status of their caste. Interestingly, all the arguments in favor of translation from Latin in general, and "holy wryt" (whether in preaching or writing) in particular, are put in the mouth of the "Dominus," and all the resistance given to the "Clericus." See further, Edwards (cf. note 3, above), p. 137: "there is one further area of research that is of particular concern to students of Trevisa. This is the question of Trevisa's possible involvement in a translation of the Bible into English, possibly the Early Version of the Wycliffe Bible." The argument for his involvement has been made most strongly by Sven L. Fristedt, ed., *The Wycliffe Bible: Part III* (Stockholm: Almqvist and Wiksell, 1973), pp. 8–58.

[35] See, e.g., the excerpts from heresy trials and anti-Lollard ecclesiatical documents collected in R. N. Swanson, trans. and ed., *Catholic England. Faith, Religion, and Observance before the Reformation* (Manchester: Manchester University Press, 1993), pp. 267–77.

[36] Commenting on the trial of Margery Baxter for heresy (Norwich, 1428–29), Hanna concludes, "the problem raised by translation is what Margery Baxter's case shows – that English texts will open the way to non-clerically supervised interpretation" (335).

[37] For a persuasive but very different reading of the narrator's mediating relationship to his inherited story see Winthrop Wetherbee, *Chaucer and the Poets: An Essay on "Troilus and Criseyde"* (Ithaca and London: Cornell University Press, 1984), Chapter One, "The Narrator, Troilus, and the Poetic Agenda."

Reading Chaucer *Ab Ovo*:
Mock-*Exemplum* in the *Nun's Priest's Tale*

Peter W. Travis

Beginning is not a beginner's game.   *Edward Said*

A povre wydwe, somdeel stape in age,
Was whilom dwellyng in a narwe cotage,
Biside a grove, stondynge in a dale.
This wydwe, of which I telle yow my tale,
Syn thilke day that she was last a wyf
In pacience ladde a ful symple lyf,
For litel was hir catel and hir rente.
By housbondrie of swich as God hire sente
She foond hirself and eek hir doghtren two.
Thre large sowes hadde she, and namo,
Three keen, and eek a sheep that highte Malle.
Ful sooty was hire bour and eek hir halle,
In which she eet ful many a sklendre meel.
Of poynaunt sauce hir neded never a deel.
No deyntee morsel passed thurgh hir throte;
Hir diete was accordant to hir cote.
Repleccioun ne made hire nevere sik;
Attempree diete was al hir phisik,
And exercise, and hertes suffisaunce.
The goute lette hire nothyng for to daunce,
N'apoplexie shente nat hir heed.
No wyn ne drank she, neither whit ne reed;
Hir bord was served moost with whit and blak –
Milk and broun breed, in which she foond no lak,
Seynd bacoun, and somtyme an ey or tweye,
For she was, as it were, a maner deye.

The *Nun's Priest's Tale* (VII. 2821–46)[1]

---

[1] *The Riverside Chaucer*, Larry D. Benson, general editor (Boston: Houghton Mifflin, 1987), p. 253.

How to begin? Indeed, how does one know what a proper beginning is? The nearly universal anxiety given voice in these and related questions carries a special set of burdens for the creators of Christian-humanist fiction. Living inside the grand narrative of salvation history at a point far removed from the Alpha and Omega, how can one settle upon any moment which pretends to be an ultimate terminus, an original beginning? And how in turn can this beginning pretend to be the initiator of an event which develops into a pattern so complete that its *finale* is as definitive an end-all as the beginning from which it sprang? Because Christ the Word's act of creation *in principio* hovers over every human artifice, medieval writers were particularly aware of the hubristic resonance of their opening words. What is immediately problematic is that such creators have no direct experience of the termini of which their own artistic boundaries are but attenuated variants. Rather, each author is positioned in a middle whose fictional representations would seem to make sense only if their beginnings and endings are grounded in some extra-fictional reality. As Frank Kermode has famously remarked, "Men, like poets, rush 'into the middest,' *in medias res*, when they are born; they also die *in mediis rebus*, and to make sense of their span they need fictive concords with origins and ends, such as give meaning to lives and to poems."[2]

One classic way of addressing the urgency of beginnings is to forestall the entire issue. Horace's advice in the *Ars Poetica* was never to begin *abo ovo* (referring to the double-yoked egg of Leda, which, producing Helen and Clytemnestra, initiated the history of Troy); a poet should rather begin, as did Homer in the *Iliad*, "in the middle of the thing," *in medias res*. With a few notable exceptions such as Milton's *Paradise Lost*, Horace's preference for the Homeric and Vergilian model has exerted only a minor influence in the composition of Western fiction. Medieval English writers, for example, never saw fit to open their narratives *in medias res*.[3] Yet the model of epic beginnings remained well known throughout the later Middle Ages and Renaissance because a variety of ways of arranging the parts of a narrative were studied and imitated in the standard school curricula. One of the most influential preceptive grammars in the late Middle Ages, Geoffrey of Vinsauf's *Poetria Nova*, a self-conscious modernization of Horace's *poetria antiqua*, both amplifies and "medievalizes" Horace's classical definitions of

---

[2] Frank Kermode, *The Sense of An Ending: Studies in the Theory of Fiction* (New York: Oxford University Press, 1967), p. 7.

[3] See Judith Davidoff, *Beginning Well: Framing Fictions in Late Middle English Poetry* (Rutherford, N.J.: Fairleigh Dickinson University Press, 1988). In Davidoff's judgment, all medieval English narrative poems begin with one of six "basic opening modes": (1) a direct plunge into the material; (2) a statement of the content of the poem; (3) a prayer; (4) an explanation of how the poem came to be written; (5) an explanation of why the audience should listen to the poem; and – the most popular – (6) a framing fiction where an initial narrative event sets the stage for the interior, "core pattern," of the poem.

the artfully constructed narrative. Geoffrey argues that there are two excellent ways of rearranging the sequence of narrative events. The poet can begin either at the end or at the middle of his material:

Let that part of the material which is first in the order of nature wait outside the gates of the work. Let the end, as a worthy precursor, be first to enter and take up its place in advance, as a guest of more honourable rank, or even as master. Nature has placed the end last in order, but art respectfully defers to it, leads it from its humble position and accords it the place of honour.

The place of honour at the beginning of a work does not reserve its lustre for the end of the material only; rather, two parts share the glory: the end of the material and the middle. Art draws from either of these a graceful beginning.[4]

In the architectonics of literary construction there are thus two narrative beginnings which "share the glory": the end of the original "material" and the middle. But Geoffrey goes on to explain that there are two additional, and "still more brilliant," ways of beginning a narrative. One may begin either with a proverb or an exemplum:

If a still more brilliant beginning is desired (while leaving the sequence of the material unchanged) make use of a proverb, ensuring that it may not sink to a purely specific relevance, but raise its head high to some general truth. . . . No less appropriately do exempla occupy a position at the beginning of a work. The same quality, indeed, shines forth from exempla and proverbs, and the distinction conferred by the two is of equal value.[5]

While honoring the classical ideal of beginning a poetic narrative elsewhere than at its "original" beginning, Geoffrey reveals himself a thoroughly medieval aesthetician when declaring his own preference for beginning with a moral exhortation, either in the form of proverb or exemplum. In thus privileging *sententia* over *mythos*, Geoffrey is suggesting that all narratives, no matter however ornate their use of rhetorical figures, are essentially a form of didactic art illustrating useful general principles. The beginning proverb or exemplum clearly signalizes the principles which obtain in the narrative that follows and thus initiates a way of reading appropriate to the work as a whole. Indeed, the introductory proverb or exemplum may be seen as the middle or an end of a work's *argumentum* in that it provides a distillation of the central point and final purpose to the narrative of which it is an integral part.[6]

---

[4] Geoffrey of Vinsauf, *Poetria Nova of Geoffrey of Vinsauf*, trans. Margaret F. Nims, (Toronto: Pontifical Institute of Mediaeval Studies, 1967), pp. 19–20.
[5] *Poetria Nova*, pp. 20–21.
[6] For the various uses of *argumentum* in classical literary theory, see Wesley Trimpi,

In this essay I intend to study in considerable detail the exemplary beginning of Chaucer's "Nun's Priest's Tale" (quoted above). I undertake this analysis in part because the *exemplum*, as Larry Scanlon has argued in his study of the genre, is the "narrative form [which] dominates later medieval culture, particularly in England." *Exemplum*, Scanlon contends, is the "dominant narrative genre of the Chaucerian tradition" as well: "Of its four most important works, the *Canterbury Tales*, the *Confessio Amantis*, the *Regement of Princes,* and the *Fall of Princes*, only the first is not [in its entirety] an exemplum collection," and yet "at least eight" of Chaucer's twenty-four tales "can be described as exempla or exemplum collections."[7] To scrutinize in detail one isolable *exemplum* by Chaucer is thus to study the fundamental genre of what Scanlon calls the "Chaucerian tradition." But the more compelling reason I have undertaken an examination of the opening scene of Chaucer's *Nun's Priest's Tale* is that Chaucer, while brilliantly in command of the *exemplum* form, was aware of the dangers of our reading each and every work of literature as if it were already processed into the *exemplum* format. In the way that it plays with the classical-medieval ideal of an exemplary, non-*ab ovo* beginning, the Nun's Priest's *exemplum* is honoring the aesthetic persuasions of Geoffrey of Vinsauf and of Horace before him. At the same time, however, through the heuristics of parody, Chaucer's *exemplum* is playing with our readerly expectations and with the prescriptive modes of decoding any narrative we presume has been arranged according to some overarching argument or *sentence*.

The *Nun's Priest's Tale* has been praised by admirers as "the most inimitably 'Chaucerian' of the *Tales*": a "virtuoso performance" and "masterpiece," it has been understood as Chaucer's unique *ars poetica* wherein the poet's own distinctive tropes and stylistic signatures are essentialized, parodied, and redeployed.[8] As Linda Hutcheon has extensively argued in *A Theory of Parody*, all literary parodies are a literary form of literary criticism, and as such they provide a heuristics of reading which attempts to co-ordinate a sophisticated aesthetics whose norms are understood, appreciated, and "created" by author and reader alike. To achieve this co-creation, it is often the case that two constructed sensibilities, that of

Muses of One Mind: The Literary Analysis of Experience and Its Continuity (Princeton: Princeton University Press, 1983), esp. pp. 296–305.

[7] Larry Scanlon, *Narrative, Authority, and Power: The Medieval Exemplum and the Chaucerian Tradition* (Cambridge: Cambridge University Press, 1994), pp. 3, 137. The eight tales Scanlon classifies as "clearly" exempla are the *Friar's Tale*, the *Summoner's Tale*, the *Physician's Tale*, the *Pardoner's Tale*, the *Monk's Tale* (an exemplum collection), the *Nun's Priest's Tale*, and the *Manciple's Tale* (p. 137. n.)

[8] Derek Pearsall, ed., *The Canterbury Tales* (London: Unwin, 1985), p. 230; Charles Muscatine, *Chaucer and the French Tradition* (Berkeley: University of California Press, 1966), p. 238; John Speirs, *Chaucer the Maker* (London: Faber & Faber, 1951), p. 142.

the inept narrator and that of the naive reader, serve as targets of the parody's subtler ironies.[9] And in the case of poetic self-parody, as in the *Nun's Priest's Tale*, the critical citation of the author's favorite practices is not meant as satiric self-deflation as much as it is meant to advertise the complexities both of the encoding and the decoding of the poet's own poetry. As the prologue to Chaucer's personal *ars poetica*, the exemplary description of the widow's humble life is a compressed experiment in the art of descrying meaning in literature.

The standard critical approach has been to treat the Nun's Priest's opening portrait of the widow as a literary exercise containing a fairly readily extrapolatable meaning. For several scholars it is an impressively accurate depiction of the socio-economic realities of fourteenth-century English subsistence farming, a specific form of marginal existence slightly below that of "half-virgater," where insufficient arable land required the cultivation of livestock to flesh out a modest living.[10] A second approach has focused upon the graphic artistry of the portrait, whose naturalism is to be appreciated in the tradition either of classical epic or of early Renaissance genre paintings.[11] A third and quite minor approach has chosen to allegorize the entire scene: for Donovan, Dahlberg and Englehardt, the widow is a representative of the Church; for D. W. Robertson, the possibility the widow engaged in winnowing underscores the Church's responsibility to separate the fruit from the chaff.[12] But the most popular critical take by far has been to emphasize the way this opening scene works as an *exemplum*. Claus Uhlig, for example, sees the widow as an emblem of "*moderatio* and temperance";[13] Charles Watkins feels the portrait underscores the virtues of good health, frugality, and fortitude;[14] John Block Friedman finds the image of the widow "a homiletic commonplace for

[9] Linda Hutcheon, *A Theory of Parody: The Teachings of Twentieth-Century Art Forms* (New York: Methuen, 1985).

[10] See especially D. W. Robertson, Jr., "Some Disputed Chaucerian Terminology," *Speculum* 52 (1977): 571–81.

[11] Robert Kilburn Root found the portrait "worthy of Tenier or Gerard Dou" in *The Poetry of Chaucer: A Guide to Its Study and Appreciation* (Boston: Houghton Mifflin, 1906), p. 214; Percy Van Dyke felt it was "Homeric in its lifelike and homely details" in *The Living Chaucer* (Philadelphia: University of Pennsylvania Press, 1940), p. 62; and Claus Uhlig saw it as "a pleasant picture, in the style of the Dutch Masters" in *Chaucer und die Armut* (Mainz: Akademie der Wissenschaften und der Literatur, Abhandlungen der Geistes- und Sozialwissenschaftlichen Klasse, Jahrgang 1973, no. 14).

[12] Mortimer J. Donovan, "The *Moralite* of the Nun's Priest's Sermon," *JEGP* 52 (1953): 498–506; Charles Dahlberg, "Chaucer's Cock and Fox," *JEGP* 53 (1954): 277–90; George J. Engelhardt, "The Ecclesiastical Pilgrims of the *Canterbury Tales*: A Study in Ethology," *MS* 37 (1975): 287–315; D. W. Robertson, Jr., "Some Disputed Chaucerian Terminology," *Essays in Medieval Culture* (Princeton: Princeton University Press, 1980): 291–301.

[13] *Chaucer und die Armut*.

[14] Charles A. Watkins, "Chaucer's *Sweete Preest*," *ELH* 36 (1969): 455–69.

expressing the eschewing of the life of vanity and the passions";[15] for William Strange she is the "model of man living in humility, free from Fortune";[16] Robertson sees her as "a model of chastity and sobriety";[17] and Trevor Whittock articulates the most widely shared sense of Chaucer's authorial intent when he asserts that the widow's portrait is "the moral ground of the poem."[18]

These four basic positions need not, of course, be mutually exclusive. One might argue that the portrait is sociologically realistic, that it is artistically part of a tradition of literary genre scenes, that tropologically the widow provides a positive moral example, and that allegorically her life may figure forth the ideals of the Christian church. But clearly these four approaches comprise two distinctly different forms of critical activity: the first two read the widow's portrait as a visual sign or icon, while the second two see the portrait as a form of moral injunction. What is interesting is that these two modes of critical response, the first emphasizing the scene's iconic power and the second emphasizing the portrait's strategies of moral exhortation, are in keeping with the two pre-eminent ways *exemplum* was originally understood by Aristotle and his Greek contemporaries. Aristotle viewed the *exemplum* as a powerful rhetorical device for producing belief in the general public about matters which do not avail themselves to absolute logical certainty. Only enthymeme vied with *exemplum* in its effective conversion of the audience to the acceptance of a general truth. An equally important understanding of *exemplum* was its close association with the word *eikon*, a pictorial form of representation, where certain details in an artistic medium (such as inlaid images in a tiled floor) foreground the argument of the scenic design.[19] Thus, the fact that Chaucer scholars have responded to the Nun's Priest's opening scene as either an iconic representation or a tropological injunction is one indication that the widow's portrait is positioned squarely within the European *exemplum* tradition.

A second indication that we are dealing with an *exemplum* in the opening scene of the *Nun's Priest's Tale* is through negative evidence: this passage has not been the site of very much critical controversy. In the Middle Ages and in the Renaissance, *exemplum* was regularly associated with and sometimes even equated with narration itself (one medieval gloss unifies

---

[15] John Block Friedman, "The *Nun's Priest's Tale*: The Preacher and the Mermaid's Song," *ChauR* 7 (1973): 250–66.

[16] William Strange, "The *Monk's Tale*: A Generous View," *ChauR* 1 (1967): 167–70.

[17] "Some Disputed Chaucerian Terminology," p. 580.

[18] Trevor Whittock, *A Reading of the Canterbury Tales* (Cambridge: Cambridge University Press, 1968), p. 230.

[19] John Lyons reviews the literature pertaining to this Greek model in *Exemplum: The Rhetoric of Example in Early Modern France and Italy* (Princeton: Princeton University Press, 1989), esp. pp. 6, 10, 246 n. 24. Scanlon reviews the Greek and Roman ways of understanding the *exemplum* genre in *Narrative, Authority, Power*, pp. 32–34.

the two activities as *exemplare narrare*).[20] And this association has of course continued into the late twentieth century, so that we often find it difficult to distinguish between an all-purpose narrative (such as the novel) and a narrative with the particular function of serving as a concrete instance of a general truth (a literary form which some critics choose to call the apologue).[21] John Lyons explains that one reason *exemplum* has rarely been an object of extended literary criticism is that, despite its seeming innocence, it is in fact a subtle threat to literary criticism itself: as a narrative with a self-inscribed explicating function, *exemplum* appears to have already used the tools and done the work of literary analysis itself. In *exempla,* the narrative's meaning is theoretically self-evident: all is apparently already made known. Standing half-way between metaphor (which purports to hide its meaning) and fable (which is "sufficiently obscure to awaken the decrypting of literary analysis"), *exempla* advertise themselves as "common property about which we can have few suspicions."[22] And so, a second indication that we are here dealing with a carefully modelled *exemplum* is, paradoxically, the fact that the widow's portrait has inspired little in the way of critical controversy.

A third indication that the Nun's Priest's *exemplum* is centrally located within the *exemplum* tradition is also the first of many clear signs that Chaucer is actually providing a critique of the dangerous effects of that tradition upon its unwary readers. This generic self-consciousness is realized in the landscape itself. A depiction of a habitation in a dale beside a grove of trees, Chaucer's type-scene is a remarkably graphic literalization of the word *exemplum*, which in medieval Latin means "a clearing in the woods." According to John Lyons, the term's radical etymology helps illustrate *exemplum*'s relationship to the other forms of discourse which surround it:

> Only the clearing gives form or boundary to the woods. Only the woods permit the existence of the clearing. Likewise, example depends on the larger mass of history and experience, yet without the "clearings" provided by example that mass would be formless and difficult to integrate into any controlling systematic discourse.[23]

---

[20] Lyons, *Exemplum*, p. 11.

[21] Sheldon Sacks, for example, in *A Study of Henry Fielding, With Glances at Swift, Johnson, and Richardson* (Berkeley: University of California Press, 1964), contrasts the apologue to the novel, or what he calls "represented action." "The informing principle" of apologues, Sacks writes, "is that each is organized as a fictional example of the truth of a formulable statement or closely related set of such statements" (p. 8). In novels, by contrast, "characters about whose fate we are made to care are introduced in unstable relationships which are then further complicated until the complications are finally resolved by the complete removal of the represented instability" (p. 26).

[22] Lyons, *Exemplum*, p. 2.

[23] Lyons, *Exemplum*, p. 3.

Lyons quite naturally assumes, in contrast to the woods, that a clearing is an orderly scene controlled by an enlightened principle of literary husbandry. However, as we are about to see, despite its attempts at domesticating decorum, the Nun's Priest's exemplary clearing is at least as unkempt as the forests which surround it.

Having just proposed a three-fold defense of the widow's portrait as a quintessential *exemplum* (it is a rhetorical, iconic, and critically uncontroversial "clearing in the woods"), for the remainder of this essay I wish to argue that an exemplary *exemplum* is precisely what it is not. Rather, it is a parody – a pseudo-quasi-mock-*exemplum* – designed to test our own reading of the *exemplum* genre while also testing our ways of reading other kinds of narrative literature. It is not a parody of the *exemplum* itself; rather, it is primarily a parody of the generic expectations of a readerly sensibility too intent on finding unitary truth in any piece of literature it reads. To see how these parodic strategies work, we need to consider a contrasting Chaucerian passage which is impressively faithful to the requisites of the *exemplum* genre. This passage is the beginning of *secunda pars* of the *Clerk's Tale*:

> Noght fer fro thilke paleys honurable,
> Wher as this markys shoop his mariage,
> There stood a throop, of site delitable,
> In which that povre folk of that village
> Hadden hir beestes and hir herbergage,
> And of hire labour tooke hir sustenance,
> After that the erthe yaf hem habundance.
>
> Amonges thise povre folk ther dwelte a man
> Which that was holden povrest of hem alle;
> But hye God somtyme senden kan
> His grace into a litel oxes stalle;
> Janicula men of that throop hym calle.
> A doghter hadde he, fair ynogh to sighte,
> And Griseldis this yonge mayden highte.
>
> But for to speke of vertuous beautee,
> Thanne was she oon the faireste under sonne;
> For povreliche yfostered up was she,
> No likerous lust was thurgh hire herte yronne.
> Wel ofter of the welle than of the tonne
> She drank, and for she wolde vertu plese,
> She knew wel labour but noon ydel ese.
>
> But though this mayde tendre were of age,
> Yet in the brest of hir virginitee
> Ther was enclosed rype and sad corage;
> And in greet reverence and charitee

Hir olde povre fader fostered shee.
A fewe sheep, spynnynge, on feeld she kepte;
She wolde noght been ydel til she slepte.[24]   (IV. 197–224)

This portrait is a masterpiece in the literary tradition of the medieval Christian *exemplum*. Here, the poverty of the humble town is nonjudgmentally counterpointed against the "honurable" but nearby palace of the marquis. Although Griselde's father Janicula is the poorest man in the village, his poverty is spiritually honorable, for, as the narrator reminds us, Christ's Incarnation occurred in a humble ox's stall. Griselde, although only moderately fair to physical sight, embraces all the beautiful inner virtues of a secular saint: virginity, love of her father, charity towards others, constant busyness, and a mature and steadfast heart. We are given just enough details to see that her virtues are consonant with the world she lives in: her "throop" is humble, yet of "site delitable"; the townspeople gain sustenance from their domestic animals (Griselde's "fewe sheep" are the only kind specified) and from their honest labor in the fields, but only to the degree that the earth is provident. Griselda's moral behavior is exemplary ("no likerous lust"); that she drinks more often of the well than of the tun (an instance of carefully controlled Christian *litotes*) offers another image of the pellucidity of her soul. Written in the plain style of low mimetic Christian pastoral, this carefully designed *sermo humilis* portrait succeeds in no small part because the camera of narrative description is held consistently at a middle distance between the universal and the particular. As in the portrait of the idealized Plowman in the "General Prologue," we are given just enough specificity to concretize the portrait's reigning spiritual and moral virtues.

What makes this passage a successful *exemplum* is not only its integration of carefully selected particulars inside a controlling sentential discourse, but the certainty embodied in the passage itself concerning the absolute rightness of this integration. In his study of the strategies of the *exemplum* genre, Bruno Gélas calls this integration an agreed-upon *theory of manifestation*:

> [W]hat the *exemplum* implies (that which it introduces) is not only or not primarily a rule, but the belief that the *exemplum*'s relationship to the rule is exactly the relationship which joins anecdotal manifestation to a transcendent truth. In this sense, no exemplarisation is possible except on the grounds of an agreement on a *theory of manifestation* which is also the theory of a reading practice.[25]

---

[24] *The Riverside Chaucer*, p. 140.
[25] Bruno Gélas, "La Fiction manipulatrice," in *L'Argumentation, linguistique et sémiologie* (Lyons: Presses universitaires de Lyon, 1981). Translated by Lyons, *Exemplum*, p. 21.

As we turn to the Nun's Priest's *exemplum*, what we find is that its theory of manifestation almost immediately calls itself into question. While controlling the relationship of anecdote to transcendent truth, this theory of manifestation, as Gélas argues, is also a theory of reading practice. Thus the *exemplum*'s rules of proper reading are also almost immediately challenged. It is necessary to recognize from the beginning that the only way of successfully tracing out both the parodied and the parodistic theory of manifestation is to read the passage with unusual care. This means we must give slow-motion attention to the smallest details in the text itself and to the roundabouts and cul-de-sacs these details generate in the reader's decoding process. A few critics have allowed that one or two phrases in the portrait of the widow's life are there for the purpose of "humorous exaggeration."[26] But I find the entire *exemplum*, including its opening lines of dutiful sobriety, a witty sendup of the art of right reading and right writing. As the widow's portrait unfolds, its edges fray, its generic outlines start shifting, metathesizing, and regrouping. Wrong ideas are allowed to come into the reader's head, various rules of interpretation sashay forth and disappear, so that the whole *exemplum* eventually plays sly havoc with the way a literary narrative is expected to settle into some form of stable significance. Whether or not all these instabilities are themselves controlled by an alternative "theory of manifestation" will be considered in due time.

Here, then, for a second time, is the way the *Nun's Priest's Tale* begins:

> A povre wydwe, somdeel stape in age,
> Was whilom dwellyng in a narwe cotage,
> Biside a grove, stondynge in a dale.
> This wydwe, of which I telle yow my tale,
> Syn thilke day that she was last a wyf
> In pacience ladde a ful symple lyf,
> For litel was her catel and hir rente.

The descriptive format with which the Nun's Priest opens his beast fable corresponds in a number of ways to the chaste, Biblical, and plain style of the *Clerk's Tale*. Various virtues of the common Christian life not only appear actualized in the tale's protagonist, but some are specifically named – poverty ("povre"), "patience" and (a bit later) "housbondrie." "[W]hilom," that most reliable of narrative opening *formulae*, immediately places the tale in an undefined literary past, an *in illo tempore* which can also be equivalent to an absolute, or "timeless," present. Spatially, the rural simplicity of cottage, grove and dale suggests, as in the *Clerk's Tale*, the salt-of-the-earth semiotics of the Christian pastoral. Not only are the details of the humble scene described in this first sentence fittingly spare, they

---

[26] See Pearsall's notes, p. 143.

appear to be controlled by a subtle yet shifting pattern of physical attitude and situation: first by angle (the widow is somewhat bent over); then by size (the cottage is "narwe"); then by contiguity (the cottage is "biside" a grove); and then by centrality of place (it is "stondynge" in a dale). These and subsequent details accord neatly, perhaps too neatly, with Aristotle's ten categories (substance, quantity, quality, relation, place, time, position, state, action, affection).[27] And they certainly appear to be arranging themselves into a stable pattern of interpretable significance even though no external norm, such as the Marquis' palace in the *Clerk's Tale*, stands as a determiner of contrastive meaning.

Moving to the second sentence, then, we are told of the widow's life of patient simplicity – a restrained life initiated on the day of her husband's death: "Syn thilke day she was last a wyf." Here, perhaps, in the narrator's intimations of the widow's former life, is the determiner of contrastive meaning we need. But are we really meant to imagine in any detail the widow's pre-widowed existence as a life of various and pointed pleasure? (The Clerk, we recall, provided his readers little opportunity to imagine an alternative Griselda – given, say, to self-indulgent mood-swings.) Having implied that the cause of the widow's present stalwart existence was her former husband's death, the Nun's Priest then explains that this "ful simple" life is also (or perhaps *rather*) the result of pressing economic circumstance: "For litel was her catel and hir rente." Although the widow's crimped vocation does not yet resonate with the Christian virtues of stoic labor and heroic poverty, like Griselda she shares her life communally with her fellow creatures:

> By housbondrie of swich as God hire sente
> She foond hirself and eek hir doghtren two.
> Thre large sowes hadde she, and namo,
> Three keen, and eek a sheep that highte Malle.

Her daughters, her only living flesh and blood, might be expected to figure as important supporting characters in the manner of Janicula, Griselda's exemplary father. Thus it comes as a bit of a surprise that the narrator chooses not to gather us around the hearth to share with these three women their bond of familial *caritas* and Christian devotion. Instead, we move hastily past the undescribed and unnamed "doghtren two" (never to be seen again) and emerge into the barnyard to meet the livestock, whom we then count with census-taking precision. These animals (all of them female) immediately gain more importance than the widow's daughters, as we measure the size of the pigs (large) and learn that the sheep's name is Malle – a plebian name (Molly), Beryl Rowland informs us, but not unusual

---

[27] *The Basic Works of Aristotle*, ed. Richard McKeon (New York: Random House, 1941), p. 8.

for a fourteenth-century English domestic animal.[28] Naming names in literature is of course an important gesture, so we might wonder why the widow ("of which I telle yow my tale") has not been accorded the honor of even a familiar first name. But perhaps this is all part of a sustained modesty trope, reinforcing the edifying *topoi* of simplicity, poverty, piety, and virtue which are waiting to be figured forth through the details of this homely scene. Despite the narrator's assurances that he has accounted for the widow's meagre livestock ("and namo"), the neatfold appears modestly sufficient rather than shockingly meagre. Indeed, the widow's life seems so far to be an unexceptional representation of lower-class English subsistance farming. So it is hardly surprising that some scholars have chosen to disagree with the Nun's Priest's own assessment of the economic standing of his tale's protagonist, preferring to judge the widow's standard of living as not "povre," but somewhat "adequate."[29] If this is the case, then poverty – with its potential attendant Christian virtues – does not yet appear to be an ideal exemplified within the Nun's Priest's *exemplum*. Indeed, to this point, the prevailing virtues of the widow's unscintillating and joyless existence remain impressively underdefined.

So we now begin to retrace our steps, returning from the barnyard to the cottage interior, glimpsing along the way a sooty hall and bower (the scene's most anti-aesthetic detail so far, although "halle" and "bour" are socially upper-class designations), to find ourselves focusing intently on the widow's food:

> Ful sooty was hire bour and eek hir halle,
> In which she eet ful many a sklendre meel.
> Of poynaunt sauce hir neded never a deel.
> No deyntee morsel passed thurgh hir throte;
> Hir diete was accordant to hir cote.

Employing a variant of the rhetorical trope Derek Pearsall calls "idealisation by negatives,"[30] the narrator describes the rich foodstuffs – the "poynaunt sauce" and the "deyntee morsel" – which the widow did not eat. What we next learn, again to our slight disappointment, is that one reason the widow's diet is simple and her meals slender is they were "accordant to hir cote" – in accordance, that is, with what her small farm could provide. Any hope that the widow's simple diet was a voluntary act of corporeal mortification and spiritual self-actualization is further undone by the narrator's assertion that these rich foods "hir neded never a

---

[28] Beryl Rowland, "A Sheep That Highte Malle," *ELN* 6 (1968): 84–87.
[29] Pearsall's extensive note on the economic status of the widow is extremely informative: Pearsall, pp. 139–40.
[30] Pearsall, p. 145.

deel" – which could mean that rich foods did not appeal to her, or in the narrator's opinion she did not deserve them.

We have moved even further from the spiritual ideals with which it could have been presumed the opening *exemplum* of the *Nun's Priest's Tale* was initially concerned. It should perhaps be noted that we have not seen the widow offering her daily prayers; nor have we seen her nurturing her daughters with maternal affection; nor have we seen her communing with her animals in a state of Fransciscan grace. Even a thin-broth version of such exemplary behavior would now seem inappropriate, for the widow's anemic spirituality has become almost antithetical to the virtues of Griselda's heroic life. What then, precisely, are the defining features of the widow's existence? Having readjusted our normative sights from matters spiritual to matters moral, we find ourselves readjusting them further from matters moral to matters physical. The primary virtue of the widow's life turns out to be her excellent physical health:

> Repleccioun ne made hire nevere sik;
> Attempre diete was al hir phisik,
> And exercise, and hertes suffisaunce.

Rather like her modern-day aerobic and calory-counting counterpart, the widow exercises, she eats right, and she enjoys her "hertes suffisaunce." This is a far cry from the norms of the Christian apologue where emblems of virtuous poverty, humble labor, stoic patience, and neighborly love grant generic steadiness to our literary vision. In place of Griselda's "rype and sad courage," we find ourselves celebrating three different kinds of physical "good." The first is the widow's moderate, well-balanced, and "[a]ttempre" diet (her meals are no longer "sklendre"). The second is her physical fitness (does Chaucer anywhere else celebrate a character's dedication to the therapeutic values of physical exercise?). The third element in the widow's healthy life-style is her "hertes suffisaunce," a phrase somewhat disturbing in its connotations. The semantic field of the one word "suffisaunce" stretches in Chaucer's poetry all the way from a generalized "good life" to the elevations of *fin amour* and the lineaments of gratified desire: "Welcome," sighs Criseyde as she draws Troilus into her arms, "my knyght, my pees, my suffisaunce!"[31] But since the two-word collocation "hertes suffisaunce" unambiguously resides inside the hot-house euphemisms of courtly love, the romantic parameters of the widow's well-being are something the circumspect reader will best avoid imagining. Let us therefore choose to understand the widow's physical activity as providing her tidy body with a high index of nonerotic cardiovascular fitness.

The widow's portrait concludes:

[31] *The Riverside Chaucer*, p. 531 (*Troilus and Criseyde*, III, 1309).

> The goute lette hire nothyng for to daunce,
> N'apoplexie shente nat hir heed.
> No wyn ne drank she, neither whit ne reed;
> Hir bord was served moost with whit and black –
> Milk and broun breed, in which she foond no lak,
> Seynd bacoun, and somtyme an ey or tweye,
> For she was, as it were, a maner deye.

Having assured us that overeating ("Reppleccioun") never made her sick, the narrator insists that the gout never prevented her from dancing nor has apoplexy succeeded in messing up her head. Preferring not to imagine an apoplectic widow swollen with gout, we replace this graphic misprision with a decorous alternative vision – that of a dancing widow with her brains intact. This merry widow *in compis mentis*, we sense, is also an errant configuration which needs to be set aside, but for what? Fortunately, the widow's meal is finally served.

If the controlling rhetorical strategy in this part of the widow's description, as Derek Pearsall insists, has been "idealisation by negatives," then negation has failed brilliantly to idealize. Rather, negation has succeeded in doing what Freud noted it is in the habit of doing: giving existence to that which is said not to exist, making present that which is putatively absent. Perhaps for this reason, when the widow's meal belatedly appears, it is a bit of a surprise. And indeed it proves to be a further surprise since, for all its apparent simplicity, it is not all that simple to understand. Thanks to the narrator's obsession with unwonted explications, the widow's diet seems to require a hermeneutic key in order to uncover its meaning. In fact, there seem to be at least two keys – the first regulated by color symbolism, the second by some principle of numerology. The widow drinks no wine, we are told, neither white nor red; rather, her board is served pretty much ("most") with white and black: e.g., milk and brown bread. Milk is white, we know, and brown bread, if not exactly black, is nevertheless closer to the end of the color spectrum opposite white than most other colors of bread. But so what? Weirdly, these propositions in color opposites recall those numerous medieval exercises in Aristotelian logic where the premise term is white (*homo est albus*), the subpremise term is black (*sortes est negrus*), and then some kind of syllogism or enthymeme is posited and extensively analyzed. But whatever syllogistic or sophistical problem subsists in the widow's nearly colorless diet would appear insoluble. (Are we faced with the pre-eminent problem of classical logic, the Law of the Excluded Middle? Should we ask whether brown, subsisting somewhere between white and black, is a *tertium quid*?) If we still are trying to decipher this meal according to some yet-to-be-explicated color code, perhaps it matters whether the color of "Seynd" bacon is brown or black (some editors suggest "Seynd" means smoked), and whether that single egg and its occasional mate are white, speckled, or brown.

Surely it is time to abandon color altogether as a code of potentially ennabling hermeneutic power. In place of color, what may just as likely serve as a ruling interpretive principle is number. Enumerating has obviously been a prominent activity throughout the portrait: we have been told the number of the widow's daughters, the number of pigs, the number of cows, the number of sheep, and the number of eggs. As the philosopher Paul Kuntz remarks in *The Concept of Order*, numbers in various patterns designate various principles of order: the principle of order of 1, 2, 3, 4, for example, is magnitude; the principle of order of 4, 3, 2, 1 is its opposite (Kuntz suggests "minitude"); the principle of order of 1, 2, 3, 3, 2, 1 is symmetry, and so on.[32] In the widow's world, we have the following number sequence: 1 (the widow), 2 (her daughters), 3 (the pigs), 3 (the cows), 1 (the sheep) and 1 or 2 (the eggs). An order of magnitude (1, 2, 3) thus gives way to a conjectured order of symmetry (1, 2, 3, 3, 2, 1), an expectation which is undone by skipping over 2 on the way back to 1, creating a disorder which is further confounded by the option of 1 egg or 2. (Need we count that piece of bacon, or is it merely a part of a whole? And does it matter that some of the creatures we are counting are human and the rest are animal, or that most are alive but the eggs are alive only *in potentia* and the bacon is dead?) The only scholars to find a pattern of significance in any of these numbers have been Levy and Adams. For them, the barnyard paradise is ruled over by three "threes" – the widow and her two daughters (3), the sows (3), and the cows (3). These three threes are not only numerically identical but also numerologically significant: that is, all symbolize the Trinity. Although the sheep is a ewe named Molly, Levy and Adams are determined to understand her to be a ram, and this ram in turn symbolizes Christ.[33] Counting and allegorizing the eggs is something Levy and Adams do not feel called upon to do.

Since numbers, like colors, lead in the direction of exegetical absurdity, what's left? One of the most obvious patterns throughout the portrait has been gender, for all living things considered in this scene (except possibly the eggs) are female – widow, daughters, sows, cows, and ewe. In a tale whose very title celebrates female preeminence, surely it is necessary to ask of its narrator-exegete what this absolute feminization of the *exemplum*'s community means. But, oddly, the narrator seems willfully to have "not seen" this all-female pattern, all the while attempting to impose rather abstract and ill-fitting patterns, like color and number, upon his original

---

[32] Paul Kuntz, ed., *The Concept of Order* (Seattle: University of Washington Press, 1968), p. xxiii.
[33] Bernard S. Levy and George R. Adams, "Chauntecleer's Paradise Lost and Regained," *MS* 29 (1967): 178–92.

material. In other words, the *exemplum*'s celibate female aesthetic seems to be awaiting some kind of masculine imaginary that the Tale has yet to supply. In due time, the widow's prosaic world will stand in stark contrast to the variegated riches of Chauntecleer's life of high adventure. As in the movie "The Wizard of Oz," we begin in a black-and-white, Puritan landscape and then wake up suddenly, as in a dream vision, inside a phantasmagoric kingdom of technicolor wonder. But how a poetics or politics of gender is instantiated in this shift in artistic register is a question that the Tale's opening *exemplum* seems not to have included in any obvious way within its implicit hermeneutic system.

One final principle of narratorial control in the Nun's Priest's opening *exemplum* is causation. Early in the portrait the narrator had felt free to provide several unnecessary explanations of why things in the widow's life are as they now are. Should we therefore at the end of the portrait descry some continuing principle of causality connecting, say, the slab of bacon, the widow, and those three fat pigs? Should we now infer some principal producer of those eggs which for some reason has been left outside the frame of this framing fiction? If causation has been a dominant principle of interpretation in this opening scene, why then does the portrait end with such a flat-out parody of causal explanations? That is, the last line, introduced by a typically oblique Chaucerian conjunction ("For"), explains that the real reason the widow's diet is made up of milk, bread, bacon, and eggs, is: "For she was, as it were, a maner deye" (For she was, if you will, some kind of dairy-maid). The syntax of this line, as Pearsall notes, is "characteristically elusive"; furthermore, "a maner deye" may possibly mean a desmesne servant, it may suggest she was not quite a "proper dairymaid," or it may be "a merely conventional construction."[34] But do we really care? Hasn't all the evidence for her mode of living been adequately presented in the preceding portrait itself, thus leaving this throwaway causal explication nothing but a mildly irritating and slightly unnecessary anticlimax?

The unsatisfactoriness of the final line is entirely appropriate, for throughout the portrait of the widow the reader has time and again been teased into a misleading sense of interpretive control. It is this presumption of interpretive control, or what Gélas calls "a theory of manifestation ruling the connection between particulars and universals," that is being parodied throughout the Nun's Priest's mock-*exemplum*. In *Authoritarian Fictions: The Ideological Novel As A Literary Genre*, Susan Suleiman argues that all exemplary, or ideological, fiction is determined by a specific end which exists "before" or "after" the story:

---

[34] Pearsall, p. 146.

The story calls for an unambiguous interpretation, which in turn implies a rule of action applicable (at least virtually) to the real life of the reader. The interpretation and the rule of action may be stated explicitly by a narrator who "speaks with the voice of Truth" and can therefore lay claim to absolute authority, or they may be supplied, on the basis of textual and contextual indices, by the reader. The only necessary condition is that the interpretation and the rule of action be unambiguous – in other words, that the story lend itself as little as possible to a "plural" reading.[35]

The opening *exemplum* of the *Nun's Priest's Tale*, although it pretends to be an authoritarian fiction, lends itself to an embarrassing plurality of readings. Profoundly multifarious are both the Truth the *exemplum* purports to exemplify and the "rule of action" it expects its readers to apply to real life. In fact, Chaucer's *exemplum* egregiously commits the three crimes which Suleiman claims are most subversive to the teleology of any ideological narrative. These crimes are: (1) the multiplication of superfluous and distracting details; (2) "Saying Too Much" – that is, reifying a moral idea to such a degree that a negative character becomes attractive or an exemplary one becomes unattractive; and (3) "Not Saying Enough," by which Suleiman means a fiction's relativizing of all truths, even those it is explicitly committed to upholding.[36] The Nun's Priest's *exemplum* is thus a fine illustration of what not to do when writing in the *exemplum* format. It is chock-full of excrescent particulars, narratorial tangents, and unasked-for editorial asides (Crime One). It so particularizes, contextualizes, and narrativizes it exemplary character, the widow, that she and her life-style become increasingly less attractive (Crime Two). And, finally, the portrait, after an initial attempt to foreground its controlling truths and virtues, succeeds only in submerging them in a welter of compromising alternative discourses, such as logic, food consumption, color, number, gender, and causation (Crime Three).

Despite its many crimes against the *exemplum* genre, and in fact precisely because of these many crimes, there is, I believe, in the experience of reading the Nun's Priest's exordium a developing sense of overall aesthetic control and purpose. Is it therefore possible or desirable to construct a non-unitary hermeneutics out of the many "theories of manifestation" at odds with each other in Chaucer's representation of the widow's life? In the remainder of this essay I want to begin, but by no means conclude, the construction of such a hermeneutics. Although no single rule of interpretation will emerge, I hope such an undertaking will begin to point toward a deeper appreciation of the craft of reading Chaucer and a deeper understanding of the craft of

---

[35] Susan Suleiman, *Authoritarian Fictions: The Ideological Novel as a Literary Genre* (New York: Columbia University Press, 1983), p. 54.
[36] Suleiman, *Authoritarian Fictions*, pp. 199–238.

reading any kind of narrative fiction. I will begin this exercise by taking my impressionistic line-by-line responses to Chaucer's *exemplum* detailed in the foregoing pages and compressing them into seven, very "minimalist," categories. These categories are as follows: (1) the representative attitude of physical space and bodily position; (2) the possible relationship of marriage and widowhood to *sentence* and *solaas*; (3) the significance of various foodstuffs and their (non-) consumption; (4) the logic of colors in fiction; (5) number sequences and the order of meaning; (6) female creatures, celibacy, and the generation of narrative; (7) causation as a principle of narrative design. Crude as they are, each of these categories is obviously freighted with a great deal of ideological and methodological baggage. While each holds promise as a viable foundation for an over-arching interpretive paradigm, each has already displaced other readings, and each promises eventually to be at odds with its paradigmatic peers.

My primary point is not to argue the greater rightness of any one of these positions, but rather to claim the potential viability of all of them. And no matter how many interpretive foundations one constructs here, the next question is the same: is there a next step? Is it possible, that is, to ascend from these low-level categorical particulars in the direction of higher-level generalities, and then to universals? In testing out the possibility of such an ascent, I will continue to tilt my scheme in the direction of Chaucer's metapoetical concerns. (1) Like the opening scene's iconic representation of *exemplum* as a clearing in the woods, the widow's being "somdel stepe in age" suggests itself as an emblem of the moralized narrative's antique age and modest vigor. (2) Marriage, as borne out in Chaucer's Marriage Group, is not only a Christian sacrament but a metonomy for the poet's dream of the ideal union of Mercury (wisdom) and Philology (language), a dream scarcely realized in this opening piece of celibate verse. (3) The consumption of food, in beast fables as well as in other literature, is a traditional metaphor for the interpretation of fiction, be it salvific or toxic, bland or spicy. (4) The critical exfoliation of colors, from *The Prologue to the Legend of Good Women* on, is one of Chaucer's pre-eminent ways of examining the basic unit of his craft, the "colours" of metaphor. (5) A major element in the design of the *Nun's Priest's Tale*, I have argued elsewhere, is the deployment of the seven liberal arts – the last four of which, the quadrivium, are mathematical arts measuring and numbering the order of all things in the universe as well as leading, in various curricular epics, to an illuminated vision of *novus homo*, or the New Reader.[37] (6) The tension in this *exemplum* between enclosures and openings, the female and her restraint, may be illustrative of what Patricia Parker has called the male narrator's failed attempts at "mastering or controlling the implicitly female,

---

[37] Peter W. Travis, "The *Nun's Priest's Tale* as Grammar-School Primer," *Studies in the Age of Chaucer: Proceedings* 1, 81–91.

and perhaps hence wayward body of the text itself."[38] Finally, (7) the narrator's awkward attempts to rationalize the wayward body of his text by supplying gratuitous cause-and-effect explications may highlight the often irresolvable tensions that subsist between the two activities of fiction-making, *exemplare et narrare*.

In beginning to amplify these seven readings, it may appear that I am beginning to move in the direction of harmonizing all the *exemplum*'s disparate parts. But in this attempt to ascend from the Many toward the One, it may also seem that I am moving in the direction of even more overt interpretive bullying. Part of us would like to believe that everything in criticism that rises must eventually converge; part of us suspects that all things that transcend the particular are forms of ideological co-optation. The epistemological debates between the nominalists and realists are thus philosophical analogues to our own disputes concerning the generic rules versus the particular instances of any literary work. In recognition of the complexity of this debate, I do not intend to undertake the extension of these seven interpretive realms into one, extremely complex, ideological synthesis.[39] Even if such a synthesis is possible,[40] the focus of this essay has from the outset been upon narrative beginnings and interpretive middles rather than ideological ends, upon, that is, the foundation of Chaucer's fictive practice and the reader-response methods we employ as we construct a series of conflicted meanings out of one exemplary narrative. This focus brings us back to the problem with which the essay began, the issue of how properly to begin a fictional narrative.

To define a narrative beginning is an extraordinary act of self-assertion. "One rarely searches for beginnings unless the present matters a great deal,"

---

[38] Patricia Parker, *Literary Fat Ladies: Rhetoric, Gender, and Property* (New York: Methuen, 1987), p. 11.

[39] One of the best studies of how authoritative discourse may contend with other discourses in the same literary text remains M. M. Bakhtin's *The Dialogic Imagination*, ed. Michael Holquist, trans. Caryl Emerson and Michael Holquist (Austin: University of Texas Press, 1981). Authoritative discourse, according to Bakhtin, is a monologic and "privileged language that approaches us from without; it is distanced, taboo, and permits no play within its framing context"; dialogism, on the other hand, is a consciousness of linguistic diversity which freely mixes "different semantic and axiological conceptual systems" by transgressing historical and social speech boundaries in order to celebrate "the living heteroglossia of language" (pp. 424, 306, 326 resp.). What is extraordinary about the Nun's Priest's exemplum is not only its heady admixture of axiological conceptual systems but the dialogical interplay of several semantic systems at once, such as the fetched-from-afar "halle and bour" and "hertes suffisaunce."

[40] The coercion involved in the pursuit of an absolute Rule even in the reading of authoritarian fictions is evident earlier in this essay, where I insisted that nothing could possibly divert one from the desired reading of Griselda's virtues: yet "No likerous lust" and "Wel ofter of the welle than of the tonne" cannot but conjure up, if only momentarily, a subversive counter-reading.

179

notes Edward Said in *Beginnings*; "It is my present urgency, the here and now, that will enable me to establish the sequence of beginning-middle-end and to transform it from a distant object – located "there" – into the subject of my reasoning."[41] In defining the beginning of his remarkable *ars poetica*, Chaucer is giving expression to an ever-present urgency in his poetic career. Put very simply, the subject of his focus, and the beginning point of his poetic art, is the reader him/herself. In this light we need to be reminded that the vast majority of his readers have readily accepted the Nun's Priest's opening *exemplum* as "the moral ground of the poem." If I have succeeded in proving that the Nun's Priest's portrait of the widow cannot serve as the moral ground of the poem, I hope I have also suggested how, as a seriocomic parody of our reception of "moral" literature, Chaucer's mock-*exemplum* mimicks the unsuccessful collusions between narrator and reader as they attempt to impose a stable significance upon the *materia* of any recalcitrant "original" text. In this parodic mimicry lies the beginning, the foundation, of a more successful collaboration between author and reader, which in turn means a more achieved theory of practice in the negotation between narrative event and its exemplary significance. While not in any obvious way the moral ground of Chaucer's *ars poetica*, the opening *exemplum* can now be understood as the originary, *in principio* principle from which the *argument* of Chaucer's craft proceeds.

In *Narrative, Authority , and Power*, Scanlon traces the power relations being fought out between two medieval *exemplum* traditions in the fourteenth century: the first is the sermon tradition, which represents the "Church's broad-based attempts to increase its institutional control of secular life"; the second is the classical and "public" *exemplum*, through which the Chaucerian tradition of poetry attempted to "establish its own authority."[42] Some of the tension between these two power bases may indeed resonate in the Nun's Priest's *exemplum*, but it is scarcely self-evident which tradition it is, the sacred or the secular, to which Chaucer is pledging his own aesthetic allegiance. If anything, Chaucer is declaring himself a poet who honors at least two aesthetic traditions at once, the Christian-humanist arts of poetry as championed by Geoffrey of Vinsauf, and the classic arts of poetry as championed by Horace. But more to the point, Chaucer is intent on writing an *exemplum* which both cites and supercedes past narrative forms, both sacred and secular, while defining itself in turn as its own distinctive point of origin. Most of all, Chaucer wants to be at the beginning of his own poetry, to make his own clearing in the woods, to compose his own master-narrative *ab ovo*. Since the middle of this essay has concentrated on Chaucer's supersession of the *exemplum* tradition, I will end with Chaucer's unique resolution of the *in medias res*/*ab*

---

[41] Edward Said, *Beginnings: Intention and Method* (New York: Basic Books, 1976), p. 42.
[42] *Narrative, Authority, and Power*, p. 137.

180

ovo debate among the humanist aestheticians. To illustrate this happy resolution, the famous lines from Horace need to be recalled in full:

> Nec reditum Diomedis ab intertu Meleagri,
> nec *gemino* bellum Troianum orditur *ab ovo*:
> semper ad eventum festinat et *in medias res*
> non secus ac notas auditorem rapit . . .

> [He (the poet) does not start the return of Diomedes from the death of Meleager nor the Trojan war from *the twin egg*: always he hurries to the outcome and rushes his hearer *into the midst of a subject* with which he is already familiar . . .][43]

Like Sterne in *Tristram Shandy*, Chaucer impishly disobeys Horace's classical prescriptive advice. Tristram, telling of his biological conception by his parents at the beginning of his life story, praises his own narrative genius: "Right glad I am, that I have begun the history of myself in the way I have done; and that I am able to go on tracing every thing in it, as *Horace* says, *ab Ovo*."[44] Chaucer, unlike Tristram, does not advertise his narrative skills nor does he name his classical authority. But he nevertheless manages to round off his opening *exemplum* in a quite eggy fashion. Whereas Horace had seen the epic of Trojan history as beginning *ab gemino ovo,* from a unique twin egg produced by the violent union of a mortal woman and a bird-god, Chaucer starts off his avian beast fable with a casual allusion to "somtyme an ey or tweye." This momentary authorial aside – in its insouciant underscoring of unity and doubleness, certainty and vagueness, creation and consumption – is a subtle narratological gesture. A pseudo-classical ovoid overture, it would seem to fit perfectly inside the beginning of a mock-epic fable which is about to recount one event in the short life of a hero who is little more, yet nothing less, than a somewhat tragic medieval chicken. And if any uncertainty remains about this as an appropriate beginning to a chicken's life (and some uncertainty surely should remain) then we are left contemplating one more issue of exemplary origins: in the best of all fictional worlds, which should ideally come first, the chicken or the egg?

---

[43] Horace, *Satires, Epistles, and Ars Poetica*, trans. H. Ruston Fairclough (Cambridge: Cambridge University Press, 1961), pp. 56, 181.
[44] Lawrence Sterne, *The Life and Opinions of Tristram Shandy, Gentleman* (New York: Oxford University Press, 1983), p. 8.

A Postmodern Performance:
Counter-Reading Chaucer's *Clerk's Tale* and Maxine Hong Kingston's "No Name Woman"

William McClellan

In this essay I want to show how a postmodern counter-reading of Maxine Hong Kingston's "No Name Woman," the first chapter in her memoir, *The Woman Warrior*, and Chaucer's *Clerk's Tale* might proceed.[1] The disciplinary and personal reasons that impel me to perform such a reading have to do with the radically new situation we are facing in our advanced technological culture of mass communication. These new conditions make it imperative that we begin to re-think our relationship to our vocation and the texts we analyze. Counter-reading means to dialogize the "olde bokes" in the provenance of the contemporary; that is, read texts written earlier in the Western tradition in conjunction with present-day texts. Counter-reading also includes revealing our personal connections to the texts we interpret in our critical practice.[2] After I show how a such a reading might proceed, I will present my rationale for it.

The texts I have chosen to compare are quite susceptible to a traditional comparative reading. Both are stories that show how patriarchal cultures subjugate and silence women. In the *Clerk's Tale*, Walter subjects Griselda to complete social and psychological domination, repetitively testing her by removing their children from her. In "No Name Woman" Kingston's aunt is raped, rejected by her family, driven to suicide, and her existence erased. Both stories reveal how patriarchal culture operates to disguise male complicity in women's repression. In Chaucer's tale the Clerk takes issue with Petrarch's religious moral that erases gender, and in an extended aside he pointedly argues that clerks, the class that controls knowledge, choose not to tell of women's suffering and forbearance. In "No Name Woman,"

---

[1] References are to *The Riverside Chaucer*, 3rd ed., gen. ed. Larry D. Benson (Boston: Houghton Mifflin, 1987); Maxine Hong Kingston, *The Woman Warrior: Memoirs of a Girlhood Among Ghosts* (New York: Random House, 1976).

[2] The practice of reading the personal in disciplinary discourse has received much attention recently. See the October 1996 issue of *PMLA* (1146–1169).

Kingston specifically mentions her mother's injunction not to repeat the story because of her father's desire to erase her aunt's existence and her own feelings of guilt for colluding with her family's denial of her aunt. Both stories make visible the connection women have to the networks of power and knowledge through the institution of marriage, and the strategies that men devise to contain, ignore and marginalize them. Finally both connect issues of knowledge and power with the construction of subjectivity, showing how these are intimately tied up with the construction of sexual difference. So there are very substantial parallel issues in both texts that bear comparison. But in order to conduct a traditional comparative reading of these texts I would also have to ignore important differences. In provenance and genre these stories are significantly incommensurable.

The provenance of the two tales is radically different in culture and historical period, and the class, gender, ethnicity, and age of their authors. Chaucer's text comes from early in the English tradition, 600 years ago. He was a white male English author, whose father was a prominent and well-connected member of the London bourgeoisie and wine butler to the royal house. He was trained and had a career as a high-level civil servant and diplomat of the King in late fourteenth-century England. Maxine Hong Kingston is a Chinese-American woman author, a daughter of Chinese working-class immigrants, whose parents, a peasant farmer and country doctor in China, ran a laundry in mid/late-twentieth-century America. Kingston took on various jobs including clerical work and teaching to survive and to write. Today she makes her living as a writer. Kingston's text was written in the latter part of the twentieth century and speaks to the dilemmas incurred by a young girl growing up in a Chinese-American immigrant tradition.

In genre the two works are also very different. Chaucer's *Clerk's Tale* is an exempleum, situated in the *Canterbury Tales*, an anthology containing virtually all the genres in late medieval culture, whose controlling fiction is the performance of storytelling by a series of different narrators. Kingston's text, on the other hand, is the first in a sequence of autobiographical stories whose controlling aesthetic conflates real and imagined childhood experiences of the author. In terms of genre and provenance, the incommensurate differences of the two narratives clearly outweigh the similarities and compel a reading at a very abstract level. Consequently, an "objective" approach ultimately misses much of what these texts can teach us. Yet I think the multiple narrative voicing in the texts offers a way out of this dilemma and suggests a clue as to how they can be more concretely read and interpreted.

The multi-voiced, decentered narrations of these stories foreground the issue of the dialogic relationship the narrator has to the tale she or he is narrating and to the previous narrator of the tale as well. The narrative structuring also reveals the narrator's extrinsic relation to himself. It is what

Lacan called the intersubjective structure of the narration that allows us to negotiate what otherwise would remain a differend (and thus occluded). However, such a reading involves more than just moving through a series of displacements in an already given structural format. The key feature here is that in order to read the stories dialogically it is necessary for the interpreter to analyze and make known his own intersubjective relation to them and the previous narrator(s). Reading how my own personal story en-counters the stories is reading my story as a counter to the two texts; it is counter-reading them. It generates a provenance, a context for interpretation; one that is both peculiar to the way I connect with them and one that is also extrinsic to my self. My analysis of how I connect with these stories reveals my "unthought" – my unconscious desires, fears, thoughts – to me, as well as my reader. As Lacan has argued, we have an extrinsic and obscure relation to our subjectivity. Revealing my personal story, then, is necessary in the interpretation of the stories.

In provenance, my story is closer to Kingston's than Chaucer's. I am a working-class university-based intellectual. My mother, Irene, who is the daughter of Hungarian immigrants, trained and briefly practiced as a nurse. My father, William, was a railroad electrician with strong union ties. Now my father did not engage in infanticide, nor was he as brutal and absolutist as Kingston's father or Walter, who subjected Griselda to the most "merveillous" and harsh testing. My mother idolized my father (and still does) and never spoke ill of him, no matter what. My father's testing of her involved an extended period of seven years in which he traveled to New Jersey to work on the railroad, returning home to Pennsylvania on the weekends, which left my mother to raise four children and care for a dying mother fairly much on her own. It was a difficult and harrowing time for her, with my father threatening to dissolve the marriage at least once during that time.

It was the event of that threatened dissolution that informs my fascination with the two tales I am interpreting here. On a fine Saturday morning in the spring when I was about ten, my father called me into the living room and announced that he was going to divorce my mother. The reason he gave in an overwrought confession was that he could no longer endure the burden of such a large family. He was overwhelmed and discouraged. His announcement terrified me and left me in tears. Though I didn't know it at the time, it became a defining event in my life. My mother, who was present during his confession, afterwards told me that she would not stop him from going because she loved him so much. Although my family crisis of abandonment has structural differences from the *Clerk's Tale* – father's threatened abandonment rather than abandonment of children – the *Clerk's Tale* resonates closely enough with my own experience so that I empathize profoundly with the grief and resignation of Griselda's acquiescence in the face of Walter's outrageous demands. That text, in turn, helps me more fully to understand my mother's despair, which as a child I could not comprehend. My life experience gives me an emotional capacity to comprehend the horror of Griselda's suffering, and the text, in turn, provides me with an intellectual understanding for the unthought of my experience. In a similar way the suicide death of Kingston's aunt and her child amplifies for me the absolute dread of Griselda's and my mother's predicaments. These stories are exempla, highlighting the suffering patriarchal culture routinely forces women to endure.

This was not the only way the *Clerk's Tale* and "No Name Woman" intertwined with my personal history. Closely associated with the suffering of women is the injunction of silence. Just as Walter demands Griselda's silent acquiescence and Kingston's mother abjured her to silence, my mother enjoined me to silence. Further, silence in and of itself is insufficient. What is demanded is willing and collaborative compliance. Walter demands that Griselda comply to all his demands "with a good herte." Kingston's mother gets her to believe that silence must be maintained to protect her father. For Kingston the silence represents collusion in her aunt's punishment: erasure of her identity. And my mother instructed me not to criticize or think ill of my father because of his threatened abandonment. In all three instances silence represents only an aspect of an expected voluntary co-operation. Yet there are some disparities here which have to do with who is demanding silence and co-operation. As I said earlier, the intersubjective structures of the narratives do not form a commensurate series. In the *Clerk's Tale* it is the hero of the story, Walter, who demands silence; whereas in Kingston's text it is a narrator, her mother who tells her the story, who demands it, and, in my instance, it is my mother, who was a co-witness to my father's confession. Although it might be useful to analyze how the differences in the structural disposition of the actors bear on the efficacy of the demand, here I want to remain focused on how my life experience contributes to my reading these texts. Reading Kingston's confession of her silent collusion with her family's punishment of her aunt made me reflect on how my own collusion with my mother affects me. Most immediately, it makes me realize more fully why I identify with the Clerk's empathy with Griselda. It also helps me to see just how strongly the Clerk rejects Petrarch's allegorical moral and erasure of the gendered moral of the "good wife."

My identification with the Clerk-narrator facilitated my unraveling the complex dialogic structure of the tale and the debate it generates on the status and position of women. What I initially admired most about the Clerk is the very sophisticated and measured way he employs his knowledge both to resist the demands of the Host for a merry tale and to conduct a polemic against Petrarch's reading of the tale. His successful resistance to these authority figures fed into my own ambivalence towards such figures and authoritative discourse. It was my ambivalence towards my father that allowed me to identify with Kingston's anger and rebellion towards her father and family.

I now understand that my identification with Kingston also has to do with the feminized position my father had accorded me because of my closeness to my mother and my literary and artistic interests. Interpellating me and my interests as feminine was his way of discounting the difference I represented which he had difficulty including in his definition of masculinity and his own self-identity. In this he was very similar to what Harry Bailley attempted to do with the Clerk. But I, unlike the Clerk, had greater difficulty in deflecting the charge. My father's interpellation of me as other than masculine affected my ability to know myself; his feminizing of me was dis-empowering. Kingston's tale also helps me more clearly see how mothers wittingly and unwittingly participate in the enforcement of patriarchal injunctions. Her mother enjoins her to silence. Yet they also transgress: Kingston's mother does tell her the secret story; my own mother encouraged me to follow my desire to learn whatever I wanted. What Kingston's and my story help me see was how completely subsumed into the patriarchal system Griselda is. She has no mother to provide an alternative, whether by example or injunction, to Walter's patriarchal demands.

The issue of feminization raises the corollary issue of sexual difference. And it is here that the *Clerk's Tale* is most loaded for me, and where I have learned the most from it. Carolyn Dinshaw's observes that the Host's interpellation of the Clerk – "Ye ryde as coy as doth a mayde" – challenges the Clerk's sexuality, and, in effect, feminizes him. Her analysis explains an important aspect of my identification with the Clerk that had been occluded from me. She argues that as a consequence of the Host's interpellation, the Clerk "reads like a woman." I agree he reads like a woman. He is sympathetic with Griselda and he takes issue with the fellowship of clerks, generalizing how the plight of women is repressed through the complicity of clerks.[3] But as I have argued elsewhere, he also rotates through other subject positions: he also reads like a man, and a scholar and humanist. The Clerk shows me the great value of his and my ability to read like a woman: it extends the range of our empathizing and consequently the scope and depth of our knowledge. Harry Bailley's reaction to the Clerk and the Clerk's response to him teach something else. Bailley queers him because he fears him. His denigrating remarks on the Clerk's sexual identity are provoked by the Clerk's knowledge and eloquence, and Bailley's ambivalent and fearful attitude towards this knowledge. The Clerk uses his knowledge and rhetorical skill to fend off the hostile remarks of the host and to tell the story he wants to tell. He also uses his skill to surmount

---

[3] See Carolyn Dinshaw, *Chaucer's Sexual Poetics* (Madison: University of Wisconsin Press, 1989).

Petrarch's moral authority and give his own moral interpretation. What both the Clerk and Kingston teach us is the value and necessity of telling the story one has to tell.

What the Clerk's, Kingston's, my own stories show is that patriarchal culture has to incessantly mobilize in order to reproduce itself and maintain control. What the tales make clear is that the three male figures – Walter, Kingston's father, and my father – also suffer because of their lack and are profoundly alienated from themselves, though, let me hasten to add, certainly not as much as women. These tales can be read as demonstration effects of how the self-alienation of men motivates them to subject women and "others" to domination and punishment for real and imagined transgressions. The *Clerk's Tale* demonstrates how monstrous this patriarchal surveillancing can be when it works well.

What these stories also suggest is that the stories we are fated to tell have a determinative effect on us, and specifically in the construction of our sexual difference. This is always other than "normal", and is always suffused with a peculiar mix of the fortuitous and contingent. Kingston's story specifically points to the intimate connection of knowledge, story-telling (the transmission of knowledge), and sexuality. Kingston tells us her mother tells her the story of her aunt as a cautionary tale, and Kingston suggests how her aunt's story and the shame connected with it cause her confusion in her sexuality. She interpellates boys as brothers to diffuse the sexual charge, and is torn between the conflicting images of Chinese feminine and American feminine. Although my father's confession of lack, and his positioning me as feminine, caused me pain and bewilderment as a child and young man, ironically it also freed me to pursue what fascinated me. And my mother's injunction not to criticize him, though it disarmed me in fending off his criticism, enhanced my identification with him. This allowed me to absorb some very positive lessons from him, such as trusting my analytic ability and being persistent in face of adversity. I bring to my reading of the *Clerk's Tale* an emotional knowledge of the lack that Lacan argues we all experience.

I realize that the counter-reading I have offered here might more accurately be described as approximating the conditions for the performance of a counter-reading. Or that this is just the beginning of a much more extensive interpretive stretch. My primary purpose has been to show how my personal history affects the way I read texts, and especially those that resonate deeply with my personal history. My theorizing about counter-reading comes out of a practical effort to better understand the *Clerk's Tale*, which, in its various forms, has occupied a large portion of my scholarly and critical work. I realize that there is a certain fortuitousness about the connection I make between Chaucer's and Kingston's works. Kingston's story precipitated my deeper better understanding of Chaucer's tale and my own story as well. The issues of the personal and gender that are explicitly elaborated in her memoir helped me see how pertinent those issues were for me and for my reading of the *Clerk's Tale*.

Triangulating texts creates asymmetries and stresses the performative aspect of reading. This keeps interpretive possibilities open. I am not the first to use such a modeling. Bakhtin uses such a triangular mode in his rhetorical model of speaker (writer)/speech (text)/listener (reader) and asserts that an interpretive reading has to account for the interaction between all three. It seems that traditional literary practice has amply examined the text and its narrator/author. What postmodern performative reading does is reveal the demonstration effects on the reader. The third term mediates the other two and prevents interpretive closure. Chaucer himself created a trilateral structure for the *Clerk's Tale*, adding a third voice in his rendition of the Griselda story. The parodic voice in the Envoi mocks the patience of Griselda and the moral views of both the Clerk and Petrarch. The effect of the third voice in this instance is to break open the closed scholarly debate between scholar and poet, displacing it into the wider social purview of late medieval culture.

Triangulating old, new, and personal texts makes possible connections between the texts that otherwise would not be possible. These connections may be fortuitous but they are important and lead to real knowledge, as I think my brief synopsis of counter-reading Chaucer's and Kingston's and my own texts shows. Another important reason for urging this practice of counter-reading traditional and contemporary texts is that I think it is the only way that traditional texts will continue to be read. This has to do with developments in our contemporary culture, which I will now address.

The New Situation of Postmodern Technological Culture

In a chapter of *The Transparent Society*, where he compares Heidegger's "The Origin of a Work of Art" with Benjamin's "The Work of Art in the Age of Mechanical Reproduction," Gianni Vattimo isolates what he thinks are the essential features of how we experience an artwork today.[4] Following Benjamin's insight that in our advanced technological culture the essence of art has been transformed, Vattimo argues that this has changed how we experience art today. Benjamin construes the change in terms of the loss of "aura," which he relates to the cult value of an artwork, or the collapsing of its "use" value to the pole of "exchange" or exhibition

---

[4] See Martin Heidegger, *Poetry Language Thought*, trans. Albert Hofstadter (New York: Harper and Row, 1971); and Walter Benjamin, *Illuminations*, trans. Harry Zohn (New York: Schocken Books, 1969).

value. Vattimo asserts that this change affects not only how we experience contemporary art *but even art works from the past*.[5]

The traditional aesthetic experience focused on the structure of the artwork and moved towards an ultimate resolution of balance and harmony. But today, Vattimo argues, we experience the work of art as *Stoss* (Heidegger) or shock (Benjamin). A major effect of this shock is that we undergo a disorientation which does not culminate in a final recuperation and grounding in an order of things. Instead, we experience an oscillatory effect, where the art work is perceived as both founding a world, but, at the same time, as provoking an ungrounding of that world. Vattimo asserts that it is an unceasing oscillation that destabilizes our subjectivity, and he links our manner of "distracted perception" of art as paradigmatic of how we experience the conditions of our existence in general.

Vattimo's argument concerns how technological culture destabilizes our subjectivity, prompting us to engage in a process of *Andenken* or (re-)thinking the past; that is, read the texts of the past in an attempt to find ourselves, to find out who we are.[6] He argues that such a (re-)grounding of our selves through the (re-)establishment of first principles never quite happens. But he is not disturbed by this non-event; for him, what is important is the search and dialogue with those messages from the past. This activity has the effect of making us aware of our mortality, paradoxically providing us with a measure of solace. Just how consoling this practice is, I am not altogether sure, but, as Vattimo suggests, this is our destiny in the sense that it offers us a "fateful opportunity" to grasp who we are, or better, the future perfect, who we will have been.

Today, because of the advanced technological culture of mass (aestheticized) communication, we have a very new relation to traditional texts and traditional cultures, whether traditional is defined as the historically other or the contemporaneous culturally other. One of the consequences of the technological apparatus, which makes possible mass culture and mass art, is to dissolve the legitimacy of the traditional. Before the advent of our society of mass communication the texts from Western European tradition served as exemplary models for us. Vattimo asserts that such is no longer the case. This loss of legitimacy coincides with two other interconnected but distinct

---

[5] Gianni Vattimo, *The Transparent Society*, trans. David Webb (Baltimore: The Johns Hopkins University Press, 1992), p. 54, my emphasis.

[6] The concept of *an-denken* or rethinking the past is a major thematic of Heidegger's which Vattimo reworks. See the chapters "An-Denken: Thinking and the Foundation" and "Dialectic and Difference" in Gianni Vattimo, *The Adventure of Difference: Philosophy after Nietzsche and Heidegger*, trans. Cyprian Blamires (Baltimore: The Johns Hopkins University Press, 1993). See also Vattimo's *The End of Modernity: Nihilism and Hermeneutics in Postmodern Culture*, trans. Jon Snyder (Baltimore: The Johns Hopkins University Press), especially the chapters, "Hermeneutics and Nihilism" and "Nihilism and the Post-Modern in Philosophy."

events: (1) the culmination and dissolution of the tradition of metaphysics, and (2) the homologation of the globe; that is, the "Westernization" of the world. The first refers to the system of philosophical thought that has governed our development for over two millenia, and the latter a result of the imperial adventure that has motivated the West for the past several centuries.

In offering a counter-argument, Vattimo draws on Heidegger's insight that the scientific/technological and the humanistic are but different aspects of the same metaphysical tradition, which is the defining philosophical framework of Western culture. They are in effect different sides of the same coin, not two different traditions. In fact, Vattimo asserts that the technological can be considered to be the most highly developed aspect of our metaphysical tradition, which has now reached a culminating stage, and is beginning to lose its force and persuasiveness, and is dissolving. One consequence of seeing the technological and the humanistic as different aspects of the same tradition is to deny humanism a privileged position "outside" to critique our technological society of mass communication. The critique has to be done from the inside, as it were.[7]

Another consequence of this culminating of the tradition is that the established historicist project of a uni-linear master history is also losing (or has already lost) its cogency and persuasiveness. Some read this as the "end" of history. The movement towards presentness exerts a strong pull in scientific/technological culture. However, Vattimo insists, the dissolution of the historicist notions of a uni-linear narrative and accompanying fantasy of recuperating the past (as it actually happened) doesn't get rid of history or the need to rethink those historical transmissions that have been dispatched to us. You can't discard history like an old coat. Nor can we just trade in our subjectivity for the newest model.

If, Vattimo argues, technological culture, with its dizzying array of inventions, manipulations, and rationalizations, creates oscillatory and disorienting effects destabilizing the normative structures of our tradition, as well as our sense of our selves, shaking up our subjectivity at the deepest levels of our being, if it does all that, it also impels us to respond to another set of imperatives, that of finding out who we are, and where we belong. The situation in which we find ourselves not only drives us to distraction, but also propels us to rethink the messages transmitted to us from our cultural past. So this crisis of humanism and the metaphysical tradition provokes a "fateful opportunity" for us to read texts from the past in a way never possible before.

One of the things that makes it possible to counter-read traditional texts is the changed sense of historical time we have. In the postmodern world,

---

[7] The ambiguity of our new positionality is suggested by the title of Gayatri Spivak's book, *Outside in the Teaching Machine* (New York: Routledge, 1993).

the synchronic and diachronic axes have become more conflated, and there has been a fluidization of historical boundaries. The boundaries of historical periodicity no longer have the absolute demarcation they once did, and the framework governing the transmission of the messages (texts) from the past has been weakened. The world has become a "vast construction site of traces and residues" of history(ies). This process of dissolution of rigid boundaries is *also* occurring in the way the messages and texts from a diversity of other cultures in our present world are transmitted and received. This arena also resembles a construction site of traces, a bricolage which has arisen as a result of the pluralization and hybridization of the world's cultures, as Vattimo claims in *The End of Modernity*.[8]

> In the process of homologation and contamination, the texts belonging to our tradition, which have always served as the measure of our humanity (the "classics" in the literal sense of the term), progressively lose their cogency as models and become part of this vast construction site of traces and residues, just as the condition of radical alterity of cultures that are other is exposed as an ideal which has perhaps never been realized and is certainly unrealizable for us. (pp. 160–161)

The boundaries governing the relationships of the traditional texts with the texts of the newly emergent groupings and with us have been changed. These texts register difference but it is a difference that now, paradoxically, enables us to begin to understand our world(s) and ourselves. The loosening of the dominance of the master narratives has enhanced the emergence of new voices from an array of previously marginalized groups, including women, people of color, gay and lesbian, and postcolonial peoples. They are producing new knowledge, new texts, and a wealth of material from our past and the world's cultures.

The effect technological culture has had on the relations that obtains between the texts of past and those of the present is to create a radically new situation that requires a new set of relations to be thought out. Re-thinking cultural texts means to re-read the traces and leftovers from our historical past in conjunction with the traces of the emerging discourses in our contemporary world. What makes this re-thinking an open-ended process is the fact that these texts contain aspects that have not been previously thought out. Again Vattimo:

> However, we can say that in history as a transmission of messages, the Same is the unthought that presents itself in each proposition as reserve, as that residuum of transcendence conserved by a proposition in every

---

[8] The quote, "vast construction site of traces and residues," Vattimo takes from the Italian anthropologist, Remo Guidieri, "Les sociétés primitives aujourd'hui," in *Philosopher: les interrogations contemporaines*, ed. Ch. Delachampagne and R. Maggiori (Paris: Fayard, 1980), p. 60.

response, and it is to this "unsaid", this "unthought", that the dialogue with the past relates, which inasmuch as it is unthought, is never past but also always yet to come. The Same understood in this sense is what historical diversity or *Verschiedenheit* allows to appear.[9]

It is because texts (messages) from the past contain the "unsaid" or "unthought" that re-thinking them is an open-ended process, one that makes possible the counter-reading and re-writing of them in a dialogic response, which is inexhaustible. Here the future perfect construction, what will have happened, captures or approximates this very new sense of historical time. What was "unthought" in the past text can be thought in the future but it still is a text from the past. This same principle of the unsaid operates in our reading of the texts from other cultures contemporary with us. In a similar fashion, Bakhtin, valorizing difference, speaks of how one culture can read another, revealing in the process meanings that otherwise would never be known.[10] In fact he argues that this dialogic exchange with foreign cultures is the only way a culture is able to know and understand itself. This dialogic process is analogous to the process that makes it possible for individuals to know and understand themselves.

Counter-reading, the process of rethinking traditional texts, should not proceed as a nostalgic recuperation of the past, nor as a reaction to the present. But neither should such a counter-reading be used solely as a justification for the present. The re-thinking of those texts should be employed as a way of destabilizing our understanding of them and the past, and, concomitantly, as a way of (re-)evaluating and (re-)orienting ourselves and the present scene we find ourselves in. This makes it imperative that we read texts from earlier in the Western tradition against texts from the diversity of the world's cultures. English is now the vehicle

---

[9] *Adventure of Difference*, p. 168. This passage occurs in a discussion where Vattimo is distinguishing between the concept of the same and the equal. The same is the sense of some continuum, without which any concept of history is possible. The equal implies some notion of totality, conceived teleological, or otherwise, within which the different aspects or elements are perceived as having some equal standing. Vattimo, following Heidegger, argues that this inhibits difference, and, in fact, prohibits emergence of true difference. Here is his discussion just previous to that which I quoted in my text:

It is only with reference to this idea of the Same that in Heidegger's view we can talk of history. For him it is not the history of things (such as works, individual existence, or forms, with their concatenations in the events of coming to birth and dying), nor is it an evolution towards a *telos*, nor a mere return of the equal. Rather, it is a history of messages, in which *the response never exhausts the call*, precisely because in some way the response actually depends upon the call. (p. 168, author's emphasis)

[10] This dialogic process of one culture engaging another is what Bakhtin calls "creative understanding." See M. M. Bakhtin, "Response to a Question from the *Novy Mir* Editorial Staff," in *Speech Genres and Other Late Essays*, trans. Vern McGee (Austin: University of Texas Press, 1986), pp. 1–7.

for a large number of national and cultural groupings in diverse parts of the globe. The rate of production of these newly emergent cultural discourses is geometric and promises within the next generation to forever change the content of English studies. Our task for the immediate future then is to transform English studies into a more heterogeneous and global discipline.

I hope this diagraming gives you some idea of how a counter-reading might proceed and how traditional works can be read against contemporary texts, without giving peremptory or privileged status of one over the other, the past over the present, or vice-versa. The fact that I feel connected to these works because of their and my peculiar singularity doesn't mean that the differences – cultural, gender, class, ethnic, historical – are erased. They remain visible, for I do not have, or want, to remove them in my reading. I don't have to eliminate their specificity in order to do a counter-reading, unlike Petrarch who moves to a high level of abstraction in order to prosecute his allegorical reading that erases the genderness of Walter's testing of Griselda.

In tracing difference in the counter-reading I also differ from traditional humanistic scholars who often resort to a concept of "eternal values" to do a reading across cultural and historical boundaries. For example, a traditional reading of the texts I have triangulated would construe the theme of silence in a more abstract and "equal" manner. In this primary act of abstraction the traditional humanistic reading would assume that the silence of one text is the silence of all. Fundamentally this approach establishes its universe of "equality" by strictly regulating the definition of silence in the three texts: the medieval Clerk's silence is equivalent to the Chinese-American woman writer's silence is equivalent to the working-class American male intellectual's silence. Such an equalizing tends to erase the differences and ignore the historical and cultural gaps between them. Within this generalized definition of silence the already reduced difference between these texts would be even further minimized. I am not denying the sophistication of the traditional way of reading texts, which often takes into account cultural and historical difference. What I am arguing against is the strong objectifying and reductive tendencies inscribed in the methodology of traditional humanists. Differences are brought under the aegis of a governing idea by a sovereign subject, thus preserving or recuperating the idea of a stable and autonomous subject that uses reason to establish the relationships of ideas and texts to one another, and to order his world. I say "his world" because the traditional humanistic subject was a (and substantially remains so) white, Euro-American, hetero male who construes a single, monologic world.

On the other hand, a counter-reading, while it pursues points of contact (what Vattimo calls the same) between the two works and my own experience, does not ignore the incommensurate differences between them and me.[11] It acts to preserve the difference which is regarded as a source of value and knowledge. The texts are different imprints, if you will, of distinct epochs in the era of patriarchy, one medieval, the other postmodern. What is important to note here is that under the old dispensation their very substantial differences would probably have disqualified them for a comparative reading, but in a counter-reading it is these differences that qualify them.

Reading these texts has inspired me to move in the direction of revealing the interconnections of the critical, personal and political. Women's writing, especially autobiographical writing and the writing about women's autobiography, I think offers a direction for critical practice to move in. I don't mean that critical writing should become only autobiographical, but that the personal should intersect the topography of our disciplinary writing. And that this intersecting should be made explicit. I collocated these texts primarily because of my "subjective" experience with them, because I am convinced that it is necessary for me to do so in order to grow as a scholar and teacher, intellectual and writer. I have known for some time that the personal is the nexus where the professional and political interact with subjective history; it is the site where the peculiar mix of voicings (Bakhtin) constituting our subjectivity happens, and it is the ethical (*ethos*) realm that most immediately affects the decisions we make as scholars and teachers and writers and intellectuals, and I might add, as colleagues and friends, lovers and companions, wives and husbands, fathers and mothers.

More recently I have become persuaded that it is important to break the bond of silence, and give voice to the personal in the disciplinary arena. Such inter-connections should be personified, made visible, made known in our critical practice. I think it is urgent that we reveal the personal process of our political and professional activities because it is crucial to our well-being and safeguards our practice. It prompts critical examination of our institutional positionality, laying bare the historically layered, overdetermined interconnections of our intellectual and discursive productions. I also think enhancing the activity of the personal offers us the possibility of countering the powerful and often destructive effects the objective structures of our technological society work (through) upon us. It is healing and convalescent. Using the personal as a locus for the practice of critical

---

[11] Vattimo, following Heidegger, opposes the idea of the "same" to that of the "equal." The same should not be understood as in the idiomatic American expression "the same thing" which implies an identity. Rather Vattimo understands "the same" as the minimum residuum which provides some notion of continuity making it possible to think of history as such. But it does not imply, as does "equal," some teleological or otherwise closed off totality. See footnote 6 above for further discussion of Vattimo's distinction of these two terms.

reading will, I suspect, begin to (re-)define the new relations evolving along the subject/object axis, and facilitate the personifying (technologizing) of our subjectness. This is a momentous project, a "fateful opportunity" for us, and for our children as well.

TABULA GRATULATORIA

Professor Malcolm R. Andrew
Professor Kathleen M. Ashley
Thomas Charles Atkinson
Stephen A. Barney
Rudy and Hanne Baum
Peter G. Beidler
Lawrence Besserman
David Bevington
N. F. Blake
Mary Carruthers
Marlene Clark
Professor Howell Chickering
Lawrence M. Clopper
Professor John Coldewey
William Emmet Coleman
Theresa Coletti
Roger Dahood
Professor Richard J. Daniels
Professor Alfred David
Clifford Davidson
Professor Vincent DiMarco
Robert R. Edwards
William F. Ekstrom
Dr Patricia Mulrooney Eldred
Professor Richard Emmerson
Garrett P.J. Epp
Alan J. Fletcher
Cathalin B. Folks
Professor Shearle Furnish
Professor John M. Ganim
Professor Warren Ginsberg
Frederick Goldin
Thomas Goodman
Leanne Groeneveld
Mia Schilling Grogan
R. W. Hanning
Professor Britton Harwood
Dr Christine Herold

Professor John M. Hill
Professor W. Speed Hill
Alexandra F. Johnston
Jean E. Jost
Professor Laura Kendrick
Pamela King
Professor Gordon Kipling
Elizabeth Kirk
Professor V.A. Kolve
Sharon Kraus
Professor Seth Lerer
Dr John J. McGavin
William McClellan
Professor Meradith T. McMunn
Dr Lister M. Matheson
Michael H. Means
Professor Benilde Montgomery
Charlotte Morse
William F. Munson
Professor Daniel M. Murtaugh
Barbara D. Palmer
In Memory of Robert O. Payne
James J. Paxson
Derek Pearsall
Scott R. Pilarz, S.J.
Robert Potter
Johanna C. Prins
Professor Liam Purdon
Esther C. Quinn
Dr G. R. Rastall
Professor Sherry L. Reames
Joseph M Ricke
Dr Margaret Rogerson
Ms Asunción Salvador-Rabaza
　Ramos
Victor I. Scherb
Anne Howland Schotter
Professor Pamela Sheingorn

197

Professor Alan Somerset
Professor Stephen Spector
Professor Susan Spector
Professor David Staines
Paul Strohm
Tammy J. Sullivan-Paxson
Dr M. Teresa Tavormina
Elza C. Tiner
Sylvia Tomasch
Professor Peter W. Travis
Professor Steven Urkowitz

Pegasus Press

Míceál F. Vaughan
John W. Velz
Professor Linda Ehrsam Voigts
John M. Wasson
Suzanne S. Webb
Professor Scott D. Westrem
E. Gordon Whatley
Professor Joseph Wittreich
Professor Stephen K. Wright
Rose Abd El Nour Zimbardo